Slavery in the Connecticut Valley of Massachusetts

Robert H. Romer

Robert H. Rome (signature)

Printed and published by
Levellers Press
Florence, Massachusetts

ISBN 978-0-9819820-0-7

To

JENNY

(ca. 1722 - 1808)

Born in Africa, captured as a young girl,
purchased in Boston in 1738 by Reverend Ashley,
for seventy years an involuntary resident of
Deerfield, buried in an unknown grave.

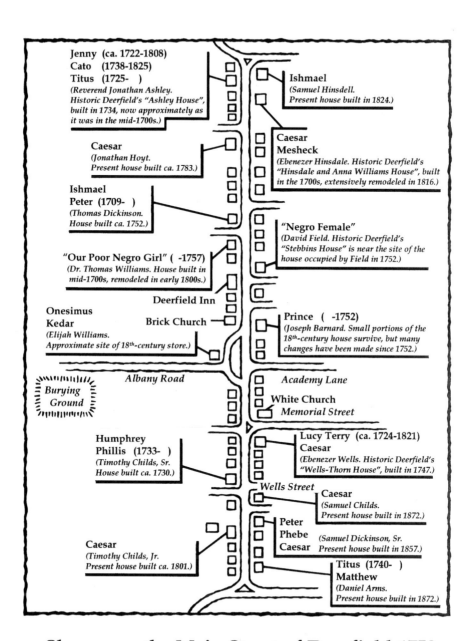

Slavery on the Main Street of Deerfield-1752

Houses indicated are on or near sites where slaves lived in 1752.
The only houses open to visitors are those identified as belonging to Historic Deerfield.

Table of Contents

CHAPTER ONE

Introduction

The Connecticut River Valley of western Massachusetts is best known now for its picturesque villages, its rich farm lands, its history as the northwest frontier of the English settlements of New England in the 1700s, and for its distinguished institutions of higher learning. What is scarcely known at all, even to those who have lived here all their lives, is that in the 18th century slavery was widespread here, that many if not most of the "important people" of the Connecticut Valley – many of them graduates of Yale and Harvard – owned a few black slaves and that slavery was just as "acceptable" here as it was in the South. When New Englanders think about slavery at all in connection with their own region, they usually think of abolitionist activities in the 1800s, of the "Underground Railroad", of the famous Massachusetts 54th – the "colored regiment" whose soldiers fought so bravely at Fort Wagner in 1863. But this book is about the previous century, the 1700s, when slaves and slave owners were found throughout Massachusetts and the other northern colonies.

That slavery existed in western Massachusetts is of course not a new discovery – even though it seems that most of those who live here are completely unaware of the fact that there was ever any slavery at all in this region. Of those who do know that there were slaves in the Connecticut Valley, most think that the numbers were so small that slavery was unimportant, that it was probably frowned upon by respectable citizens. What is astonishing to most people is the number of prominent people, especially the college-educated ministers, who owned slaves and the size of the enslaved population. Not just an occasional one or two slaves – by the middle of the 18th century there were a very significant number of black slaves in prosperous valley towns such as Deerfield.

That is a major result of my own research. On the main street of Deerfield, for instance, there lived about twenty-five black slaves in the mid-1700s. But how important was the institution of slavery in colonial western Massachusetts? Was slavery perhaps more benign here than it was elsewhere? Who were the owners? Who were the slaves, where did they come from? What did the slaves do, how did they live? What was the nature of their interactions, with each other and with their white owners? Where did they go, what happened to them and their descendants after slavery ended? Some, indeed many, of these questions are ones that cannot be answered in more than a very partial and unsatisfying way.

I myself first looked closely at slavery here in my own neighborhood when I began to study the life of Jonathan Ashley, minister at Deerfield throughout much of the 18th century. Slavery was not on my mind when I began. I chose to learn about Ashley because of his prominent position in a colonial town, because I hoped to learn more about the role of religion in colonial Massachusetts. Also, I must admit, I was interested in Deerfield because I have probably never outgrown my childhood fascination with the rigors of life on the frontier, with savage warfare between the English settlers and the Indians, with the French and Indian attacks for which Deerfield is so well known.

One of the first things I learned about Reverend Ashley was that he owned three black slaves. This was in no way an original discovery on my part. But it was a surprise to me (the minister!), and I began to look more carefully at slavery in the valley. At first, I was simply collecting all the information I could find about Ashley and his slaves, then about other slaves in Deerfield and other Connecticut Valley towns, from the time of the earliest English settlements in the mid-1600s until the last decades of the 1700s when slavery gradually came to an end in Massachusetts. Trying to organize my data, trying to make sense of what I was learning, it occurred to me to construct what I call a "snapshot" of slavery. I picked a particular place and a particular time and asked – "Who lived here at that time, to whom did they belong, and what do we know about them?" The place I picked was the main street of Deerfield (simply because so many Deerfield documents are readily available), and I arbitrarily chose a date of 1752, about two and a half centuries ago and roughly midway between the beginning of significant English settlements in this area and the time that slavery ended in Massachusetts. To the best of my knowledge, no one has ever looked at a New England street in this way before.

The map of the main street of Deerfield shown at the beginning of the book is the 1752 snapshot that resulted from this work. This map has revolutionized my own thinking about slavery in the valley. Twenty-five slaves on this mile-long street, a street that I had seen many times but which I now see in a very different way. A large enough number of slaves so that there surely was a black community embedded in the majority white community. Twenty-five black slaves belonging to fifteen different families, 8% of the total population of about 300 on that street. Although the numbers were smaller in outlying areas (and though the numbers were of course much larger in the southern colonies), the enslaved blacks were a very significant presence in many western Massachusetts towns, not just Deerfield but also in other relatively prosperous towns along the Connecticut River such as Springfield, Hatfield, Hadley, and Northampton.

The territory under discussion is the Connecticut Valley of western Massachusetts, approximately the area that now includes the three Massachusetts counties of Hampshire, Hampden, and Franklin, together with a few towns such as Suffield, now part of Connecticut but part of Massachusetts until 1749.[1] Slavery was also important in the lower Connecticut River Valley, in the province of Connecticut. In fact, some Deerfield slaves were purchased from Connecticut towns such as Windsor and Middletown. Slavery in Connecticut, however, will have to be left for another book.

In Chapter Two I explore the early (*very* early) beginnings of slavery in Massachusetts and describe some aspects of the history of slavery throughout Massachusetts. In Chapter Three I address the question that I am often asked – "Was it really slavery here or was it not something much more benign?"

In Chapter Four, "Slavery in Deerfield, 1752", I look carefully at the main street of Deerfield as it was in 1752. As you will see, though the information presented represents a large fraction of what is known about the slaves who lived on that street at that time, what is known about their *lives* is really very little. None of our information comes directly from the slaves themselves, all of it comes from their white owners, almost all from

---

1 Berkshire County, in the far western part of the state, was formed as a county in 1761, and Franklin and Hampden Counties, north and south of present-day Hampshire County, were set off from Hampshire County in 1811 and 1812, respectively.

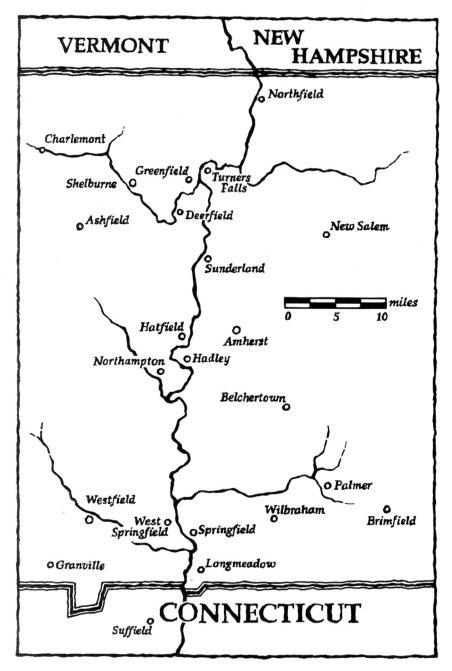

The Connecticut River Valley
of Western Massachusetts

*Shown with modern state boundaries and most of the towns
mentioned in the text.*

merchants' account books, church records, and legal documents such as bills of sale, wills, and estate inventories.[2] This chapter is important not because Deerfield is unusual – on the contrary, the story I relate about Deerfield, the amount of detail and the absence of true information about the lives of the enslaved members of the population, is probably very similar to the story that could be told about other valley towns. "Slavery in Deerfield, 1752" could serve as a model for what might be learned about Hadley or Hatfield or Northampton. In an Addendum to Chapter Four I give some highlights of the story of slavery in Deerfield before and after 1752 – information that was not directly relevant to the 1752 snapshot – and in Chapter Five similarly abbreviated information about other towns in the valley. These two chapters, Chapters Four and Five, are really the core of the book, with their detailed information about slavery in the valley, much of it by way of quotations from original documents and reproductions of portions of those documents.[3]

In Chapter Six I address the question of why it was that so many of the prominent citizens bought slaves. In Chapter Seven, a regrettably brief chapter, I describe some of the doubts that western Massachusetts citizens expressed about slavery. In Chapter Eight I explore the murky question of when and how slavery came to an end in Massachusetts, and in Chapter Nine I discuss what happened after the end of slavery

---

2 I use the terms *estate inventory* and *probate inventory* interchangeably. In colonial Massachusetts, inventories were frequently made after the death of a property owner, especially of the estates of relatively affluent citizens. Many of the originals of these inventories are kept at the Hampshire County Registry of Probate in Northampton. These inventories were copied into an official record book, also kept at the Registry of Probate. Microfilm copies made from this record book are available in the library of Historic Deerfield and at other locations as well. Typewritten transcripts of many Deerfield inventories are also available in the Deerfield library, transcripts made from the microfilms, not from the original documents. Errors can of course arise in any copying process, and the typewritten transcripts, in particular, should be used with caution.

3 In transcribing colonial-era documents, I have tried as well as I can to be faithful to the original spelling (which, from a modern point of view, is often very creative), as well as to the seemingly random use of punctuation and capitalization. There are also many abbreviations and spellings that seem at first to be mysterious. The most common one is y for the sound *th*. Thus ye should be read as *the*, not *ye*. Another peculiarity that occasionally arises is the writing of *u* for *v*, and vice versa – *riuer* rather than *river*, *vpon* instead of *upon*, for instance. And writers were fond of saving space – on gravestones as well as on paper – with superscripts that often represented several letters. Thus y^t for *that*, L^d for *Lord*, $pleas^d$ for *pleased*, dec^d for *deceased*, sh^d for *should*, s^d for *said*, $serv^t$ for *servant*, etc. And ministers in composing sermons often used X for *Christ* and *Xtianity* or simply *Xy* for *Christianity*. Some

and how the people of Massachusetts managed for the most part to forget that slavery had ever existed here. Then in Chapter Ten I offer some final thoughts on the motivation for writing this book.

In discussions of slavery, it is all too easy to get lost in statistics – so and so many slaves in Hampshire County at this date, this many in Suffolk County at some other time. Even though in many cases all we know is the name of an owner and perhaps a purchase price, it is important to remember that these were human beings, forced to live their lives as property.

The institution of slavery played a central role in the founding and continuing history of this country. Slavery was by no means an institution peculiar to the South. Massachusetts was in fact the very first colony to legalize slavery, in 1641. Even at the end of the American Revolution in the 1780s, slavery was practiced everywhere in the new nation. This country continues to live with the legacy of slavery. I am convinced that knowledge of our history, of the history of slavery and of its importance in the history of our nation, can help us come to terms with the legacy of this dreadful institution. This book deals with one small part of this history, but my hope is that it will increase in some measure the awareness of how pervasive slavery has been in this country.

---

words in old documents are partially or totally undecipherable. An undecipherable word will be indicated by a question mark in square brackets separated by spaces from other words. A word or words that are simply omitted will be indicated by an ellipsis (...). Two books that are sometimes helpful in reading 18th-century documents are Sperry (1998) and Sperry (2003).

Another problem with understanding documents from the first half of the 18th century has to do with the *calendar*. See Appendix II for further discussion. Although the Gregorian calendar was first introduced in 1582 and soon adopted in most of the Catholic regions of Europe, England and her colonies remained on the Julian calendar until the fall of 1752. Between 1700 and 1752 dates on the Julian calendar differed by eleven days from dates on the Gregorian calendar. More confusingly, for various purposes two different days were considered to mark the start of a new year – January 1 and March 25. A date given in a document as, say, March 7, 1743 may have been written by someone using the "March 25 convention"; someone else, using the "January 1 convention", would refer to the same day as March 7, 1744. (On the Gregorian calendar, that date would be March 18, 1744.) In quoting from documents, I will follow the document as written, but – especially if the date is of some significance – I will often add an explanatory comment giving the date in "dual-year notation" – March 7, 1743/44. References in the text to events prior to October, 1752 will be given using the Julian calendar. Dates between January 1 and March 25 in the years before 1752 will be given either according to the "January 1 convention" or in "dual-year notation".

This study of slavery in the Connecticut Valley is a work in progress. I am constantly in search of new data. Nearly every time I visit the Hampshire County Registry of Probate or the Deerfield library I learn something new. When I write, for instance, that "No other information about Ishmael is known to have survived", I mean, of course, *known to me, at this time*. I welcome comments, additions, and corrections. (Write to me at my Amherst College email address – rhromer@amherst.edu.) And I hope that others will study Hadley and Hatfield and other towns in the valley in the way that I have examined Deerfield.

CHAPTER TWO

The Beginnings and Rise of Slavery in Massachusetts – Early Days in the Connecticut Valley

The Beginnings of Slavery in Massachusetts

Slavery began very early in Massachusetts. The Pilgrims landed at Plymouth in 1620, and the first Puritans who began to settle in what became the Massachusetts Bay Colony (administratively distinct from Plymouth until 1691) arrived on Cape Ann in 1629 at what is now the town of Gloucester. By 1636 there were English settlements at Salem, Charlestown, Watertown, Lynn (originally Saugus), Roxbury, Cambridge (originally Newtown), Dorchester, and Boston (John Winthrop's "City Upon a Hill"). And at least by 1638, English settlers in Massachusetts were owners of African slaves.[1] As John Winthrop (governor of the colony at various times between 1629 and 1648) recorded in his Journal entry of February 26, 1638[2] –

> Mr. Peirce, in the Salem ship, the Desire, returned from the West Indies after seven months. He had been at Providence,[3] and brought some cotton, and tobacco, and negroes, etc., from thence, and salt from Tertugos. Dry fish and strong liquors are the only commodities for those parts. He met there two men-of-war, set forth by the lords, etc., of Providence with letters of mart, who had taken divers prizes from the Spaniard, and many negroes.

Only a few years later, writes Lorenzo Greene (author of an important 1942 history of blacks in colonial New England), there was a

---

[1] It is possible, though unlikely, that African slaves had been brought to Massachusetts before 1630. See, for example, Moore (1866), pp. 8-9 and Greene (1942), p. 16.

[2] Winthrop (1630-1649). *The Journal of John Winthrop* (1996 edition), p. 246. (Entry of February 26, 1638.)

[3] Providence Island, an island off the coast of Nicaragua, site of a small and unsuccessful Puritan settlement in the 1630s. See Kupperman (1993).

serious shortage of labor in New England, efforts to solve the problem by enslaving whites and Indians seemed unpromising, and "Negroes were regarded by many as the solution".[4] As Emmanuel Downing, John Winthrop's brother-in-law, wrote to Winthrop in 1645[5] –

> A warr with the Narraganset is verie considerable to this plantation. ... If vpon a Just warre the lord should deliver them into our hands, wee might easily haue men woemen and Children enough to exchange for Moores [i.e., blacks], which wilbe more gaynefull pilladge for vs then wee conceive, for *I doe not see how wee can thrive vntill wee gett into a stock of slaves suffitient to doe all our buisines.* ... And I suppose you know verie well how wee shall maynteyne 20 Moores cheaper then one Englishe servant. [Italics added.]

And indeed, during the ensuing decades, the number of black slaves in Massachusetts steadily increased, the slaves playing an increasingly important part in the Massachusetts economy.

The Massachusetts Body of Liberties and the Legalization of Slavery

Although there were already African slaves in Virginia by 1619 (only twelve years after the first English settlement at Jamestown in 1607), of all the thirteen colonies that would win their independence from England and form the United States a century and a half later, Massachusetts was the first to explicitly legalize slavery, with the adoption by the General Court of the "Body of Liberties" in 1641, with Article 91 devoted to "bond slaverie".[6]

Body of Liberties – 1641 (Article 91)

> There shall never be any bond slaverie villinage or Captivitie amongst us, unles it be lawfull Captives taken in just warres, & such strangers as willingly selle them selves *or are sold to us*. And these shall have all the liberties & Christian usages wch ye law of god established in Israell concerning such persons doeth morally require. This exempts none from servitude who shall be Judged there to by Authoritie. [Italics added.]

---

4 Greene (1942), p. 60.
5 *Winthrop Papers* (1929-1992), Vol. 5 (1645-1649), p. 38.
6 *Colonial Laws,* pp. 52-53.

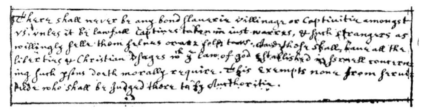

Article 91 of the 1641 "Body of Liberties". (*Colonial Laws*, p. 52)

"... or are sold to us." Until one reaches those words, it seems as if one is reading a *prohibition* of slavery. But at most this article appears to forbid Massachusetts residents from going out and *capturing* slaves, from raiding African villages, taking slaves without payment, while leaving them free to *purchase* slaves from others – a seemingly hypocritical distinction. (And the final sentence – whatever it was originally intended to mean – seems to leave the way open for "Authority" to assign the status of slave to anyone at all.)

There was some concern that because of the restriction to *strangers*, children born in Massachusetts to enslaved parents would not be subject to enslavement. (The children, having been born in the colony, would not be considered as *strangers*.) And so that article in the 1641 "Body of Liberties" (first *printed* in 1648[7]) was soon amended to eliminate the word *strangers*, and the revised version was printed in 1660. In the process of deleting the word *strangers*, other changes in wording and punctuation changed the meaning of the article so that the 1660 version (if read literally) appears to refer *only* to "Lawfull captives, taken in just warrs" and thus *could* be interpreted as a prohibition of most forms of slavery.[8]

Body of Liberties – 1660

It is Ordered by this Court & Authority thereof; That there shall never be any bond slavery villenage or captivity amongst us, unles it be Lawfull captives, taken in just warrs, as willingly sell themselves, or are sold to us, and such shall have the liberties, & christian usuage, which the Law of God established in Israel, concerning such persons, doth morally require, provided this exempts none from servitude who shall be judged thereto by Authority.

---

7 Moore (1866), p. 14.
8 *Colonial Laws*, p. 125.

George Moore (who wrote the first history of slavery in Massachusetts in 1866) points out, though, that corrections were made to this version by a committee of the General Court in 1670, so that the article, as amended to remove the word *strangers*, should in fact read as follows, with the 1670 corrections indicated in italics.[9]

Body of Liberties – 1670

It is Ordered by this Court & Authority thereof; That there shall never be any bond slavery villenage or captivity amongst us, unles it be Lawfull captives, taken in just warrs, *or such* as *shall* willingly sell themselves, or are sold to us, and such shall have the liberties, & christian usuage, which the Law of God established in Israel, concerning such persons, doth morally require, provided this exempts none from servitude, who shall be judged thereto by Authority.

With the additional words *or such*, it seems from the 1670 wording that bond slavery is not in any way restricted to "Lawfull captives, taken in just warrs" but that anyone who is "sold to us" may be enslaved. It is almost certain, though, that 17th-century legislators were not as careful with their punctuation as we may be now as we try to decipher their exact intentions – commas do matter, as do little words such as *or*. With or without the corrections, with commas or without, it seems clear that the point of the various revisions was to eliminate the word *strangers*, to continue the legalization of slavery while also letting it be known that children born to enslaved parents would themselves normally be regarded as slaves. As Moore writes[10] –

If under the original law the children of enslaved captives and strangers might possibly have claimed exemption from that servitude to which the recognized common law of nations assigned them from their birth; this amendment, by striking out the word "strangers," removed the necessity for alienage or foreign birth as a qualification for slavery, and took off the prohibition against the children of slaves being "born into legal slavery in Massachusetts".

Most authors agree that the Massachusetts "Body of Liberties"

---

9 Moore (1866), pp. 15-16. "The Court, hauing pervsed & considered of the returne of the committee, to whom the revejw of the lawes was referred, &c, by the Generall Court in May last, as to the litterall erratars, &c, do order, that in ... Bondslauery, read 'or such as shall willingly,' &c." (*Massachusetts Records*, Vol. 4, Part 2 (1661-1674), pp. 453, 467.)
10 Moore (1866), p. 17.

did indeed legalize slavery and that legislators intended that children of slaves should inherit the status of their parents. Such is the view not only of Moore but also of more recent authors such as Greene[11] and of many others, for instance John Hope Franklin in his classic 1947 book.[12] As Moore concludes[13] –

> Thus stood the statute through the whole colonial period, and it was never expressly repealed. Based on the Mosaic code, it is an absolute recognition of slavery as a legitimate status, and of the right of one man to sell himself as well as that of another man to buy him. It sanctions the slave-trade, and the perpetual bondage of Indians and negroes, their children and their children's children, and entitles Massachusetts to precedence over any and all the other colonies in similar legislation. It anticipates by many years anything of the sort to be found in the statutes of Virginia, or Maryland, or South Carolina, and nothing like it is to be found in the contemporary codes of her sister colonies in New England.

Some revisionist authors, though, writing in the 19th century, went to great lengths to interpret the "Body of Liberties" as a *prohibition* of slavery in Massachusetts. Even in the 20th century, some authors continued to make such claims, often focusing on a 1645 case that supposedly demonstrates the illegality of slavery in colonial Massachusetts. Spector, for instance, asking whether the intention of the "Body of Liberties" was to establish slavery or, on the other hand, to abolish slavery in Massachusetts, writes – apparently ignoring the wording of the article – that the latter interpretation "would seem to be more logical" and somehow manages to interpret the words "or are sold to us" as applying *only* to "indentured servants from England placed in servitude for crimes".[14] He goes on to say that –

> the clear intentions of [the 1641 "Body of Liberties"] are demonstrated by events occurring shortly thereafter. When two Negroes were brought to the colony in 1645 by slave-traders who had captured them in a raid on an African village, and sold, the General Court obtained possession of the Negroes and had them returned to Africa at the

---

11 Greene (1942), pp. 63-65.
12 Franklin (1947), p. 101. "The law of 1641 was as explicit an approval of the institution as energetic traders in human chattel could desire. They only had to take care to see that the slaves they brought in were taken in wars, or that the slaves either willingly sold themselves or were sold to them by someone else."
13 Moore (1866), p. 18.
14 Spector (1968), pp. 18-19.

colony's expense. And the following year [1646], the General Court passed an act "to bear witness against the heinous and crying sin of manstealing as also to prescribe such timely redress for what is past, and such a law for the future as may sufficiently deter all others belonging to us to have to do in such vile and most odious courses, justly abhorred of all just men." ... Taken together, section 91 of the *Body of Liberties* and the act of 1646 certainly indicate the wish of the early Puritans to abolish slavery in Massachusetts.

But the offense for which charges were brought in the 1645 case was not for slave ownership, for slave selling or purchasing, but for *man-stealing*.[15] With its focus on stealing rather than on slavery itself, the 1645 case and the General Court's action in 1646 seem to lead not to Spector's conclusion but rather to the opposite interpretation – the Puritans had no objections to slavery as long as Massachusetts citizens *purchased* slaves (though never on Sunday[16]) and – whether in Massachusetts or in Africa – did not *steal* them.

It is difficult to justify the significance attributed by Spector and many other authors[17] to the 1645 man-stealing case. As summarized by Greene[18] –

Some New England historians would have us believe that the Puritans abhorred slavery. They based this supposed anti-slavery feeling upon

---

15 What the General Court actually did in 1646 was not to "pass an act" but simply to express its opinion of man-stealing ("yᵉ haynos & crying sinn of man stealing ... justly abhored of all good & just men") and to order that those captured in 1645 be returned to Africa ("sent to his native country of Ginny, & a letter wᵗʰ him of yᵉ indignation of yᵉ Coᵗte thereabouts ..."). (*Massachusetts Records*, Vol. 2 (1642-1649), p. 168 and Vol. 3 (1644-1657), p. 84.)

16 The charge was not only for man-stealing, but also for murder and Sabbath breaking! In 1645 Richard Saltonstall presented a petition to the General Court "in the case concerning the Negers taken by captain Smith and Mr. Keser; wherein it is apparent, that Mr. Keser *upon a sabbath day* gave chace to certaine Negers; and upon the same day tooke divers of them; and at another time killed others ... The act of stealing Negers, or of taking them by force, (whether it be considered as theft, or robbery) is (as I conceive) expressly contrary both to the law of God, and the law of this country. The act of chacing the Negers (as aforesayde) *upon the sabbath day* (being a servile work and such as cannot be considered under any other heade) is expressly capitall by the law of God." [Italics added.] (Winthrop (1630-1649). *The Journal of John Winthrop* (1853 edition), Vol. 2, pp. 462-463.)

17 For instance, Alden Bradford, who wrote – "The general court of Massachusetts showed their abhorrence of the slave-trade in 1645, by ordering a Captain Smith to send back, at his own charge, some negroes, which he had brought to Piscataqua that year." (Bradford, Alden (1835), p. 51.) [Alden Bradford (1765-1843), historian and clergyman, served as clerk of the Massachusetts Supreme Court and as Secretary of State of Massachusetts.]

18 Greene (1928), p. 500.

the return by Massachusetts, of two Negroes stolen from Africa and brought to the colony in 1645. There was not a trace of anti-slavery sentiment in this action. It was done solely because of the Puritans' due regard for the Biblical prohibition of manstealing. The Puritanic law, based upon the Old Testament, had made manstealing a capital crime, and the Puritan conscience revolted against this unjust method of securing property.

The action in the 1645 case can only be interpreted as a true expression of "the wish of the early Puritans to abolish slavery" if one closes one's eyes to the following century and a half of slave ownership and slave dealing, as well as to the slave trading that brought in healthy profits for many Massachusetts ship owners.

Whatever the intended meaning of Article 91 may have been, whether one chooses the original 1641 version or its 1660 or 1670 revisions, neither the "Body of Liberties" nor the Puritans' supposed abhorrence of slavery prevented Massachusetts residents from purchasing slaves nor from keeping in servitude the children of those slaves nor – for that matter – from engaging in the slave trade. More will be said in Chapter Eight about when and how slavery came to an end in Massachusetts. Let us just note here that although there were a number of relevant court cases (but no court *decisions* outlawing slavery) near the end of the 18th century, it was not until the state ratified the 13th Amendment to the United States Constitution in 1865 that any *legislative* action was taken to forbid slavery in Massachusetts.

Enslaving Indians

New Englanders had no compunctions about enslaving captured Indians ("taken in just wars").[19] Most commonly, the majority of the captured men (and some of the women) were sent to the West Indies and exchanged there for black slaves, just as Winthrop's brother-in-law, Emmanuel Downing, recommended in 1645. Indeed, at the time Downing wrote, the English had already had a "just war" with the Indians, the

---

19 Useful general references on the relations between the English and the Indians include Newell (2003), Philbrick (2006), and (especially for "King Philip's War") Lepore (1998). As for the terminology – "Indians" or "Native Americans" – one visiting speaker at Deerfield, herself an Abenaki, assured me that most Indians (or Native Americans) do not particularly care which label is used.

Pequot War in the 1630s. At the conclusion of that war, largely fought in Connecticut, numerous captured Pequots were sold into slavery in the Indies.

Here, for instance, is Governor Winthrop, writing to his fellow governor, William Bradford of Plymouth Plantation in 1637.[20]

> WORTHY SIR: ... My desire is to acquainte you, with the lords greate mercies towards vs, in our preuailing against his, and our enimies; that you may rejoyce, and praise his name with vs. About 80 of our men ... mett hear, and ther, with some pequents [Pequots], whom they slew or tooke prisoners. 2 sachems they tooke, and beheaded ... Vpon the 13 of this month, they light vpon a great company of them viz. 80 strong men, and 200 women, and children ... The prisoners were devided, some to those of the riuer,[21] and the rest to vs; of these *we send the male children to Bermuda , by mr. William Peirce*, and the women and maid children are disposed aboute in the townes. Ther haue been now slaine and taken in all aboute 700. The rest are dispersed, and the Indeans in all quarters so terrified, as all their freinds are affraid to receiue them ... [Italics added.]

We noted earlier that it was the Salem ship Desire, with Mr. Peirce as captain, that brought the first known cargo of black slaves to Massachusetts in 1638, bringing from the West Indies "some cotton, and tobacco, and negroes, etc." On the outward trip of the very same voyage, as indicated in Winthrop's letter ("we send the male children to Bermuda, by mr. William Peirce"), the Desire had taken Pequot captives to be sold into slavery. According to an entry in Winthrop's journal, the captives were supposed to be sent to Bermuda and sold, but Captain Peirce overshot Bermuda (by about 2,000 miles) and took them to Providence Island, the "other" Puritan colony, instead. ("We sent fifteen of the boys and two women to Bermuda, by Mr. Peirce; but he, missing it, carried them to Providence Isle."[22])

Most of the female Indian captives, at least those in this group, were apparently kept and enslaved in Massachusetts. Winthrop himself

---

20 *Winthrop Papers* (1929-1992), Vol. 3 (1631-1637), pp. 456-457.

21 "The river", i.e., the Connecticut River.

22 Winthrop (1630-1649). *The Journal of John Winthrop* (1996 edition), p. 227. (Entry of July 13, 1637.) Kupperman quotes a mysterious reference to these Indian captives from the contemporary records of the Providence colony – "The Pequots sold into slavery on Providence Island appeared in the company records only once as 'the Cannibal Negroes brought from New England'." (Kupperman (1993), p. 178.) See also Moore (1866), p. 6.

owned Indian slaves. In a will drawn up in 1639, he wrote[23] –

> I give to my sonne Adam my Iland called the Gouernours Garden, to
> haue to him and his heires forever: not doubting but he will be dutyfull
> and loving to his mother and kind to his brethren in letting them par-
> take in such fruits as grow there. I give him allso my Indians there and
> my boate and such household as is there.

Several decades later, at the conclusion of "King Philip's War"
which engulfed New England in 1675-76, the English once again were
in possession of a large number of captive Indians, many of whom were
shipped off as slaves to the West Indies, where they were almost sure to
die an early death on the sugar plantations. Chief Metacom (known to
the English as King Philip) was killed and his head placed on a pole at
Plymouth, where it remained for many years, becoming something of a
tourist attraction long before anyone thought of the commercial ex-
ploitation of Plymouth Rock.[24]

Meanwhile, the colonists debated the fate of Philip's son and his
wife, Wootonekanuske. Philip himself was the son of Massasoit, famous
for befriending the Pilgrims soon after their arrival at Plymouth. Moore
quotes "a passage of surpassing eloquence" from Edward Everett's 1835
"Address at Bloody Brook".[25]

> What was the fate of Philip's wife and child? She is a woman, he is a
> lad. They did not surely hang them. No, that would have been mercy.
> The boy is the grandson, his mother the daughter-in-law of good old
> Massasoit, the first and best friend the English ever had in New En-
> gland. Perhaps – perhaps now Philip is slain, and his warriors scat-
> tered to the four winds, they will allow his wife and son to go back –
> the widow and orphan – to finish their days and sorrows in their na-
> tive wilderness. They are sold into slavery, West Indian slavery! An

---

23 *Winthrop Papers* (1929-1992), Vol. 4 (1638-1644), pp. 146-147. Two years later, his estate
"becoming since much decayed", Winthrop had to revoke this will and "leave all to the
most wise and gratious providence of the Lorde".

24 Lepore (1998), p. 174.

25 Moore (1866), pp. 42-44. Everett's speech was given to mark the 160th anniversary of
the "Bloody Brook Massacre", which took place during the early days of King Philip's War,
in September, 1675. As a wagon train escorted by soldiers was crossing a previously nameless brook in what is now South Deerfield, they were attacked by Indians, with much loss
of life. Edward Everett (1794-1865), governor of Massachusetts from 1836 to 1840 and a
United States senator in the years 1853-54, is now most often remembered as the orator
who gave a very long speech at Gettysburg in the fall of 1863, during the same ceremony
at which Lincoln gave a very brief speech.

Indian princess and her child, sold from the cool breezes of Mount Hope, from the wild freedom of a New England forest, to gasp under the lash, beneath the blazing sun of the tropics!

In fact, Lepore concludes that though Philip's son, whose name we do not know, was indeed sold to the West Indies, the fate of Wootonekanuske is unknown.[26] In all probability, she either died in a Massachusetts prison or, like her son, was sold away into slavery as Everett had proclaimed.

A 1678 record of expenses and income for the whole war (from June 1675 to September 1676) included, as an expense item, £7 for bounties for *scalps* and the following item as income.[27]

> Captives; for 188 prisoners at war, sold,   397.13.00

Earlier, in a "counsell of warr" held in August, 1675, it was decreed that a number of captives should be sold away.[28]

> In reference vnto a companie of natiues now in costody, brought in to Plymouth, being men, weomen, and children, in number one hundred and twelue, ... the conclusion is as followeth: ... the councell adjudged them to be sold, and deuoted vnto servitude, ... and the Treasurer is appointed by the councell to make sale of them in the countryes behalfe.

The next month, reports Moore, "one hundred and seventy-eight were put on board a vessel commanded by Captain Sprague, who sailed from Plymouth with them for Spain".[29] During and after the war, public auctions of hundreds of Indian captives were held at Plymouth.[30] Even "Friendly Indians" or "Praying Indians", those who had been converted to Christianity, were not immune from kidnapping and sale.[31]

In the decades following King Philip's War, enslavement and export of war captives declined, while *de facto* enslavement, what Newell[32] terms "judicial enslavement", sentencing Indians to long terms of involuntary servitude for a variety of reasons, became the favored method of holding Indians in bondage.

---

26 Lepore (1998), pp. 150-154.
27 *Plymouth Records*, Vol. 10 (1653-1679), pp. 399-401.
28 *Plymouth Records*, "Court Orders", Vol. 5 (1668), p. 173.
29 Moore (1866), p. 36.
30 Newell (2003), p. 112.
31 Lepore (1998), pp. 136, 156-162.
32 Newell (2003), p. 108.

By the early decades of the 18th century, blacks represented an increasing fraction of the enslaved population of the colony. Lauber, in a general discussion of "The Decline of Indian Slavery", attributes the decreasing number of Indian slaves – at least of those with obvious "Indian features" – to intermarriage between black slaves and the less numerous Indians.[33] But he goes on to opine that – "By his very constitution ... the Indian seemed unfitted for servitude." Lauber goes on to make some rather sweeping generalizations about the Indians' capacity for "civilization" and "the inability of the Indian to develop beyond the stage which he had already reached when discovered by the Europeans". "The general conclusion", Lauber writes, "is that Indian slave labor ... was not, as a rule satisfactory". Mason,[34] writing in the 1730s at the time of the Pequot War, comments on the (quite understandable) inclination on the part of Indian slaves to run away – "The Captives we took were about One Hundred and Eighty; whom we divided, intending to keep them as Servants, but they could not endure that Yoke; few of them continuing any considerable time with their masters." It would surely have been easier for an enslaved Indian than for an African to slip away into the woods. (Not without risk, however – Indian runaways might well encounter Indians from tribes hostile to their own.) Thus there was strong motivation for sending Indian captives off to the West Indies, where escape would probably be as difficult as it would be for an African captive brought to New England.

Indians, though, continued to be enslaved in Massachusetts. Although advertisements for black slaves became more numerous, listings of Indians for sale continued in Boston newspapers well into the 1700s. Sometimes blacks and Indians were offered in the same advertisement.

An Indian Boy aged about sixteen Years, and a Negro Man aged about twenty, both of them very likely, and fit for any Service; they speak very good English to be Sold: Enquire at the Post Office in Boston.
Boston News-Letter   May 3 to May 10, 1714

A Lusty Indian Man Servant, aged about 20 Years, that speaks very good English, and fit for any Service in Town or Country, to be Sold on reasonable Terms, by Mr. Jonathan Williams over against the Post-Office in Cornhill, Boston.
Boston News-Letter   March 25 to April 1, 1717

---

33 Lauber (1913), pp. 287-288.
34 Mason (1736).

A Young Indian Woman to be Sold by John Brewster, at the End of Cross-Street Boston.

    Boston Gazette   July 8 to July 15, 1728

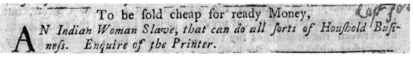

Boston Evening-Post May 17, 1742
(Courtesy of the American Antiquarian Society.)

Massachusetts Slavery in the 1700s

Although an occasional large shipment of slaves arrived in Boston directly from Africa, more commonly a ship from Africa would go first to the West Indies, where the bulk of the "merchandise" would be sold, the remainder being sent on to be sold in Boston. New Englanders often described the blacks sold to them as "refuse Negroes". Governor Dudley, reporting from Boston to the London Board of Trade in 1708, wrote[35] –

> ... And I find by the best Computation that I can make (which cannot faile me to any Degree)
> That there are in Boston Negro Servants to the Numb'r of 400 above halfe of them born here...400
> In One hundred Towns and villages in this Province....................150
>
>   Total 550
>
> ... Every Body is sensible of the Absolute necessity and great benefit of [the slave] trade for the West Indies, but it is not so Serviceable for these Northern Plantations. Because the Winter halfe year Admits of little Service from them, but Demands a great deal of Clotheing, which is very dear in these Provinces. The Negroes so brought in from the West Indies, are Usually the worst Servants they have, which are therefore Sent [to Boston] to be Solde.

On the other hand, slaves who had already spent time in the West Indies or possibly in the southern American colonies were sometimes preferred to "raw" captives directly imported from Africa because they had been "seasoned". They were perhaps more resigned to being enslaved, accustomed to western practices and to the arduous labor demanded of slaves, and might speak some English.

---

35 *Documents Illustrative of the History of the Slave Trade to America* (1930-1935), Vol. 3, pp. 23-25.

A French traveler writing about slaves in Boston in the late 1600s observed, with considerable exaggeration[36] –

> You may also own Negroes and Negresses; there is not a House in Boston, however small may be its Means, that has not one or two. There are those that have five or six.

Though there never came a time when every home owner in Boston owned one or more slaves, the number of black slaves in the colony, never greater than about 2% of the total population, steadily increased during the early 18th century, as did – of course – the total population. A modern estimate[37] puts the total black population of the colony (both free and enslaved) in 1700 as about 800 (most of whom were probably slaves), about 1.4% of the total population of 56,000. (Governor Dudley, in his report to the Board of Trade just cited, estimated the number of slaves in the colony in 1708 as about 550.) Recent estimates put the total "Negro and mulatto" population of the colony, both free and enslaved, seventy years later at the beginning of the Revolution in 1776, at about 4800, some 1.6% of the total of 291,000.[38]

Did the children of slaves necessarily become slaves?[39] Whether the automatic enslavement of children of slaves was ever explicitly writ-

---

36 Shurtleff (1872), p. 48.

37 *Historical Statistics of Black America* (1995), Vol. 2, pp. 1540-1541.

38 *Historical Statistics of Black America* (1995), Vol. 2, p. 1828. See also *Historical Statistics of the United States* (2006), Vol. 1, Part A, p. 5-659. Sweet asserts (Sweet (2003), p. 61) that as of 1750, the number of slaves in New England as a whole amounted to 5% of the total population; however, the source he refers to (Wells (1975)) provides no support for that figure. (The percentage was higher in Connecticut than in Massachusetts – and higher yet in Rhode Island – but not nearly high enough to support a figure of 5% for the whole of New England.) I have also heard the claim that "recent research" shows that as of 1776, about 4% of the total population of Massachusetts were enslaved. The person who made that statement was unable to provide references to support the figure. Skepticism seems in order with regard to any figure greater than about 2% for the slave population of Massachusetts at any date.

39 Hart says that by a 1698 law "children of slaves were definitely declared to be slaves". Neither Moore nor Greene mention such a law nor have I been able to find any such law from the 1690s or from the following decade. (Hart (1927-1930), Vol. 2, p. 262). [Albert Bushnell Hart (1854-1943) was a professor of history at Harvard and served as president of both the American Historical Association and the American Political Science Association.] In several recent papers (e.g., Minkema (1997), p. 829) there appear statements that a Massachusetts "Law of 1670" established that a child's condition was determined by that of its mother. Such authors are probably referring to the 1670 revision of the "Body of Liberties", which was intended to have that effect but which does not include any explicit reference to children.

ten into law or not, it is clear that many 19th-century statements on this issue were simply incorrect. John Palfrey, for instance, apparently referring to the "Body of Liberties", wrote[40] – "One feature of the law of servitude deserves especial mention. The child of slaves was as free as any other child. No person was ever legally held to servitude in Massachusetts as being the offspring of a slave mother." And in 1854 our passionate antislavery senator, Charles Sumner, declared in a speech in the United States Senate that – "In all her annals, no person was ever born a slave on the soil of Massachusetts."[41] But in fact, children of slaves were almost always, if perhaps not universally, treated as slaves. And the status of a child born to parents of whom one was a free black, the other a slave, generally was taken to be that of the mother, at least by the late 1600s.[42]

Did Christian baptism perhaps automatically grant freedom to an enslaved person? Could one be a slave and simultaneously a baptized Christian in good standing? In 1641 Winthrop noted the baptism and admission to the church of a Negro "maid".[43]

> A negro maid, servant to Mr. Stoughton of Dorchester, being well approved by divers years' experience, for sound knowledge and true godliness, was received into the church and baptized.

In the following years quite a number of slaves were baptized and some, like Mr. Stoughton's maid, received into full membership in the church. (We will see some Connecticut Valley examples later.) In 1694 a group of ministers petitioned the legislature to specifically write into law the understanding that Christian baptism did not require emancipation.[44]

> A Memoriall Humbly offered unto His Excellency The Governour & ye Generall Assembly of ye Province of ye Masachuset-Bay, Convened At Boston May 30. 1694. By Many Ministers of ye Gospel, In ye said

---

40 Palfrey (1883), Vol. 1, p. 282. [John Gorham Palfrey (1796-1881) was a professor in the Harvard Divinity School, a representative in Congress (1847-49), and editor of the *North American Review*.]

41 Sumner (1854).

42 Greene (1942), p. 126.

43 Winthrop (1630-1649). *The Journal of John Winthrop* (1996 edition), p. 347. (Entry of April 13, 1641.)

44 *Acts and Resolves*, Vol. 7, "Being Volume 2 of the Appendix, Containing Resolves, etc.", 1692-1702, p. 537.

Province, then Meeting in Boston ... It is Desired That yᵉ wel-knowne Discouragemᵗ upon yᵉ endeavours of many masters to Christianize their slaues, may be removed by a Law which may take away all pretext to Release from just servitude, by receiuing of Baptisme.

It does not appear that any such law was ever enacted. In 1706, Cotton Mather (a prominent Massachusetts minister and theologian, well known for his role in the Salem witch trials and himself a slave owner[45]) published a lengthy pamphlet on the subject, *The Negro Christianized*, which seems to have set the matter to rest.[46] After exhorting slave owners to convert their slaves to Christianity, Mather gets to the point, addressing the hypothetical objection that a baptized slave will become free.

Truly, to Raise a *Soul*, from a dark State of Ignorance and Wickedness, to the Knowledge of GOD, and the belief of CHRIST, and the practice of our Holy and Lovely RELIGION; 'Tis the noblest Work, that ever was undertaken ... And such an opportunity there is in your Hands, O all you that have any NEGROES in your Houses; an Opportunity to try, Whether you may not be the Happy *Instruments*, of Converting, the *Blackest* Instances of *Blindness* and *Baseness*, into admirable *Candidates* of Eternal Blessedness ...

Well; But if the *Negroes* are *Christianized*, they will be *Baptised*; and their *Baptism* will presently entitle them to their *Freedom*; so our *Money* is thrown away ...

But it is all a Mistake ... What *Law* is it, that Sets the *Baptised Slave* at *Liberty*? Not the *Law of Christianity*: that allows of *Slavery* ... *Christianity* directs a *Slave*, upon his embracing the *Law of the Redeemer*, to satisfy himself, *That he is the Lords Free-man*, tho' he continues a *Slave*.

In no way was Mather calling for an end to slavery. And he was probably less interested in persuading his fellow slave owners to do good works by converting their slaves and educating them in the ways of Christianity than in showing owners how they could make their slaves more useful – "Your *Servants* will be the *Better Servants*, for being made *Christian Servants*." Mather certainly believed that blacks were inferior, but he was ahead of many of his contemporaries in stressing that they possessed souls, that they were humans, and must be treated decently – "There is a *Reasonable Soul* in *all* of them ... They are *Men*, and not *Beasts*

---

45 For example, Silverman (1984), pp. 263-264, 451.
46 Mather, Cotton (1706). The excerpts quoted are taken from Ruchames (1969), pp. 59-67. [Italics as in Ruchames.]

that you have bought and they must be used accordingly. 'Tis true; They are Barbarous. But so were our own *Ancestors*."

At least by 1695, slaves were treated for tax purposes together with horses, sheep, cattle, swine, and other personal property.[47] Slight revisions of the relevant Province Law were adopted from time to time. A 1707 version specified the value to be put on each slave, ox, cow, horse, etc.[48]

> ... And said commissioners and trustees shall estimate Indian, molatto and negro *slaves*, proportionably as other personal estate ... each male negro above fourteen years of age, at twenty pounds value; each female negro of fourteen years of age and upwards, at fifteen pounds value; except said trustees, by reason of their age or infirmity, shall see just cause to make any abatement of said value, which they are hereby allowed. And all Indian, molatto male *servants* shall be numbred and rated as other polls, not as personal estate; and every steer or ox at the age of four years old and upwards, at forty shillings value; and every cow or heifer of three years old and upwards, at thirty shillings value; and every mare or horse of three years old and upwards, at forty shillings value; and every swine of one year old and upwards, at eight shillings value; and every sheep of one year old and upwards, at four shillings value. [Italics added.]

Notice the italicized words here – *slaves* and *servants*. In colonial documents, the word *servant*, when applied to a black, mulatto, or Indian, almost always meant *slave*. For the purposes of this particular law, however, it was important to draw a distinction between *slaves* (property) and *servants* (with *servants* here meaning those who were *not* slaves), who were treated not as property but as *polls* (persons). For the purposes of this law, the word *servant* meant an indentured servant[49] or someone hired for a short period of time, a meaning closer to the modern sense of the word.

---

47 *Acts and Resolves*, Vol. 1 (1692-1714), pp. 213-214.
48 Ibid., pp. 614-615.
49 Indentured servants (usually white) were sometimes treated almost as if they were slaves. Their indenture was supposedly voluntary, but many, even young children, were kidnapped from England and Ireland into their American indenture. But indenture, no matter how brutal it often was, was different from slavery in significant ways – indentured servants were not "servants for life", though it is true that, not infrequently, indentured servants died before achieving the freedom to which they looked forward. See, for instance, Jordan and Walsh (2008).

Although there are no known instances of marriage between blacks and whites, such marriages were not explicitly forbidden until 1705, with the adoption of a severe anti-miscegenation law.[50]

AN ACT FOR THE BETTER PREVENTING OF
A SPURIOUS AND MIXT ISSUE

Be it enacted ... (SECT. 1.) that if any negro or molatto man shall commit fornication with an English woman, or a woman of any other Christian nation within this province, both the offenders shall be severely whip'd ... and the man shall be ordered to be sold out of the province, and be accordingly sent away... and the woman shall be enjoyned to maintain the child (if any there be) at her own charge ... (SECT. 2.) And if any Englishman, or man of other Christian nation within this province, shall commit fornication with a negro, or molatto woman, the man so offending shall be severely whip'd ... and be enjoyn'd to maintain the child, if any there be. And the woman shall be sold, and be sent out of the province as aforesaid ... And be it further declared ... (SECT. 4.) that none of her majesty's English or Scottish subjects, nor of any other Christian nation within this province, shall contract matrimony with any negro or molatto.

This act refers only to fornication between blacks or mulattoes, on the one hand, and English, on the other. No concern is expressed about the possibility of "mixt issue" as a result of unions between blacks and Indians, and indeed there was considerable sexual contact and marriage between blacks and Indians.[51]

Section Three of the same law provided penalties for any black person who struck a white person.

And if any negro or molatto shall presume to smite or strike any person of the English or other Christian nation, such negro or molatto shall be severely whip'd, at the discretion of the justices before whom the offender shall be convicted.

An act adopted in 1694 banned the serving of alcohol to slaves, apprentices, and servants who did not specifically have permission from their owners or masters, with a severe fine of ten shillings for a violation.[52]

---

50 *Acts and Resolves*, Vol. 1 (1692-1714), pp. 578-579.
51 See, for instance, Greene (1942), pp. 198-201.
52 *Acts and Resolves*, Vol. 1 (1692-1714), p. 154.

And that no person who is or shall be licensed to be an inholder, tav-
erner, common victualler, or retailer, shall suffer any apprentice, servant, or negro to sit drinking in his or her house, or to have any manner of drink there, otherwise than by special order or allowance of
their respective masters, on pain of forfeiting the sum of ten shillings
for every such offense.

An act adopted in 1703 prohibited Indians, blacks or mulattoes,
whether slaves or servants, from being abroad after 9 P.M.[53]

AN ACT TO PREVENT DISORDERS IN THE NIGHT

WHEREAS great disorders, insolencies and burglaries are ofttimes
raised and committed in the night time by Indian, negro and molatto
servants and slaves, to the disquiet and hurt of her majesty's good
subjects; for prevention whereof,– Be it enacted ... That no Indian,
negro or molatto servant, or slave, may presume to be absent from
the families whereto they respectively belong, or be found abroad in
the night time after nine a clock, unless it be upon some errand for
their respective masters or owners. And all justices of the peace, constables, tythingmen, watchmen, and other her majesty's good subjects ... are hereby respectively impowred to take up and apprehend ...
any Indian, negro or molatto servant or slave that shall be found abroad
after nine a clock at night, and shall not give a good and satisfactory
account of their business, make any disturbance, or otherwise misbe-
have themselves, and forthwith convey them before the next justice
of the peace (if it be not over-late in the night) ...

There were many other laws pertaining to blacks. At a 1723 meeting of Boston citizens it was decreed "that no Indian, Negro, Mulatto or
Slave (even though he had obtained permission of his Master to visit the
Common on days of public Celebrations) should remain there after sun-
set, under penalty of a severe whipping at the House of Correction".[54]

Massachusetts laws restricting the activities and movements of
slaves were less severe than those that existed in the South in the 1800s.
And slaves did have rights that slaves in the South did not enjoy. As Greene

---

53 Ibid., pp. 535-536. In the 1707 tax valuation law quoted earlier, the authors needed to
make clear the distinction between *enslaved* blacks (property) and *free* blacks ("rated as other
polls", i.e., *not* as property), and thus the words *slave* and *servant* were used with distinct
meanings. Similarly here, the intent was to prohibit all blacks, both free and enslaved, from
being abroad after 9 P.M., and in order to make this clear, both words were also used in
this 1703 legislation.
54 Lawrence (1927), p. 97.

puts it – "The Negro slaves of New England occupied a dual status: they were considered both as property and as persons before the law. ... As a person, the New England slave had a right to life. ... Although a master might reasonably and moderately correct and chastise his servant or slave, the deliberate murder of his bondman was a capital crime."[55] The testimony of slaves (even for or against whites) was admissible in court, and if brought to court, slaves had a right to trial by jury. (Blacks, whether free or enslaved, did not serve on juries, though it is not clear whether jury service was explicitly prohibited.) Slaves could enter into contracts and could sue for their enforcement.[56] To what extent slaves really had these rights and were able to exercise them is open to question.

Section Five of the 1705 miscegenation law cited earlier provided that owners must permit their slaves to marry (but only "with one of the same nation").[57]

> And no master shall unreasonably deny marriage to his negro with one of the same nation, any law, usage or custom to the contrary not withstanding.

Slaves were allowed to own property,[58] usually small items that they were able to purchase at a town store, often in exchange for the performance of odd jobs for the store owner or with cash they had received for small jobs done for other owners in town. But very occasionally a slave came into possession of real estate, usually bequeathed by an owner who gave him his freedom in his will.[59] In a very few known cases, however, slaves came into possession of a piece of land while still legally enslaved.[60] Greene even discovered a 1656 case in which a free black in Massachusetts owned a slave.[61]

An act adopted in 1703 prohibited the manumission of any slave unless the owner provided security to ensure that the freed slave would not become a financial burden to the town.[62]

---

55 Greene (1942), pp. 167-177.
56 Greene (1942), pp. 179-186.
57 This provision was inserted at the instigation of Samuel Sewall. (See Sewall (1674-1729), Vol. 1, pp. 445-446. (Diary entry of December 1, 1705).)
58 Greene (1942), p. 177-179.
59 Greene (1942), p. 177-178.
60 Carvalho (1984), p. 12; Greene (1942), p. 179. See also the discussion of Peter Newport in Chapter Five.
61 Greene (1942), pp. 98, 310-311.
62 *Acts and Resolves*, Vol. 1 (1692-1714), p. 519.

AN ACT RELATING TO MOLATO AND NEGRO SLAVES

WHEREAS great charge and inconveniences have arisen to divers towns and places, by the releasing and setting at liberty molato and negro slaves; for prevention whereof for the future, – Be it declared and enacted ... That no molato or negro slave shall hereafter be manumitted, discharged or set free, until sufficient security be given to the treasurer of the town or place where such person dwells ... to secure and indempnify the town or place from all charge for or about such molato or negro, to be manumitted and set at liberty, in case he or she by sickness, lameness, or otherwise, be rendred uncapable to support him- or herself.

An act adopted in 1768 required the assessor of each town and district in the province to make a list of all the property owned by every adult male – dwelling houses, real estate, servants for life between fourteen and forty-five years of age, horses, oxen, cows, swine, etc.[63]

AN ACT FOR ENQUIRING INTO THE RATEABLE ESTATES OF THIS PROVINCE

Whereas the rateable estates of the several towns and districts in this province are much altered since the last valuation, – Be it enacted ... That the assessors of each town and district within this province ... shall ... take ... a true and perfect list ... agreeable to the following list: ... Number of polls rateable ... number of dwelling-houses, and the annual worth; ditto of tan-houses ... number of iron-works and furnaces, and their annual worth; other real estate, and the annual worth; servants for life, between fourteen and forty-five years of age; ... number of horses and mares, three years old and upwards; number of oxen at four years old and upwards; number of cows and heifers at three years old and upwards; number of goats and sheep, one year old and upwards; number of swine, one year old and upwards; number of acres of pasturage ...

Many well known and important people of colonial Massachusetts were slave owners, dealers, or traders.[64] Governor John Winthrop owned no black slaves[65] but he left his Indians to his son Adam in the will that he

---

63 *Acts and Resolves*, Vol. 4 (1757-1768), pp. 985-987. A similar act was passed in 1771. The surviving portions of these province-wide assessments are kept at the Massachusetts State Archives. Microfilm copies are available in some libraries. The results of the 1771 assessment have recently been collected and published. (Pruitt (1978).)
64 There are various sources for the names in this paragraph; only a sampling of these sources are given here.
65 Greene (1942), p. 109.

drew up in 1639.[66] Another slave owner was Governor Jonathan Belcher, who was heavily involved in the slave trade, as was his father, Andrew.[67] Andrew and Peter Faneuil (whose family name lives on in Faneuil Hall – the "Cradle of Liberty" – given to the city of Boston by Peter Faneuil in 1742) were important slave traders.[68] The Belchers and Faneuils were only two of the families that sent ships to Africa to purchase slaves. Throughout the 18th century, an increasing number of Boston ship owners – as well as those of Bristol and Newport, Rhode Island, for instance – were turning handsome profits in the slave trade. James Bowdoin, governor of the state after the Revolution, had been a slave owner.[69] John Hancock, prominent signer of the Declaration of Independence and also a governor of Massachusetts after the Revolution, had been an owner and slave merchant.[70] Cotton Mather was an owner,[71] as were Harvard presidents Increase Mather,[72] Benjamin Wadsworth,[73] and Edward Holyoke.[74] Other Massachusetts slave owners whose names are still familiar include Bulfinch, Cabot, and Endicott.[75] Even Dr. Joseph Warren, hero of the Battle of Bunker Hill in 1775, was an owner – a 1770 bill of sale records his purchase of a "Negro Boy".[76]

> Boston June 28th: 1770. I the Subscriber having this day purchas'd a Negro Boy of Joshua Green, have made the follow[g] : conditions with him viz[t] . That I will add Ten Pounds Lawfull Money to be paid in Potter's Ware manufactur'd in this Town in three years to the Thirty pounds first agreed for if in 3 months from this date I shall think the negro worth the money & if I do not think him worth the additional ten pounds I will reconvey him to s[d] Green, he returnin[g] the two Notes I gave him for the negro, one for 17 £, & the other for 13 £, both of them bearing date herewith.
>
> JOSEPH WARREN

---

66 *Winthrop Papers* (1929-1992), Vol. 4 (1638-1644), pp. 146-147.
67 Greene (1942), p. 28; Twombly and Moore (1967), p. 239.
68 Greene (1942), pp. 28, 36, 42, 353.
69 Sweet (2003), p. 164.
70 Greene (1942), p. 58; McCullough (2001), p. 132.
71 Silverman (1984), pp. 263-264, 451.
72 Hall (1988), pp. 291, 357.
73 Greene (1942), p. 47.
74 Greene (1942), p. 354.
75 Greene (1942), pp. 22, 28, 42.
76 *Proceedings of the Massachusetts Historical Society*, Vol. 14 (1875-76), p. 101; Greene (1942), p. 45.

Benjamin Franklin – a Bostonian by birth – owned one or two slaves for most of his life, though he became a strong opponent of slavery after the constitutional convention of 1787.[77] And out in western Massachusetts, the slave owner whose name is best known now was Jonathan Edwards, minister of Northampton from 1729 to 1750.[78]

Sam Adams was not an owner. In fact, in 1764 he refused the gift of a Negro girl.[79] Nor was his cousin John Adams, though John's father-in-law, William Smith, was.[80] In several cases shortly before the American Revolution in which slaves took their owners to court, suing for their freedom, John Adams served as counsel for the owners.[81] (In the majority of those cases, the slaves were successful, for various reasons, in their suits.[82]) Adams, believing that even the most unpopular defendant had a right to a fair trial, also served as counsel for the British soldiers brought to court for their role in the 1770 "Boston Massacre".[83]

Early Days in the Connecticut Valley

Although the first English settlements in New England were concentrated along the coast, by the 1630s the English were moving up the Connecticut River. By 1635 there were English settlements in Connecticut at Wethersfield, Hartford, and Windsor. And in Massachusetts, English settlements began at Springfield by 1636, Northampton in 1654, Hadley in 1659, Deerfield in 1670, and Northfield in 1673.

As English settlers moved up the valley, African slaves came with them. William Pynchon, founder of Springfield, fur trader, and a frequent negotiator of land purchases from the Indians – who probably had little understanding of what the English meant by a land sale – probably did not own slaves but his son John did. Hadley was first settled in 1659 by a group of religious dissidents from Wethersfield, Connecticut, who moved up the river with their minister, John Russell, the first of four successive Hadley ministers who owned slaves.

---

77 Isaacson (2003).
78 Marsden (2003).
79 Greene (1942), p. 109.
80 McCullough (2001), p. 56.
81 *Legal papers of John Adams* (1968), Vol. 2, pp. 48-67.
82 An exception was the suit brought by Amos Newport of Hatfield, whose unsuccessful freedom suit will be discussed in Chapter Five. (This was one of the cases in which Adams was involved as counsel to the owner.)
83 *Legal papers of John Adams* (1968), Vol. 3.

Though there were probably one or more black slaves in Deerfield before 1690, the earliest surviving record of slavery in Deerfield dates from 1695, a document referring to the death of Robert Tigo, a slave of the minister. By the middle of the 18th century, there were approximately twenty-five black slaves living and working on the main street of Deerfield. In Chapter Four we will take a closer look at slavery in what is now the popular tourist destination, "Old Deerfield".

CHAPTER THREE

"Was it really slavery?"

"They weren't really slaves. They were just servants. They were always well treated and happy, and they were just like members of the family."

Though that is not a direct quote from a published source, remarks like this are ones that I have heard many times from those who hear about my research. In particular, "just like members of the family" is a phrase that I have heard again and again. Consider the following remark, from a recent book about colonial Massachusetts – "African slaves, like white servants, were usually considered part of the family, and they ate and lived with their master's family."[1] The idea that northern slavery (if it existed at all) was really a benign institution and that "our slaves" were happy slaves is by no means new. Consider this striking passage from an 1893 book – "In the main, New England slaves were not unhappy, for they were well treated, and the race has the gift to be merry in the worst of circumstances."[2] And here is Nathaniel Hawthorne (an extreme example, to be sure) – "The sable inmates of the mansion were not excluded from the domestic affections: in families of middling rank, they had their places at the board; and when the circle closed round the evening hearth, its blaze glowed on their dark shining faces, intermixed familiarly with their master's children."[3]

But Massachusetts slaves were not "just servants". They were not "just like members of the family". They were property – bought, sold, and taxed just like real estate, like cows and horses and chairs and kitchen utensils. They were often sold away from their parents or their spouses or their children. Some were born here, many had been kidnapped in Africa. There was nothing in the least bit voluntary about their bondage. They were slaves for life, and if they had children, the children would become slaves like their parents.

---

1 Burgan (2005), p. 66.
2 Earle (1893), p. 91.
3 Hawthorne (1835). (Earle's phrase, the "gift to be merry ... ", is taken directly from Hawthorne.)

African slaves *were* often referred to in legal documents as "servants" – and sometimes as "Negroes", or "servants for life", and sometimes simply as "slaves". In fact, "servant" *was* the most common term for black slaves in colonial Massachusetts. When the word *servant* applied to a black person appears in a colonial document, one must assume – unless there is good reason to believe otherwise – that the person referred to is what we in the 21st century would describe as a *slave*.[4]

Some of the misunderstanding, the misconception that northern slaves were not really slaves, may be simply the result of wishful thinking, but some, undoubtedly, arises from a linguistic accident – the changing connotation of the word *servant*. In colonial times the words *slave* and *servant* were in many circumstances almost interchangeable; nowadays no one is likely to think of those two words as synonymous, and so referring to Massachusetts slaves as "servants" can have the unfortunate consequence of giving false comfort to modern readers who would like to believe that slavery here in the North was a more benign institution than it really was. Use of the term *servant* for a slave is unavoidable if one is to quote from contemporary documents, but because of the change in meaning over the last two centuries, one should not use "servant" in referring to New England slaves unless one is also careful to explain the 18th-century meaning of the word.

Another issue of terminology is worthy of comment. In recent years, there has been an increasing tendency, in writing about slavery, to refer to the slaves not as *slaves* but as *enslaved persons*. There are good intentions behind this idea. To label someone a "slave" is, some believe, to think of that person as *only* a slave, whereas "enslaved person" or "enslaved African American" may suggest that this is a *person*, who is – among other things – a slave but who is also a father, a mother, a carpenter or a seamstress, a farm worker, a fiddler, or a blacksmith. But there is another,

---

4 There were indentured servants (usually white) in colonial times, bound for a period of years, and young white women employed for short periods of time as maids (in the Deerfield household of Reverend Ashley, for instance). Very occasionally, a black person might be an indentured servant, or a free black employed in the role of what we, too, would call a "servant". Although the word *servant*, when applied to a black person, almost always meant slave, it was occasionally important in a law or regulation to draw a distinction between a slave and a free black who really *was* a servant (and not a slave), and so in such cases the meaning of the word *servant* was closer to modern usage – meaning someone who was not a slave, who was in fact free. Some examples of such laws were quoted in Chapter Two.

unintentional, consequence of using the term *enslaved person*. By avoiding the direct one-syllable word *slave*, using the term *enslaved person* tends to soften the harsh reality of what we are writing about. Another choice of words that is often made by those who write about northern slavery, a choice that has a similar softening effect, is the frequent use of the word *master*, rather than *owner*. To be sure, "master" was often used in colonial times as well, yet "owner" more accurately describes the relationship of an owner to his slave, his property.

It really was slavery. Slaves in western Massachusetts were slaves, they were property, by no means were they "just members of the family" as some would like to believe. To disabuse one's self of the notion that slavery in the North was "not really slavery", one need only peruse a few documents – tax lists with columns for "Negroes" or "slaves" or "servants for life" as well as for "cows" and "sheep", a bill of sale in which ownership of a nine-year old girl is conveyed to a purchaser with exactly the same sort of language that would be used to sell a piece of real estate, or a will in which "my Negro woman servant" is left to a beloved wife along with "my two cows and ten sheep". Here are a few excerpts from some of these documents, which will be quoted more fully in subsequent chapters.

> I do bargain, sell and Deliver ... one negro man named Titus, aged thirty-one years ... to have and to hold, the said bargained negro ...

> To my beloved Wife Sarah Williams I give and devise the use and Improvement of one Third of my real Estate during her Natural Life and also all my houshold Goods and within Door moveables (except my Silver Tankard) also my Negro Woman named Phillis my Cows and Sheep for her own use and Benefit for Ever.

> I Samuel Kendall of New Salem ... have sold & Delivered to him the Said Ashley a Certain Negro Man ... to have & to hold to him the Said Ashley his heirs & assigns During the term of his Natural life and I do hereby ... warrant Secure and Defend to him the said Ashley his heirs & Assigns the Said Negro against the Claims and Demands of any person or persons what Soever. ... In witness whereof...

> I the Subscriber Do assign & Deliver the above mentioned Negro man Titus to be his property During the term of his Natural life to Mr Elijah Williams of Stockbridge as witness my hand ...

> I give to my Son, Chileab-Brainerd, ye one half of my Negro Boy, named, Scipio, in Conjunction, with his Mother; – – my brown horse, my newest Saddle & Bridle; A Yoke of oxen ...

I John Cook Do freely and Absolutely, Bargain, Sell & Dispose of my Negro man Peter to him the Said Thomas Wells, and to his Heirs and Assignes forever, To Have and to Hold to his and their proper use Benifit & Behoof forever, Warranting hereby that at the time of the Delivery hereof, I am Lawfully Seized of Said Negro man, and that I have Good Right full power, and Lawfull authorety to Dispose of him. ... In witness where of I have here unto Set my hand and Seal ...

Know all Men that I Matthew Tallcott have Sold unto Thomas Dickinson of Deerfeild one Certain Niegro Man Named Hartford and do by these present Sell and Convey the S^d niegro unto the S^d Thomas Dickenson his heirs & assigns as a Slave for Life and do Contract and agree with the S^d Dickenson his heirs and assigns that ye S^d nigro is in a State of Sound body & helth and that I have Good Right to sell and Convey the S^d Nigro ... hearby acknowledging the Receit of Sixty pounds Lawfull Money p^d To me in full Satisfaction for the Nigro in witness whereof ...

I do hereby Assign Sell & Convey to him a Certain Negro Boy Named Prince aged about nine years, a Servant for life to hold to him his heirs ag^t ye Claims of any Person whatsoever as Witness my hand ...

In the name of God Amen. I Ephraim Williams ... give and bequeath unto my beloved brothers my homestead at Stockbridge, with all the Buildings and Appertenances therunto belonging, with all the Stocks of Cattle and Negro Servants now upon the place, to be Equally Divided between them ...

I will warrant and secure the s^d Negro During his Natural Life against the claim and chalange of any other person and all Rightful Pretentions of his own to Freedom, by any Law or right whatsoever. Witness my hand & seal ...

And one can examine advertisements that appeared in Boston newspapers. (There were no regularly published newspapers in western Massachusetts in colonial times; news came from Boston or perhaps from Hartford.) It is hard to remember as one peruses the advertisements on the next few pages that one is looking at Boston newspapers rather than those of, perhaps, Charleston, South Carolina.

A Negro Man Slave about 35 years of Age, who speaks good English, to be Sold & seen at Cap. Samuel White's house at the North-end of Boston, where you may know further.

    Boston News-Letter[5]   January 1 to January 8, 1704,5

---

5 This newspaper is unusual in that the date on page 1 is given in dual-year notation.

A Lusty, strong Negro Woman to be sold; Enquire at Mr. Callender's in Sudbury Street near the Orange-Tree, Boston.

> Boston News-Letter July 16 to July 23, 1716

Two Negro Girls and a Negro Woman to be Sold, Inquire at Mr. Fanuel's Warehouse in King-street, Boston.[6]

> Boston News-Letter May 25 to June 1, 1719

A Likely Negro Girl, of about seventeen Years of Age, to be disposed of, by Mr. John Greenough Builder, at the North End in Boston.

> Boston Gazette July 25 to August 1, 1720

Eight Choice Negro Men, One Negro Woman, and an Negro Girl to be seen, and Sold at the Salutation, by Mr. Benony Waterman at the North End, Boston.

> Boston News-Letter May 19 to May 26, 1726

Several choice Gold Coast Negros lately Arrived, To be Sold at Mr. Bulfinch's, near the Town Dock, Boston.
A Likely Young Negro Boy, to be Sold by Mr. Samuel Sleigh, in Boston.

Boston News-Letter November 11 to November 17, 1726.
(Courtesy of the American Antiquarian Society.)

Two likely Young Negro Men, of about Eighteen Years, and a Negro Girl of about Fifteen Years of Age, who can speak good English, To be Sold, Inquire of the Printer hereof.

> New-England Weekly Journal May 1, 1727

A parcel of very likely Negro Boys & Girls lately Arrived, To be Sold by Mr. Samuel Royal, at Dorchester.

> New-England Weekly Journal June 12, 1732

TO BE SOLD, A Likely Negro Wench about 26 Years of Age, Inquire of Capt. Elias Jarvis at the North-End of Boston, or of the Printer hereof.

> New-England Weekly Journal September 2, 1734

---

6 Notice the name of the warehouse owner. "Mr. Fanuel" was probably Andrew Faneuil, of the family that gave Faneuil Hall to the city of Boston.

JUST Imported from Guinea, A Parcel of likely young Negroes, Boys and Girls: To be Sold by Thomas Jenner, Esq; at his House in Charlestown.
    Boston Weekly News-Letter   May 19 to May 26, 1737

A likely healthy strong Negro Boy about 15 Years of Age To be disposed of, Inquire of the Publisher of this Paper
    Boston Gazette   July 3 to July 10, 1738

Two likely Negro Men, who can work well at the Blacksmith's Trade; also a strong healthy Negro Woman, to be Sold; Inquire of Wm. Owen Taylor, near the Market Boston.
    Boston Gazette or Weekly Journal   October 29, 1745

To be sold, a very likely young Negro Woman, with a healthy Male Childd at her Breast, about six Weeks old; Inquire of the Printer.
    Boston Gazette or Weekly Journal   December 1, 1747

A D V E R T I S E M E N T S.
TO BE SOLD, by *Samuel Hendly* and Company, at his House in *Charlestown*, A likely Parcel of Negro Boys and Girls, and two fine Negro Men, juft imported from *Africa*.

Boston Weekly News-Letter   October 19, 1749.
(Courtesy of the American Antiquarian Society.)

A Strong healthy Negro Girl, about 18 Years of Age, fit for either Town or Country Business, to be sold; Inquire of the Printer.
    Boston Gazette or Weekly Journal   December 22, 1747

TO BE SOLD by John Banister at his House in Newport, also at Middleton on Connecticut-River, A fine Parcel of Negro Men, Women, Boys and Girls, imported directly from the Gold Coast, and are esteemed to be the finest Cargo of Slaves ever brought into New-England. – Likewise to be Sold by said Banister, European Goods, at the Places aforesaid.
    Boston Post-Boy   May 11, 1752

To be SOLD, A likely negro woman, about 25 years of age, has had the small-pox, and been in the country about ten or twelve years, understands all houshold work, and will do either for town or country; inquire of the printers hereof.
    Boston Gazette or Country Journal   May 12, 1755

Just imported from Africa, and to be Sold at No. 19 on the Long Wharf,
A Parcel of likely, healthy Negro Slaves.
>   *Boston Gazette and Country Journal*   June 22, 1761.

> **JUST Imported from AFRICA,**
> **A Number of prime young Slaves, from the Windward Coaft : To be feen at Mr. *Blanchard's* Store at New-Bofton.**

Boston News-Letter and New-England Chronicle   May 20, 1762.
(Courtesy of the American Antiquarian Society.)

TO BE SOLD   A fine Negro Girl, about 15 Years of Age. Enquire of
the Printers.
>   *Massachusetts Gazette*   January 16, 1766

One likely Negro BOY, and Three GIRLS, also a Negro MAN about 25
Years old, that has been in this Country some Months, to be sold. –
Enquire of HENRY LLOYD, at Warehouse No. 5, on the Long-Wharff.
>   *Boston Gazette and Country Journal*   June 20, 1768

TO BE SOLD, A young NEGRO WENCH, capable of doing most
Sorts of House-Work. Inquire of the Printers.
>   *Independent Chronicle and Universal Advertiser*   January 23, 1777

TO BE SOLD, An extraordinary likely Negro Wench, 17 years old, she
can be warranted to be strong, healthy, and good-natur'd, has no notion of Freedom, has been always used to a Farmer's kitchen and dairy,
and is not known to have any failing, but being with Child, which is
the only cause of her being sold: – Enquire of the printer.
>   *Continental Journal and Weekly Advertiser*   March 1, 1781

It might be some small comfort to think that at least New Englanders were sufficiently humane so that they did not break up families by sale.
Unfortunately, that is not the case. Husbands and wives, parents and
children, were often separated by sale. Think about that "parcel of very
likely Negro Boys & Girls lately Arrived". Where were their parents? And
if some of them were brothers and sisters, what were their chances of

remaining with their siblings? Sometimes the possibility of separate sale ("either with or without the child") was explicitly mentioned.

A likely Negro Woman about 19 Years, & a Child about 6 months of Age, to be Sold together or apart, enquire of the Printer.
    New-England Weekly Journal   May 1, 1732

☞ A *Very likely Negro Woman that has a Child of about Six Weeks old, to be Sold, either with or without the Child, Inquire of the Printer hereof.*

New-England Weekly Journal   April 9, 1733.
(Courtesy of the American Antiquarian Society.)

TO *be Sold together, or a-part, A Negro Woman about* 24 *Years of Age, fit for Town or Country Business ; and a Negro Girl about* 7 *Years of Age, both healthy, and had the Small-Pox ; enquire of the Printers hereof.*

Boston Gazette and Country Journal   January 22, 1759.
(Courtesy of the American Antiquarian Society.)

Sometimes unwanted children were simply given away.

A Negro Child to be given away lately Born in A Family where the Small-Pox hath not been, nor is at present in the Neighborhood, Inquire of the Printer of this Paper.
    Boston Gazette   June 8 to June 15, 1730

A Negro Child a few Days old, to be given away, Inquire of the Publisher.
    Boston Gazette   June 4 to June 11, 1739

To be given away, two Negro Children, one a Boy, the other a Girl, neither of them a Fortnight old; Inquire of the Printers hereof.
    Boston Gazette or Country Journal   February 23, 1756

A Very fine likely Male Negro Child, of an extraordinary Breed, to be given away ; inquire of the Printers hereof.

Boston Gazette and Country Journal   April 20, 1761.
(Courtesy of the American Antiquarian Society.)

To be given away, a Negro Child of an excellent Breed. Inquire of the Printers.
> *Boston Gazette and Country Journal*   June 15, 1761

A Negro Female Child to be given away, without Danger of the Small Pox, and is six Weeks old: Inquire of the Printers.
> *Boston Gazette and Country Journal*   July 2, 1764

A Negro Child, foon expected, of a good breed, may be owned by any Perfon inclining to take it, and Money with it. For further Information apply to the Printer.

Independent Chronicle and Universal Advertiser   December 28, 1780.
(Courtesy of the American Antiquarian Society.)

Some believe that at least sales were always carried out in private, in one-on-one discussions between buyer and seller, rather than at public auctions. We might like to think that at least in that respect New England Yankees were superior to southerners. But although many notices of slaves for sale did end with instructions such as "Inquire of the Printer" or "Enquire at Mr. Callender's in Sudbury Street", even in the North slaves were frequently sold at auction (or, to use the other common contemporary term, *By Public Vendue*), often mixed in with other goods. Rather than being sold from outdoor auction blocks of the sort that we have all seen in heart-rending scenes in movies about the antebellum South, auctions were most often held indoors, in smoky taverns or in warehouses, where the prospective buyers could gather to inspect the merchandise and offer bids.

A D V E R T I S E M E N T.
¶▐¶ On *Wednesday next the* 22d *of this Instant Sept.*
will be *Sold by publick Vendue at the Sun Tavern on Dock.*
Square, *at Three a Clock Afternoon, sundry sorts of English*
Goods, *a fine Coach Bed, Feather Beds, Mens wearing Ap-*
parel, *fine gilded Sconces of several Sizes, good Bohee Tea,*
and *sundry Negro Boys and Girls.*

New-England Weekly Journal   September 20, 1731.
(Courtesy of the American Antiquarian Society.)

On Wednesday next, at the Sun Tavern, at Three of the Clock in the
Afternoon, Will be SOLD BY PUBLICK VENDUE, a parcel of very
good Knives and Forks, Mens Neckcloths, strip't Kentons, a parcel of
very good Threds, a box of fine flanders Lace, some good Chairs, a
Bed &c. Also three or four Likely Negroes, just arrived, all to be seen
at the place of Sale.
       New-England Weekly Journal   September 9, 1734

THURSDAY 13th Instant, Will be Sold by PUBLIC AUCTION at the
Bunch of Grapes Tavern, in King-Street, A great Variety of ENGLISH
GOODS, Viz. Purple and Gold Sarsnetts, blue, pink and white ditto,
Shaded Grizets, White Tabby, Sattin Shoes and Clogs, Handsome
Chints, Sewing Silk, black Alamode, Sattins, a Variety of Ribbons,
Lawns, Paper Hangings, Kippin's Snuff, Broad Cloth, Thicksetts, a few
neat Firelocks. – Also a NEGRO BOY, that has been us'd to a Family. –
And a very valuable Collection of BOOKS, by the best Authors, on a
Variety of Entertaining Subjects, &c. &c. &c.
N.B. The Sale to begin at 10 o'Clock, and to be continued from Day to
Day till all is Sold.
M. Deshon
       Boston Post-Boy and Advertiser   September 10, 1764.

Thursday 23d Instant at Eleven o'Clock, Will be sold by PUBLIC VEN-
DUE By Moses Deshon At his Vendue Room; A Likely strong NE-
GRO GIRL, about 22 Years of Age, who has had the Small Pox, can do
any Family Business, and is fit for Town or Country.
N.B. Any Person that has a Mind to purchase the said Negro at private
Sale, may treat with said Deshon at his Auction Room.
       Massachusetts Gazette   January 16, 1766

NEW AUCTION ROOM,
In Royal-Exchange Lane,
To be Sold by PUBLIC VENDUE, by
ELIAS DUPEE,

Tuesday, Wednesday, and Friday.

A Curious Wheel Engine for cutting Tobacco, Mahogany Desks, Tables, Looking Glasses, Feather Beds Harrateen Curtains and Chairs, a Negro Man, European Goods, Watches, Books, &c

Boston Gazette and Country Journal   August 18, 1766.
(Courtesy of the American Antiquarian Society.)

On Thursday next, the 7th inst. At THREE o'Clock Afternoon, Will be Sold by PUBLIC VENDUE, at the Auction Room in Queen-Street. A variety of English Goods, —— among which are Broad-Cloths, Irish Linnens, Blankets, Duffils, &c. &c. – Also, a NEGRO MAN about 25 Years of Age, warranted healthy and sound, has been 8 Months from the Coast of Guinea, can do many sorts of House-Work very well, and is sold for no Fault.   J. Russell, Auctioneer.
Sale to begin exactly at Three o'Clock.
     Boston Post-Boy & Advertiser   January 4, 1768

On Wednesday the 21st Instant at ONE o'Clock, Will be Sold by PUBLIC VENDUE, At the Bunch of Grapes in King-street, Five stout able-bodied Negro MEN, that are healthy and strong. Also, a Negro Boy about 17 Years of Age, and 2 Negro Women, suitable for Town or Country. Any Person minded to purchase any of the above Negroes at private Sale, before the Time fixed for public, may apply to
J. RUSSELL, Auctioneer/
     Boston Evening-Post   June 19, 1769

Thursday the 14th of this Instant, at 10 o'Clock Beforenoon, will be sold by PUBLIC AUCTION at the Dwelling-House of Mrs. Doreas Ingraham, Widow, in Auchmuty's Lane, South-End, viz. Feather Beds,

Bedsteads and Bedding, Chairs, Looking Glasses, Tables, sundry Pieces of Plate, a Negro Man and Woman, Copper, Brass, Pewter and other Kitchen Furniture, &c.

M. DESHON, Auctioneer

N.B. The Goods may be seen the Day before the Sale.

Boston Gazette and Country Journal   February 11, 1771

Although the newspapers were filled with "Slaves for Sale" advertisements, sometimes prospective buyers placed their own notices, specifying the characteristics they desired in their slaves.

If any Person has a likely Negro Boy to sell between the Age of fourteen and twenty Years, may hear of a Purchaser, by inquiring of the Printer hereof.

Boston Gazette or Weekly Journal   October 29, 1745

WANTED a Negro Boy of the following Age and Qualifications, not under Thirteen Years and not above Twenty, born in the Country, or sent into it young, bred to Country Work, or taught the Shomaker's or Carpenter's Business: Also a Negro Girl not under the Age of Fourteen nor exceeding Twenty, used to Houshold Work, that can make and mend Servants Linnen, &c. both of them well made and recommended, healthy and strong; none need apply but them that has such of the above Descriptions. Enquire of the Printers hereof.

Boston Gazette and Country Journal   February 6, 1758

WANTED, a Negro Boy, 5 or 6 Years of Age. Likewise, some second hand Household Furniture that is tolerably good. Any Person having either of the above may hear of a Purchaser by enquiring of the Printers.

Boston Post-Boy and Advertiser   March 24, 1760

Like slaves everywhere, Boston slaves ran away in search of freedom. Only three of the many runaway notices will be shown here.

RAN away from her Mistress Margaret Robinson, on the 2d Inst, Nancy, a Negro Girl of a middling Stature, mark'd in her Face with the Small-Pox: She had on when she went away, a white Linnen Jacket, and a large check'd Petticoat: Whoever shall take up said Run away and convey her to her Mistress at Mr. Joseph Marion's opposite to the North Door of the Town-House, Boston, shall be well rewarded and have all necessary Charges paid. – All Masters of Vessels and others are hereby forbid harbouring or carrying off said Negro.

Boston Weekly News-Letter   August 22, 1745

Twenty-one year old Cajo was barefoot when he left his owner but wore an iron collar.

RAN away from Mr Benjamin Aftills, now of Bofton, on Friday the 17th of September Inftant, a Negro Man named Cajo about 21 Years old, with an Iron Collar about his Neck, with the Name of his Mafter engraven upon it in Capital Letters. He had on a double breafted Jacket of a greenifh Colour, an Oznabrigs Frock and Trouzers, but no Hat or Cap, Shoes or Stockings. Whoever fhall take up the faid Negro, and bring him to Mr. James Gordon, Merchant, living in Cornhill in Bofton, fhall have Twenty Shillings Reward, befides all neceffary Charges paid.

Boston Evening-Post   September 20, 1736
(Courtesy of the American Antiquarian Society.)

RAN away from Admiral Montagu, on Saturday Evening last, a Negro Man, named JOHN POLITE, about 23 or 24 Years of Age, well made, about 5 Feet 8 Inches high. Had on when he went away, a green Livery Coat, and red Waistcoat, both with Brass Buttons, a New Pair of Leather Breeches, and a New Hat with a Brass Button. Whoever will apprehend the above Negro, and bring him to Admiral Montagu, shall have EIGHT DOLLARS Reward.
Massachusetts Gazette and Boston Post-Boy and Advertiser
May 10 to May 17, 1773

Finally, lest there be any doubt that Boston merchants were involved in the African slave trade, here is one more advertisement, this one offering "a Number of Shackles and Hand-Cuffs suitable for a Guineaman" (a common term for a slave ship).

To be Sold by public AUCTION on Thursday next, at Store No. 19 on the Long-Wharff, TWO Tierces of Irish Beef, 6 small Casks Sugar, 2 old Still Heads, 1 Cask damaged Barley, 4 3-pound Cannon, 15 Small Arms, some Cutlasses, 2 Boxes Tortoiseshell very good, 1 small Cask Gun Powder, a Number of Shackles and Hand-Cuffs suitable for a Guineaman, and sundry Sorts of Ship Carpenters and Joiners Tools. The Sale to begin at Eleven o'Clock.   WILLIAM GREENLEAF, Auctioneer.
Boston Gazette and Country Journal   January 6, 1777

Despite the numerous examples, these are but a very small sample of the advertisements that appeared during the time of slavery. It was a rare issue of the *Boston Gazette*, for instance, that did not carry one or more "Slaves for Sale" advertisements or notices seeking "Runaway Slaves". There was nothing hidden about this commerce; it was all out in the open.

But still one might ask – "Was not slavery in the North a 'gentler' form of slavery than it was in the South? Were not northern slaves often better treated?" The answer to that question is "perhaps", though *evidence* for such a conclusion is not easy to come by. Evidence for the claim quoted at the beginning of this chapter, for instance, that in Massachusetts, slaves usually "ate and lived with their master's family" is really nonexistent. In any event, any system in which some human beings own other human beings as property, in which families can be and are separated by sale, in which babies automatically acquire the same enslaved status as their parents, can only be described as slavery. Once these basic obscenities are in place, other aspects are details. Important details, to be sure, but details nonetheless. Northern slavery – whether in New York City, Boston, or the Connecticut Valley of western Massachusetts – was undeniably slavery.

CHAPTER FOUR

Slavery in Deerfield, 1752

Introduction

In this chapter, we take a close look at the slaves who lived on the main street of Deerfield in the year 1752. By presenting a significant amount of the available information about the slaves who lived here at that particular moment, limited though that information is, I hope to get as close as one can to understanding the realities of life for Deerfield's slaves. Such a snapshot of slavery can convey much more clearly the nature and extent of slavery on this street than would be given by a listing of *all* the known slaves who lived in Deerfield throughout its history. Of course a treatment of those who lived here in 1752 will necessarily include quite a bit of information about events before and after that time. In an Addendum to this chapter I discuss some of the slaves who lived here before and after 1752, those whose stories did not receive mention in the discussion of that year.

I will also discuss the sources of our information – and the limitations of those sources. Even determining who lived here at that time and who they belonged to is not a simple matter but one that requires a good deal of digging through old documents, putting together information from various sources, and indeed indulging in some necessary speculation and guesswork. One must work from a variety of documents – bills of sale, the occasional tax list or fragment of a tax list that has survived, wills, probate inventories, church records, account books of Deerfield merchants, etc., realizing all the time that there are many documents that simply have not survived the 250-year lapse of time or that I myself have not discovered.

Deerfield has profited greatly from the work of its 19th-century historian, George Sheldon – not only from his excellent history of the town (Sheldon (1895)) but also from his admirable habit of collecting and preserving documents from colonial times. Sheldon's book contains a wealth of information, and though one can identify a few errors –

hardly surprising in a book of this size, some 1400 pages – it is obvious that the book was written with great care. His Deerfield history is probably far more reliable than most of the many town histories that were written in the late 19th century. Frustratingly, though, Sheldon almost never gives information about the sources of the information that he provides. Sheldon made his adamant opposition to the institution of slavery very clear in his writings. His history is remarkable for the inclusion of a lengthy section on "Negro Slavery" (pp. 888-905), in contrast to so many other late 19th-century town histories in which scant mention – if any – is made of slavery.

Sheldon's work led to the creation of the Deerfield library, whose collections are preserved, organized and increased by the continuing professional work of the library's staff. The Deerfield library officially comprises two libraries under a single roof, with a single staff – the Pocumtuck Valley Memorial Association ("PVMA") Library and the Henry N. Flynt Memorial Library of Historic Deerfield, Inc. And a great deal of information, not only about Deerfield but also about the other towns in the valley, is kept at the Hampshire County Registry of Probate in Northampton in the form of wills and estate inventories.

Now, referring to the 1752 street map shown at the beginning of the book, let us make a circuit of the street, stopping at each house where slaves lived in 1752. We begin at the south end of the street, at the home of Titus and Matthew, property of Daniel Arms. (The house in which Titus and Matthew lived in 1752 no longer exists; the house that is now on the lot is near the site of the earlier house.) We will then proceed up the east side of the street to the home of Ishmael (property of Samuel Hinsdell), cross to the west side of the street, and return, ending at the home of Caesar (property of Timothy Childs, Jr.)

Titus (1740-) and Matthew
Property of Daniel Arms (1719-1784)

Titus, one of two slaves owned by Daniel Arms, was born about 1740. Titus was baptized in 1762, at the same time as Humphrey, a slave of Timothy Childs, Sr.[1]

> Decem 5 1762　Baptized Humphry Servant to Timothy Childs &
> 　　　　　　　　　Titus Servant to Daniel Arms

The minister's records provide no indication of his age at the time he was baptized. Nine years later, however, in 1771, when Arms sold him to a new owner in Charlemont, the bill of sale described him as "aged thirty-one years", which fixes his date of birth as 1740 and his age when baptized as twenty-two.[2] Like many of the slaves who were baptized in the Deerfield church, Titus was baptized as an adult.

> Know All Men by these Presents, that I, Daniel Arms of Deerfield in the County of Hampshire, yeoman – for and in consideration of the sum of twenty shillings, lawful money, to me in hand paid by Jonathan Taylor of Charlemont, in said County, yeoman – have bargained, sold and delivered, and by these Presents, do bargain, sell and Deliver, unto the said Jonathan, one negro man named Titus, aged thirty-one years, and which I bought of Samuel Smith, of Hatfield, gentleman dec'd. To have and to hold, the said bargained negro, to the said Jonathan, his Executors' Administrators and Assigns, to his and their only property forever, – And I, the said Daniel, shall and will, warrant and defend the said Negro, to the said Jonathan, his Executors, Administrators and assigns, against all, and all manner of persons. – In witness, whereof, I have hereunto set my hand and seal, the twenty-seventh day of June, in the eleventh year of his Majesty's Reign, Annoque Domini 1771.
>
> 　　　　　　　　　　　　　DAN'L ARMS
>
> Signed, sealed and delivered, in presence of Joseph Barnard, Junr., Sam'l Barnard, Jr.

---

1 Deerfield minister's record book, PVMA Library. This record book is labeled "Copy of Deerfield Church Record Kept by Rev Jonathan Ashley to His Death in 1780"; it includes, however, references to some ministerial affairs from before and after Ashley's time. (Filed at PVMA under "Meeting House and Church, First Church, Business Affairs".)

2 A transcript was published in the *Greenfield Gazette & Courier*, September 5, 1881. The bill of sale refers to Titus' previous owner, Samuel Smith, as deceased, but this only means that Smith had died sometime before 1771, not that he was already deceased at the time that Arms bought Titus. In fact, the most likely "Samuel Smith of Hatfield" died in 1767. (See Wells and Wells (1910), p. 437.)

Titus was twelve years old in 1752, so in order to place him on my 1752 map of Deerfield, I had to assume that he had been purchased from Samuel Smith as a child. As we have seen in Chapter Three, children were often bought and sold at a very early age, but it is impossible to know with certainty whether or not Titus was in fact living in Deerfield in 1752.

Titus plays the central role in the only surviving account of a Deerfield whipping, an account passed down to us by Pliny Arms, a descendant of the Arms families who lived in Deerfield in the mid-1700s. Probably writing around 1840, Pliny Arms wrote a manuscript history of Deerfield and also left the texts of several speeches he gave on Deerfield's history that cover much the same ground as his history.[3] In his history, Arms writes –

> There was an affair which took place in Deerfield just before or just after the commencement of the revolution. It is a subject frequently conversed on in our family circles. It has no relation to the political events of the times. But as it has met with the censures of some at the time and since, I will venture to mention it. The story runs thus, that some half a dozen negroes belonging some of the most respectable people, set out to have a frolic. They pilfered rum from the store of Maj Williams eggs butter and bread from some pantry and chickens from some henroost and met at some place of resort to cook their meal and enjoy themselves. They were detected and without judge or jury sentenced to the whip. In other words they were lynched. Maj Catlin was selected to carry into execution the sentence. Titus Danl Arms's negro was first drawn up. His back laid bare and the Maj^r plied with all his force the woodchuck. It was rather hotter than poor Tite liked to soup[4] it. Every stroke drew blood. Tite cried out "O Lord blessed Massa Catlin, do stop and let us take bres". The condemnation and punishment of these poor negroes was had without law or authority. But they were slaves and none to stand up for them.

---

3 Arms, Pliny (ca. 1840). Arms' *Deerfield History* is in the PVMA Library. A transcript made by Robert H. Romer in 2005, together with a copy of the manuscript, is available in the library of Historic Deerfield.

4 "Soup". Though the meaning is fairly clear, the verb "to soup", used in the sense that is implied here, does not appear to be in any dictionary. The *Oxford English Dictionary* does give "soup" as a variant of "swoop", and two possibly relevant definitions – "To make a rapid sweeping descent through the air upon its prey, as a bird", and "To come down upon suddenly with a sweeping movement". With this meaning of "soup", though, it was Major Catlin who was doing the souping, not Titus.

At that time, the word *lynch* did not have the connotation that it now has, of summary *execution*, but rather the infliction of punishment of any kind without benefit of judicial process. Some of the curious words (*woodchuck* and *bres*) in this account are clarified by comparison of this passage with a slightly different account in Arms' "Bloody Brook Address", which is preceded by a description of the construction of the meetinghouse that was in use in the 1760s and some clues as to the location of the town whipping post, which – Arms speculates – was the site of the whipping of Titus and his friends.[5]

> The first allusion I find on the records to a meeting house is in the year 1693 when the town voted to new seat the new meeting house and to appoint tything men. In '94 they voted to build a meeting house of the bigness of Hatfield house & £140 payable in corn & pork was raised for the purpose John Hawks, David Hoyt & John Sheldon to let out the falling hewing framing shingling & clapboarding. It was located on the hill south west of the present brick house.[6] You will understand this sign-post[7] was a place for posting up notifications & also served as a whiping post. It was not the indication only of a public house. On one occasion there is a tradition that this post or a similar one was used for lashing the negros to, who pilfered rum from Maj Williams store. Several were engaged, found out & sentenced to the whip. Maj Catlin was the execution officer on the occasion. Titus Dan Arms negro[8] was drawn up. His back laid bare and Maj Catlin plied the woodchuck.[9] It was rather hotter than poor Titus[10] liked to soup it and he cried out Lord blesser Master Catlin do stop & let us take breath.[11]

5 PVMA Library. The transcript of Arms' *Deerfield History* includes a transcript of the relevant portion of his "Bloody Brook Address".

6 The "present brick house" is what is now referred to as Deerfield's "Brick Church", built in 1824.

7 In spite of the reference to "*this* sign-post", there is no previous mention of this post in the Arms manuscript.

8 In the manuscript, the words "Pomp or Caesar" were originally written. They have been crossed out and replaced by "Titus Dan Arms negro". There were many black slaves in Deerfield to whom the name "Caesar" had been assigned, and slaves named "Pompey" appear in Deerfield history at various times, so the crossed out words "Pomp or Caesar" do not serve to pin down the date of the incident.

9 The original was "cat-gut", which has been crossed out and replaced by "woodchuck". This makes it clear that a woodchuck skin was being used as a whip.

10 The original was "Pomp", which has been crossed out and replaced by "Titus".

11 "Breath". Use of the word "breath" here confirms my guess that "bres" in the *Deerfield History* (the version quoted earlier) represents an attempt by Pliny Arms to represent "Negro dialect".

Curiously, in his voluminous history of Deerfield, George Sheldon makes no mention of this incident, though he was surely familiar with Arms' manuscripts – his initials, "G.S.", appear in the margins. It is likely that this whipping incident took place in the 1760s when Titus was in his twenties, but there is no way to be certain. It is possible that it was this incident that prompted Daniel Arms to sell Titus in 1771.

As to where the whipping took place, perhaps it was simply at the "scene of the crime" but perhaps, as Pliny Arms suggests, Titus and his friends were taken to the town whipping post – on what is now the town common, in the middle of Deerfield Academy. Many towns had such whipping posts, and of course its use for applying the "Discipline of the Post" was by no means restricted to slaves.

We also know that on at least one occasion in 1764 Titus was treated by Dr. Williams and that he received credit on his account by cutting tobacco.[12] If it was at that time that the whipping was inflicted, perhaps his need for medical treatment was the result of the punishment that he had suffered at the hands of Major Catlin.

Occasionally Arms used work by Titus to pay for his own medical treatments.[13]

March 14, 1760	trimming orchard 1 day & Titus ½ a day
July 3, 1767	2 Days Mowing & Titus

There is another item from Deerfield history that probably refers to Titus. On Sunday, May 31, 1767, "Titus negro" confessed in church to "Stealing & lying".[14] But which Titus was this? Because of the profusion of identical names for various slaves, a simple "Titus negro" does not suffice for identification. Jonathan Ashley's Titus had been sold in 1760, but there may have been other Tituses in town in 1767. It does not seem likely, though, that this particular confession referred to the "frolic" for which Arms' Titus was whipped, for none of his companions on that spree were forced to confess in church.

---

12 Account books of Dr. Thomas Williams, PVMA Library.
13 Ibid.
14 Deerfield minister's record book, PVMA Library. Sheldon reports the same confession with an additional charge – "Lying, Stealing & Disobedience to his Master". Sheldon also reports the date incorrectly, as May 21. (Sheldon (1895), p. 896.)

In addition to Titus, Arms also owned Matthew, of whom our knowledge comes exclusively from the account book of Daniel Arms.[15] There are many entries in Arms' account book from the late 1750s and early '60s that show debts owed to Arms by various Deerfield men for work done by Titus and Matthew. Some representative entries from that account book follow.[16]

a days work by Titus	– 2 –
Matthew & Titus plowing half a day	– 3 –
Matthew & teem one Day	– 4 –
Matthew Titus & teem one day	– 6 –
Titus one day Cuting wood	– 2 –
Titus one day Cuting wood and two Days thrashing & Caning	– 6 –

---

15 Account book of Daniel Arms, PVMA Library. Many "account books" and "day books" have been preserved in the PVMA Library. A *day book* consists of a chronological day-by-day listing of sales, payments made, and other transactions, whereas an *account book* (or *ledger*) generally has a separate page for each person with whom the keeper of the accounts had business transactions. A store owner, for instance, would keep a running record of the day's transactions in his *day* book and then, at the end of the day (or after several days or a week) transfer the information to his *account* book. Some of the surviving account or day books from colonial times are mixed in character, with some sections recording accounts with separate pages for particular individuals and other sections giving chronological listings in the style of a day book. For simplicity, I will refer to all of these books as "account books". Account book entries often contain the terms *to*, *by*, D^r, and C^r. Thus, for instance, one entry on a left-hand page in an account book of Elijah Williams reads – "1756 Abijah Negrow Dr March 22 To 1 Knife - - 8, June 22 To 1 Drum Rim - 2 8", indicating that "Abijah Negrow" (actually Abijah *Prince*), the debtor, owes eight pence for a knife and two shillings and eight pence for a drum rim. Then on the right-hand page, the "Contra" page, the notation "1756 Contra C^r May 14 By 1 Salmon - 7 -11" shows that Abijah received credit of seven shillings and eleven pence for a salmon. For more comments on account books, see, for example, Wilson, Robert J. (1981).

16 Amounts of money are usually given in colonial documents in pounds, shillings, and pence – occasionally including the pound sign (£) but more often not. (Even *farthings* are occasionally shown.) Thus an amount listed as "5–8–7" should be read as "five pounds, eight shillings, and seven pence". A simple dash usually indicates a zero, and thus "– 6 – ", for instance, indicates six shillings. Sometimes, when it was obvious that the amount was less than one pound, only two figures might be given – thus "-1-6" (or sometimes "1/6") would denote one shilling and sixpence. Sometimes one finds amounts written with periods instead of dashes – "£53.6.8", for instance. In addition to the problem of notation, there are serious difficulties in learning what a sum of money really meant, especially if, for instance, one wishes to compare an amount paid in 1745 with one paid in 1760. For an exploration of the devaluations that occurred in colonial times, the mysteries of "Old Tenor", "New Tenor", and the like, see, for instance, Felt (1839); Davis (1900), Vol. 1; McCusker (1978); McCusker (1992).

Titus one day work	– 2 – 4
Matthew Drawing wood	– 3 –
Matthew and teem ½ day	– 3 – 6
Titus 3/4 of a day	– 1 – 4
2 ½ Days by Matthew & Titus	– 5 –
Titus 4 Days Scoaring timber	– 10 – 8
Titus a Day loading Dung	– 2 – 4
a Days Work by Titus	– 1 – 4
two Days by titus	– 4 – 8
one by titus	– 2 – 4
two Days works by titus	– 4 – 0
Titus Caning 3/4 of a Day	– 1 – 4

Further reinforcing the identification of both Matthew and Titus as slaves belonging to Daniel Arms is the disparity between the value placed on work by Matthew and Titus and that on work by Consider Arms, Daniel's much younger brother. In November of 1759, for instance, when Consider was twenty-three years old, a day's work by Titus or Matthew called for payment of about two shillings, but other entries in Arms' account book show that a day's work by Consider was valued at fifteen shillings.

Unfortunately, these account book entries contain the total of our surviving knowledge about Matthew. At least with Titus, we know that he was purchased (at an unknown date) from a Hatfield owner, that he was baptized, that he was treated at least once by Dr. Williams, that he was whipped, that he was rented to various Deerfield farmers, and that he was sold in 1771 – not much, but more than we know about Matthew and some of the others on the street.

Peter, Phebe, and Caesar
Property of Samuel Dickinson, Sr. (1687-1761)

It is quite certain that Samuel Dickinson, Sr. owned slaves in 1752, but identifying them by name is difficult and requires a bit of guess-work. From the various records cited below, I think it is reasonable to list Peter, Phebe, and Caesar as those he owned as of 1752.

On June 22, 1737, Reverend Ashley baptized "Fortune Serv[t] Sam Dickinson on his mistress' account".[1] Fortune (a name often assigned to male slaves) may still have belonged to Dickinson in 1752, but no record remains beyond that of his 1737 baptism.

In 1742, Dr. Richard Crouch of Hadley charged Dickinson 12 shillings for "med. & plaster for Negro girl with visit", the "Negro girl" – as is so often the case – not being identified by name.[2] And there are several entries in the account book of shoemaker Joseph Stebbins that may refer to this young woman.[3]

March 1746	A pare of Shoes for your maid	1 – 4 – 0
August, 1746	a pare of shoes for your wench	1 – 7 – 0

As the next few account book entries show, Peter was a young boy who belonged to Dickinson in 1752. In December, 1745 Stebbins charged Dickinson for a pair of shoes.

A pare of Shoes for your negro Boy   0 – 13 – 0

And in 1748 Stebbins made three pairs of shoes for Dickinson's slaves.

Three pair of Shoes for your negros   3 – 5 – 0

On several occasions, Dr. Williams charged Dickinson for medical treatments.[4]

---

1 Deerfield minister's record book, PVMA Library. It is not clear why Fortune was bap-tized "on his mistress' account". Sheldon incorrectly lists the date as 1787. (Sheldon (1895), p. 895.)
2 Judd Manuscripts, Forbes Library. (Judd's notes on Crouch's accounts.)
3 Account book of Joseph Stebbins, PVMA Library.
4 Account books of Dr. Thomas Williams, PVMA Library. Phlebotomy (often abbrevi-ated as "phleb" or "phlebot"), bloodletting, was a common medical intervention of doubtful positive effect.

September 4, 1749   To Vis^t y^r Negroe Boy & Phleb   – 8 –
September 23, 1749 To vis^t Peter   – 4 –

And in May, 1754, Dr. Williams treated "Peter's arm", and later that year he prescribed a "Pil" for Peter.

A surviving document pertaining to the settling of Dickinson's estate in 1761 reads in part as follows[5] –

> We the Subscribers Have Made a Distribution of Part of the Real Estate of Saml Dickinson Late of Deerfield Dec^d as follows: viz Nathaniel Dickinson Part of Real Estate the whole farm at Mill River ... and a Negro man: viz: Ceser ... Saml Dickinson part of Real Estate The Home Lot and Buildings ... Hannah Dickinsons Part of Real Estate The home lot called Mun Lot ... and the Negro girl Called Phebe.

Nathaniel (who inherited Caesar[6]), Hannah (who inherited Phebe), and Samuel, Jr. were Dickinson's three living children. (Dickinson's wife, also named Hannah, and another daughter, Hepzibah, had drowned together "while fording Deerfield River on horseback" in 1740.[7]) Dickinson's daughter Hannah married and left town in 1765, while brothers Nathaniel and Samuel continued to live in Deerfield but on an outlying farm rather than on the main street. Peter, owned by Dickinson at least as recently as 1754, is not mentioned in this document.

In 1771, Nathaniel Dickinson's Caesar was brought into court on a charge of stealing a gallon of rum from John Williams (son of store keeper Elijah Williams and grandson of the Reverend John Williams).[8]

> To Thomas Williams one of his Majesties Justices of the Peace for the County of Hampshire, John Williams of s^d County, Gentleman, against Cesar a laborer, a servant of Nathaniel Dickinson of Deerfield aforesaid that on the last day of November A. D. 1771, he s^d Cesar did at Deerfield aforesaid, feloniously take steal and carry away one gallon of West India Rum, of the value of four shillings Lawful money, the property of y^r complainant and other enormities there and then did against the peace & contrary to law. Wherefore y^r complainant

---

5 Hampshire County Registry of Probate.

6 The Roman name that we usually write as "Caesar" appears in colonial documents in a wide variety of forms – sometimes as "Caesar", but also as "Cesar", "Cezar", "Ceser", "Cesser", "Sezor", and other variations as well. In quoting from an original document, I will copy whatever form is used there, but otherwise I will use "Caesar".

7 Sheldon (1895), Genealogy Section, pp. 145-146.

8 Sheldon (1895), p. 895. The rum was presumably stolen from the store of John Williams, son of Elijah Williams who had died in June, 1771.

prays that a warrant may issue against s^d Cesar, that he may be apprehended and dealt with according to law & as in duty bound.

JOHN WILLIAMS.

Hampshire S.S.   To the Sheriff of the County of Hampshire, his under sheriff, or Deputy, or either of the Constables of the Town of Deerfield Greeting
In his Majesty's Name you are commanded forthwith to apprehend the above named Cesar & him convene before me or some other Justice of the Peace for s^d County, to answer to the above complaint & that he may be dealt with according to Law.
Given under my hand & Seal at Deerfield the second day of December A. D. 1771, & in the twelfth year of his Majesty's Reign.

Thomas Williams Justo Pace.

On this document there is an interesting endorsement.

Hampshire S.S.   Dec. 3, 1771   In obedience to this writ I arrested the body of the within-named Cesar and have him before this Honorable Court for Trial.

JOHN RUSSELL, Constable of Deerfield.

Sheriffs fees for service		1–4
one assistant one day		4-
Two witnesses 1 day each	Titus negro	1–6
	John Linsey	1–6
Comp^t & warrant		1–6
Entry &c.		3–4
		———
Total		13-2
Threefold damages		12-
		———
		£ 1 – 5 – 2

Examined and allowed
THOMAS WILLIAMS Justo Pace.

Inevitably, questions arise, questions that cannot be answered. Did the case actually go to trial? If so, was Caesar punished or fined? If he was fined, who paid the fine, Caesar or Nathaniel? Who was Titus, who appeared as witness? Arms' Titus had been sold earlier that year, and Ashley's Titus had been sold in 1760. Did Titus receive the fee of one shilling and sixpence for his appearance, and if so, did he get to keep the money or did it go directly to his owner?

Nathaniel, who had inherited Caesar, was "a violent and active Tory" who left town hurriedly in the mid-1770s for New Brunswick.[9] At that time, those of Nathaniel's possessions (including Caesar) that were not confiscated passed into the hands of his brother Samuel (also a Tory but apparently not as "violent and active"), as we learn from this final entry, describing the only marriage between Deerfield slaves during the entire 18th century that was listed together with other marriages in the Deerfield records.[10]

> Married by Rev. Ashley, January 16 1778   Caesar & Hagur Servt[s] / Sam Dickinson

Nothing certain is known about Hagur, the woman Caesar married in 1778. And except for the entries in the account books of shoemaker Joseph Stebbins, Doctor Crouch, and Doctor Williams and the record of Caesar's brush with the law in 1771, we know nothing about the lives they all led in Deerfield.

When Samuel Dickinson, Jr. died in 1780, the lengthy inventory of his estate included the following sequence of items.[11]

1 p[r] of Saddle Bags	0 – 12 – 0
1 Horse Collar	0 – 3 – 6
1 Black Negro Wench & 2 Children	30 – 0 – 0
2 Bushels & 3 pecks of Wheat	– 11 – 0
1 Draught Chain	0 – 6 – 8

Very possibly the "Black Negro Wench" was Hagur and the two children had been born since Hagur's marriage to Caesar two years earlier.[12] There is no mention of Caesar in this inventory; he may have died

---

9 Sheldon (1895), p. 752 and Genealogy Section, p. 146.

10 Deerfield minister's record book, PVMA Library. In the 1920 printed volume of the *Vital Records of Deerfield*, in the "Unidentified and Negroes" section, this marriage is incorrectly listed as that of "Cesar and *Oscar*, servants of Samuel Dickinson, Jan. 16, 1778". Frank and Parthena, slaves of Reverend John Williams, were married in 1703, but, as Sheldon points out, that marriage was recorded "not on the page where marriages were regularly entered, but stands by itself on the fly leaf of the volume". (Sheldon (1895), p. 889.)

11 Hampshire County Registry of Probate. The figures shown here are taken from the original document kept at the Registry of Probate.

12 The word *wench* now has a rather pejorative significance, but that was not necessarily true in colonial times. Among the definitions of "wench" in the *Oxford English Dictionary* are: (1) "A girl, maid, young woman"; (2) "A wanton woman"; (3) "A female servant"; (4) "In America, a black or colored female servant, a negress". When we see the word today, it is probably some variation on "wanton woman" that first comes to mind, but that was not always the case.

Three excerpts from the 1781 estate inventory of Samuel Dickinson, Jr. (Hampshire County Registry of Probate.) Samuel's sister, Hannah, who had married a Williams in 1765, was one of the administrators.

or been sold in the interval. Although slaves were almost always listed by name in wills, they were much less frequently identified in estate inventories, even though the men who compiled those inventories knew or could very easily determine their names. Such an anonymous listing seems all the more surprising in this case, for in the very same inventory some of the *horses* were listed by name.

Nancy Dawson a Bay Mare	13 – 0 – 0
Jo Miller a Sorrel Horse	18 – 0 – 0

This estate inventory provides important lessons for those who read old documents – "Use primary sources if at all possible, and never rely on someone else's transcript."[13] When I first looked at this estate inventory, I was using a typewritten transcript,[14] a transcript taken from a microfilm of the record book into which the original document had been copied. In that transcript (and in the record book), the line "1 Black Negro Wench & 2 Children" appears simply as "Negro Wench & 2 Children" and those horses were listed as "Nancy Dawson Bay Mare" and "Jo Miller Sorrel Horse". The omission of the word "Black" does not change the meaning significantly, though the difference between "Negro" and "Black Negro" is interesting. I have seen African slaves referred to both as "Black" and "Negro", but this is the only instance I have seen where the two words appear together – "Black Negro". The omission of the one-letter word "*a*", though, can change the meaning in a significant way. When I first read the listing "Nancy Dawson Bay Mare", I thought that the mare's name was probably Nancy Dawson but that it might instead be a *breed* of horse, a "Nancy Dawson mare". But the actual listing, "Nancy Dawson *a* Bay Mare" (even without the comma that I would have put in), makes it clear that the horse was *named* Nancy Dawson. ("Nancy Dawson", by the way, is the name of a tune that was popular in England in the mid-1700s, named for a well known dancer, a tune that is still familiar as the tune of "Here we go 'round the mulberry bush".)

Much more seriously, the typewritten transcript of this 1781 inventory mistakenly identifies it as that of the father, Samuel Dickinson, Sr. (who died in 1761), rather than that of Samuel Dickinson, Jr. (who died in 1780). Having first come across this inventory in the collection

---

13 I have not myself been able to follow these rules as faithfully as I would have liked.
14 At the library of Historic Deerfield.

of typewritten inventory transcripts, I was initially fooled by this error. In 2002, when I first began to compile my map of "Slavery on the Main Street of Deerfield – 1752", I mistakenly showed "Negro Wench & 2 Children" as the property of Samuel Dickinson, Sr.[15]

---

15 The typewritten transcript also includes an incorrect version of a note just below the "Black Negro Wench" section. The note in the original reads – "This List of Aprisal was Made Agreable to the Current prizes of produce In the year 1774." That is, those who made this inventory in 1781 were estimating the value of the slaves, the horse collar, and other "produce" according to prices as of 1774.

Caesar – Property of Samuel Childs (1679-1756)

Just to the north of the home of Peter, Phebe, and Caesar is the home of another Caesar (property of Samuel Childs), one of six Caesars on the street in 1752. The only thing we know about Caesar is that he served in the military in the 1750s. Sheldon writes[1] – "Still another Cesar, servant to Samuel Childs, served in the same war." A number of the slaves who lived in Deerfield in 1752 served one or more terms in the French and Indian War later in that decade. Those who served, in addition to Samuel Childs' Caesar, were Cato and Titus, slaves of Jonathan Ashley, and the Caesars who belonged to Timothy Childs, Jr., Ebenezer Hinsdale, and Jonathan Hoyt.[2] In several cases, little else is now known about these individuals – in the case of Samuel Childs' Caesar, it is all the information we have.

It is not clear how these slaves came to serve in the armed forces. Blacks and Indians (along with ministers, schoolmasters, and the president and students of Harvard College) were by law excused from military training. Throughout the colonial period, slaves were legally excluded from the militia, but this did not protect them from military service when bodies were needed in time of war.[3] They may have been part of a town's regular quota or perhaps sent as substitutes for the owners or the owners' sons. (Jonathan Ashley, as minister, would have been exempt from regular duty, though his oldest son, Jonathan, Jr., born in 1739, might have been called up by the late 1750s.) Possibly owners were moved by a sense of civic responsibility to volunteer their slaves. Or perhaps, as Fred Anderson has suggested, if an owner could send a slave off to serve in the military for the winter months when there was less need for his labor on the farm, he would be fed and clothed at no expense to the owner, who could in addition collect all or most of the soldier's pay that was due.[4]

---

1 Sheldon (1895), p. 894.

2 Sheldon (1895), pp. 894-898. In Sheldon's essay on Deerfield in Everts' 1879 *History of the Connecticut Valley*, in a long list of Deerfield men who served in "The Last French War", he accidentally inserted an erroneous Caesar, this one a supposed Ashley slave. (Everts (1879), Vol. 2, p. 609.)

3 Greene (1942), pp. 127, 187-188.

4 Fred Anderson, private communication.

What were their military duties? It seems likely that their owners would have been reluctant to have their slaves become proficient in the use of firearms and bayonets, although slaves in frontier towns such as Deerfield did sometimes have the use of firearms for hunting. They may have been used simply as laborers – building fortifications and digging latrines – or as servants to the officers.

Lucy Terry (ca. 1724-1821) and Caesar Property of Ebenezer Wells (1691-1758)

Lucy Terry is unique among the Deerfield slaves. Not only is her story very different from those of all the other slaves, but so also is the extent of our knowledge – both of Lucy and the man she married, Abijah Prince.[1] Lucy was born in Africa about 1724, captured and brought to Boston where she was purchased by Samuel Terry in 1728.[2] Terry had lived in Bristol, Rhode Island, but by this time he was probably living in Mendon, Massachusetts, and when Terry ran into financial problems and had to sell many of his assets, Lucy was sold and came to Deerfield in 1734 or 1735 as the young slave of Ebenezer Wells.

Home of Lucy Terry and Caesar in 1752. The house, built in 1747, is now Historic Deerfield's "Wells-Thorn House". (Author's photograph.)

---

1 Proper (1997); Gerzina (2008).

2 Gerzina (2008), p. 65. Thus the surname *Terry* became associated with Lucy, who probably acquired her "given" name from Samuel Terry as well.

On June 14, 1735, Lucy – together with four other Deerfield slaves, including Caesar, who also belonged to Ebenezer Wells – was baptized in the Deerfield church.[3]

> Names of Children Baptized
> June 14 1735
> Pompey Servant to Justice Jonathan Wells, Adam & Peter Servants to Justice Thomas Wells, & Caesar Servant to Ebenezer Wells assented to the articles of ye xtian faith Entered into Covenant and were Baptized, & Lusy Servant to Ebenezer Wells was Baptized upon his account.

Nine years later, Lucy, now about twenty years old, was "Admitted to Full Communion".

> Names of Persons Admitted to Full Communion
> August 19 1744 Lusey Servant to Ebenezer Wells was admitted to the fellowship of the chh.

In the summer of 1746, a war party of Indians attacked a Deerfield group in the meadows south of town, in what became known as the "Bars Fight".[4] Four Deerfield men and a nine-year old boy were killed, an eight-year old boy was captured and taken to Canada, and Eunice Allen, a thirteen-year old girl, was tomahawked and left for dead but somehow survived. This was the last time that Deerfield settlers were killed by raiding Indians. It was the Bars Fight that led to Lucy's fame as a poet – she composed a poem about the attack. It seems that Lucy never wrote down the words, but she repeated them, others repeated them, finally the poem was put in writing,[5] and Lucy eventually became known as "America's First Black Poet". As far as anyone knows, the "Bars Fight" was Lucy's only venture into poetry.

Lucy was occasionally treated by Dr. Williams. In November, 1748, for instance, Williams charged Ensign[6] Wells for treating his "Negro girl" and in July, 1754 he charged Wells for extracting one of Lucy's teeth.[7]

---

3 Deerfield minister's record book, PVMA Library.
4 "The Bars" was a place a few miles south of town where a set of bars in the fence enclosing the town meadows provided access to the road to Hatfield.
5 Probably for the first time by Pliny Arms about 1840. (Arms, Pliny (ca. 1840).) The words are given in Sheldon (1895), pp. 548-549; Sheldon (1893), p. 56; Proper (1997), pp. 18-19; and Gerzina (2008), p. 79. Proper's version contains two lines that are not included by Gerzina or Sheldon. (Sheldon does mention those two lines but does not include them as part of the poem. (Sheldon (1895), p. 899; Sheldon (1893), p. 56.))
6 "Ensign", a title for Ebenezer Wells that appears frequently in Deerfield records.
7 Account books of Dr. Thomas Williams, PVMA Library.

Like nearly all the male slaves in town, Lucy made purchases at Elijah Williams' store.[8] I have not, however, come across any records of store purchases by other *female* slaves in Deerfield. Among Lucy's purchases during the 1750s were these –

December 3, 1751	$1/8$ y^d Cambrick & 3 sheets paper
October 17, 1754	$1/8$ y^d of Cambrick
May 3, 1755	1 y^d of Ribband
May 26, 1755	Sundries
May 29, 1755	a thimble
June 7, 1755	Cake of Chocolate
November 25, 1755	a Sheet of Cartridge paper

The purchases of *paper* are especially interesting. Later in life Lucy surely knew how to read and write, but these purchases suggest that already as a young woman she was literate.

Abijah Prince, born about 1706, was for many years a slave of Reverend Benjamin Doolittle of Northfield. Doolittle died in 1749 (January 9, 1748/49 in dual-year notation), and though Abijah was never freed by Doolittle, he did eventually gain his freedom. Sometime during the next two years, Abijah became the property of Aaron Burt of Northfield, though exactly when and how this happened is still unclear. Abijah Prince was freed by his new owner on May 9, 1751, and the manumission document is now on file at the Hampden County Registry of Deeds in Springfield.[9] (In that document, Abijah is referred to as "my Negroman Servant or Slave named Abijah Alias Prince".)

For some years before and after his manumission, Abijah was in and around Deerfield from time to time and arrived there to settle in about 1754. He had surely met Lucy before that time, perhaps they had already courted, and Lucy and Abijah were married in 1756.[10]

Abijah Prince and Lucy Terry Servant to Ens. Ebenr Wells were married May ye 17, 1756 by Elijah Williams, Justo Pace

Lucy and Abijah were married by Justice of the Peace Elijah Williams, not by Reverend Ashley. One cannot conclude from that fact that Ashley had any objection to marrying a black couple – many marriages

---

8 Account books of Elijah Williams, PVMA Library.

9 Gerzina (2008), pp. 44-50.

10 Town records of "Births, Intentions, Marriages, and Deaths", as quoted by Proper (1997), pp. 23, 44.

Abijah Prince's manumission document, dated May 9, 1751. This is not a copy of the original document but of the entry in the record book into which land deeds and other documents were copied. (Hampden County Registry of Deeds, Book U, p. 221.)

at this time were performed by justices of the peace rather than by ministers. Lucy, like Abijah, became free, but how she became free and when (whether before or after the marriage) is still not clear.

Lucy and Abijah lived in Deerfield for some time and had six children,[11] all of whom were baptized by Reverend Ashley. Caesar Prince,

---

11 According to the 1821 obituary of "Mrs. Lucy Prince" (in *The Franklin Herald* of Greenfield, Massachusetts, reprinted by Proper), Lucy had been the mother of seven children. (Proper (1997), p. 6.) Whether this was an error or there was another child who died in infancy is not known.

born in 1757, was almost certainly the first black child born into free-dom in Deerfield. In baptizing Caesar, Ashley used *Negro* as the sur-name for his parents – thereafter he used the correct surname, *Prince*.[12]

1757	Feb 13	Caesar S Abijah & Lusey Negro
1758	July 30	Duroxa D Abijah & Lusy Prince
1760	Sep 7	Drusilla D Abij^h & Lusy Prince
1763	Jan 9	Festus S Abijah & Lusy Prince
1765	Sep. 22	Tatnai S Abij^h .. Lucy Prince
1769	Aug 6	Abijah S Abijah & Lusy Prince

The Princes later moved to Vermont, where Abijah died in 1794 and Lucy in 1821. The story of their life there, of their not always friendly reception by their Vermont neighbors, must be left to Gerzina's book.[13] One thing that is disappointing about the story of Lucy and Abijah Prince is that in spite of the extensive efforts of researchers Anthony and Gretchen Gerzina, we do not know of any living descendants. The chal-lenge of finding descendants of any black slaves from colonial times is daunting. The Princes, with a known surname and six children, all of whom grew to adulthood (itself an unusual statistic), would appear to provide a very promising case, and perhaps something will still turn up and let us identify some of their descendants or descendants of other Deerfield slaves.

Ebenezer Wells owned two slaves, not only Lucy but also Caesar. Unfortunately, we know very little about Wells' Caesar. As mentioned earlier, Caesar was baptized in 1735, on the same day as Lucy and three other slaves – Pompey (a slave belonging to Jonathan Wells), and Adam and Peter (who belonged to Thomas Wells). A year and a half later, Caesar was fully "taken into ye church".[14]

Names of persons Taken into ye Church
Feb 27   1736/7   Cesar Servant to Eben^{er} Wells

Caesar was frequently treated by Dr. Williams, most often by phle-botomy (i.e., bloodletting). There were frequent entries of the follow-ing sort in Williams' account books.[15]

---

12 Deerfield minister's record book, PVMA Library.
13 Gerzina (2008).
14 Deerfield minister's record book, PVMA Library.
15 Account books of Dr. Thomas Williams, PVMA Library.

May 5, 1749   To Extract 1 Tooth 4/Caesar - - 4
June 22, 1751   To Phlebot Caesar 8
June 24, 1756   To Phlebot. Caesar 8

On July 3, 1754, Dr. Williams extracted one of Caesar's teeth and then bled him the same day.

July 3 1754   Ens^n Eben^r Wells D^r to Extract Den Cesar 0/8
              Ens^n Eben^r Wells D^r to Phlebot Cesar 0/8

Like many other Deerfield slaves, Caesar ("Ensign Wells Negro") occasionally made purchases at Elijah Williams' store.[16]

1745   Cesar En^s Wells Negro D^r
Octr 12   to a pair of Shoe buckels0 6 0

He then paid off some of his debt with half a fox skin.

Cesar C^r by ½ fox   £ 0 4 - 0

And on December 18, 1745, *two* Caesars, Caesar who belonged to Widow Wells[17] (and later to Timothy Childs, Jr.) and Caesar who belonged to Ebenezer Wells, paid for some of their purchases at the same time.

Cesar Wid^o Wells and En^s Wells
    C^r by 2 foxes

Most interesting, though, is Caesar's purchase of a psalm book.

May 10, 1756   Ens Wells D^r To 1 psalm Book (Cesar)

Together with Lucy's purchases of paper, this suggests that perhaps Ebenezer Wells or his wife, Abigail, had taught both Lucy and Caesar to read.

It is fortunate that we know so much about the life of Lucy Terry, especially of her life after slavery, her marriage, and her family. But there is a curious downside to her inspiring story and the fact that we know so much about her. Modern tourists who visit "Old Deerfield" and take guided tours of the historic houses that line the street may leave town without having heard a word about the many black slaves who lived there in the 1700s. If they do hear about slavery, it often happens that

---

16 Account books of Elijah Williams, PVMA Library.
17 "Widow Wells", Mary Hoyt Wells, was the widow of Jonathan Wells, Jr., a first cousin of Lucy and Caesar's owner, Ebenezer Wells.

they hear *only* about Lucy. But this is even more misleading than hearing nothing at all. Lucy's life was far from typical. Lucy learned to read, became free, was happily married, and had six children. Her life is especially unusual in that we know so much about it. For a visitor to leave thinking that, curiously, there was *one* black slave who lived in Deerfield – a slave who became literate,[18] composed a poem, became free, had a marriage and a family and died in freedom, and about whom we know so much – gives a completely false picture of colonial Deerfield and further obscures the existence of the many other slaves for whom none of those things is true. It is disappointing that we know so little about Lucy's fellow slave, Caesar, who has, so to speak, lived for years in her shadow.[19] And Caesar is just one of many such Deerfield slaves, most of them now almost hidden from view.

---

18 Gerzina observes that in the years shortly after their marriage, Lucy and Abijah Prince purchased a "secretary's guide" and several primers – probably to help their children learn to read. (Gerzina (2008), pp. 99-100, 107, 123, 227.) See also the account books of Elijah Williams, PVMA Library.

19 In Proper's book about Lucy, there is just one sentence about Caesar – "[Ebenezer Wells] was evidently well off, and owner of two slaves: Cesar, about whom little is known, and Lucy." (Proper (1997), p. 10.)

Prince (– 1752)
Property of Joseph Barnard (1717–1785)

Prince (not to be confused with Abijah Prince, Deerfield's one free black) belonged to Joseph Barnard and lived on the site now occupied by the house called "The Manse", the official residence of Deerfield Academy's head of school. (Parts of the structure that were on this site in Prince's time remain, but the house has been extensively remodeled and enlarged since the 1700s.[1])

In the early 1740s, Prince belonged to Dr. Thomas Wells.[2] In May 1741, for instance, Joseph Barnard rented Prince from Wells to clear some land.[3] Then on May 27, 1743, Barnard purchased Prince from Dr. Wells.

> then Bought of Doct Wells his Negro fellow at £160

Barnard soon began renting Prince to others. In July of that year, for instance, Barnard rented him to Samuel Bardwell for "one Day to reep".

Two years later, after the death of Doctor Wells, Barnard bought from "Widow Wells" the bed and other items that Prince had used.

> then Reckn[d] With Wi[d] Sarah Wells and Ball all acct[s] including prince[s] Bed & Bedsted and Cord and a Blankit and there is Due to her 60/
>
> W[d] Sarah Wells Cr by y[e] old Blankit of princes 1-0-0

Barnard also purchased clothes for Prince from time to time. In May, 1744, he paid tailor Samuel Childs for a coat for Prince.

> pd Sam[l] Childs Jun[r] For Cuting Prince[s] Coat & Brushes & Other things

And in 1746 he paid Jonathan Taylor for "a pair of Shoes for Prince".

Prince, like many other Deerfield slaves, occasionally bought small

---

1 McGowan and Miller (1996), pp. 159-160.

2 There was more than one Thomas Wells living in Deerfield at about this time. Another Thomas Wells (a first cousin of Prince's first owner), who died in 1750, was an owner of several slaves, including Peter. We will have more to say later about Peter, who had become the property of Thomas Dickinson by 1752.

3 Information in this section on Barnard's payments and income comes from his own account books. Information about the medical treatments of Prince comes from the account books of Dr. Thomas Williams, and the entries showing the debts that Barnard incurred for Prince's shoe repairs come from the account book of Ebenezer Arms. (PVMA Library.)

items from Deerfield merchants, as indicated, for instance, by the following account book entries[4] –

Prince D^r to a knife	0 – 3 – 6
to a pocket book	0 – 3 – 6
to a pair of Sleave buttons	0 – 1 – 6
to 1 pair D^o	0 – 1 – 6

When Thomas Wells died on March 7, 1743/44, his widow, Sarah, rented Prince from Barnard to dig a grave for her husband, Prince's previous owner.

Mr^s Sarah Wells to Prince digging a grave

In subsequent years, Barnard received income from Prince's grave digging skills on at least four other occasions, but it is only for Wells that I have identified an existing gravestone. Thomas Wells' gravestone

Gravestone of Thomas Wells near the southwest corner of the Deerfield burying ground. Here in March, 1743/44 Prince dug the grave of his former owner. (Author's photograph.)

---

4 Account book of Elijah Williams and David Field, PVMA Library.

can still be seen in the old Deerfield burying ground with the following epitaph.[5]

> Here lyes Buried the Body
> of Doct^r THOMAS WELLS
> Who Departed this Life
> March the 7th Anno Dom
> 1743 in ye 51 Year
> of His Age.

Barnard rented Prince to many Deerfield residents, including store owner Elijah Williams and Reverend Jonathan Ashley, both of whom owned slaves of their own. Tasks that Prince performed while working for others included mowing, sowing peas and oats, fanning flax seed, mending fence, "making a bridge", and spreading dung.

Toward the end of May, 1744 Barnard charged the town of Deerfield sixteen shillings for "Myself & Prince a Day to Scoare timber for the Mounts". Then a few days later, Barnard spent a day working on the mounts without Prince ("a Days Work at the Mounts, my selfe"), for which he charged the town eight shillings. (He apparently put the same value, eight shillings, on a day's work by Prince and on a day of his own.)

What were these "mounts"? From the time of King Philip's War (1675-76) when Indian uprisings throughout New England devastated many English settlements until 1763 when the Treaty of Paris was signed and the French finally relinquished control of Canada to the English, there was scarcely a moment when Deerfield was free from the threat of attack by Indians or the combined forces of French and Indians. In 1744, the town's citizens, feeling that their defenses needed strengthening, voted to build several "mounts" or "watch towers" at several sites in town. Sheldon writes that "Mounts were primarily square towers with a strong post at each corner, built for watch boxes. I find them from fourteen to forty feet high, according to location. The top story, about eight or ten feet square, was usually planked and made a bullet-proof sentry box." One such site was at Reverend Ashley's house, at the north end of

---

5 The epitaph on Wells' gravestone reads "March the 7th Anno Dom 1743". Before 1752, both January 1 and March 25 were, for different purposes, considered as the dates on which a new year began. With the former choice, it was already 1744; using March 25, it was still 1743. See Appendix II for more explanation of this calendar problem, the confusion that it can cause, and the dual-year way of writing dates between January 1 and March 25.

the street, looking out toward the meadows across which the French and Indians had attacked in 1704.[6]

Joseph's uncle, Samuel Barnard, originally lived in Deerfield but moved to Salem about 1720, where he became quite wealthy.[7] Samuel owned a slave, Titus,[8] and also – it appears from Joseph Barnard's account books – another slave, Pompey. Samuel still owned property in the Deerfield area and sent Titus and Pompey to Deerfield for long periods of time, where they apparently lived with Joseph. Joseph kept track of the work that Titus and Pompey did for his uncle, as well as of the work they did on his own property. Prince, too, often worked on Uncle Samuel's property, sometimes along with Joseph, his owner.

One can see in the account books of Joseph Barnard some of the complexities that arose in the transactions between Deerfield residents, especially when the labor of slaves was being exchanged. In 1741 Barnard was renting Prince *from* Thomas Wells, and soon thereafter he bought Prince, then rented him back to his former owner's widow to dig her husband's grave. Joseph provided room and board and purchased some clothing for Titus and Pompey, slaves who belonged to his uncle Samuel and worked on Samuel's property in and near Deerfield. Samuel had to reimburse Joseph for those expenses. And, on occasion, Barnard in effect rented *himself* out, along with Prince, as when he and Prince together worked for Barnard's uncle Samuel or "scoared timber" for the town's watch towers. Joseph presumably had to supervise the work done by Titus and Pompey, even when they were working on Samuel's property. At the same time, Joseph sometimes rented Titus and Pompey *from* his uncle to do work on his own property, even while they were living in Joseph's Deerfield house. Meanwhile, Barnard was renting his own slave, Prince, to many others – including the town of Deerfield. And occasionally there were what appear to have been private transactions with slaves who belonged to others. In 1749, for instance, Barnard reported – "Paid Peter Negro for Cabling one acre oats." To top it all off, Deerfield residents occasionally squared their accounts with one another with cash but often with goods ("two bushels wheat", for instance), or with work by one of their own slaves. Truly an accountant's nightmare.

---

6 Sheldon (1895), pp. 529-530; Miller (1962), p. 16.

7 Sheldon (1895), Genealogy Section, p. 66.

8 Sheldon (1895), p. 896.

On April 20, 1749 (and then again on May 7) Dr. Williams charged Barnard four shillings to "Phleb. Prince". We know that Prince survived Dr. Williams' phlebotomies, for one of the most interesting things about Prince is that later that year he ran away. Joseph Barnard offered a reward for his return, placing a notice in the *Boston Weekly Post-Boy* that appeared for several weeks in the fall of 1749. (This is one of only two known "runaway notices" for a Deerfield slave.)

R AN-away from his Mafter, *Jofeph Barnard* of *Deerfield* a Negro Man named *Prince*, of middling Stature, hisComplection not the darkeft or lighteft for a Negro, flow of Speech, but fpeaks good Englifh ; He had with him when he went away, an old brown Coat, with Pewter Buttons, a double-breafted blue Coat with a Cape, and flat metal Buttons, a brown great Coat with red Cuffs and Cape, a new brown Jacket with PewterButtons, a Pair of new LeatherBreeches check'd linnenShirt andTroufers, tow fhirt andTroufers, a redCap, two CaftorHats, feveral Pair of Stockings, aPair of Pumps, aGun andViolin. Whoever fhall apprehend faid Fellow and convey him to his Mefter, fhall have *Ten Pounds* old Tenor, and all neceffary Charges paid by
Deerfield, Sept. 18, 1749. *Jofeph Barnard*
All Mafters of Veffels and others are caution'd not to conceal or carry off the faid Negro, as they would avoid the Penalty of the Law.

Boston Weekly Post-Boy   October 16, 1749.
(Courtesy of the American Antiquarian Society.)

Ran-away from his Master, Joseph Barnard of Deerfield a Negro Man named Prince, of middling Stature, his Complection not the darkest or lightest for a Negro, slow of Speech, but speaks good English; He had with him when he went away, an old brown Coat, with Pewter Buttons, a double-breasted blue Coat with a Cape, and flat metal Buttons, a brown great Coat with red Cuffs and Cape, a new brown Jacket with Pewter Buttons, a Pair of new Leather Breeches check'd linnen Shirt and Trousers, tow shirt and Trousers, a red Cap, two Castor Hats, several Pair of Stockings, a Pair of Pumps, a Gun and Violin. Whoever shall apprehend said Fellow and convey him to his Master, shall have Ten Pounds old Tenor, and all necessary Charges paid by
Deerfield, Sept. 18, 1749   Joseph Barnard
All Masters of Vessels and others are caution'd not to conceal or carry off the said Negro, as they would avoid the Penalty of the Law.
Boston Weekly Post-Boy   *October 16, 1749*

The idea that because northern slaves were in close contact with their owners ("just like members of the family"), living under the same roof, often working alongside their owners rather than under an overseer on some distant plantation, they were especially contented and happy with their lot is surely belied by the example of Prince. Not only did Prince probably live in the same house as his owner, but on page after page of Barnard's account books we read about the many occasions on which Prince and Barnard worked side by side all day long.

Yet Prince ran away. We do not know why he ran away, where he went, or where he was trying to go. But Prince was extremely well dressed when he escaped! He was probably hoping to acquire some cash for the extra clothing and the gun, perhaps to earn some money with the violin. Freedom-seeking slaves had a much greater chance of making good their escape if they lived closer to port cities such as Boston. The wording at the end of the advertisement, warning "masters of vessels not to conceal or carry off the said Negro" was a standard part of such notices.

Prince's attempt to escape did not succeed. We do not know how or when he was recaptured. Barnard's advertisement appeared in the *Post-Boy* not just once but in several issues, from September 25 to October 16. This may indicate that Prince was free for some time. He was recaptured, though, and once again he appears in Deerfield account books, as Barnard continued to rent Prince to others. In July, 1750, for example, Barnard charged the town for work that he and Prince did together.

> myself & prince a Day at the high way in the Street

And during the following year, Barnard had Prince's shoes repaired on several occasions. In February, 1750/51 shoemaker Ebenezer Arms charged "Ensign Barnard" for repairing Prince's shoes.

> Ens^n Barnard D^r to Soleing & Caping Princes Shoes 0-2-4

In October of that year, Arms again charged Barnard for shoe repairs.

> Ens^n Barnard D^r To mending y^r negros Shoes   0-0-4

And in December he repaired Prince's high-top shoes.

> Ens^n Barnard D^r to y^r Negros Hi^{tp} Shoes 0-7-9

The conclusion of the story of Prince's life in Deerfield is marked by an entry in Barnard's account book for June, 1752, showing that Barnard hired James Couch, a Deerfield carpenter, to build "a Coffen for Prince". Prince had dug several graves for white residents of Deerfield. Who dug a grave for Prince? And where was it? In spite of the voluminous entries in Barnard's account books, the dozens of times that Prince's name appears there, no one knows the answers to these questions.

"Negro Female"
Property of David Field (1712-1792)

In July, 1749, Dr. Williams treated a "Negroe" belonging to David Field.[1]

> July 12th   1749   David Field Dr to [?] [?] 3 / for y[r] Negroe

And the following winter Dr. Williams charged Field five shillings to treat his "Negro Female", probably the same person, extracting a tooth.

> March 14   1749/50   To Ext. Dent. y[r] Neg. Fem. 5/

I have not been able to find any other evidence of this woman's existence.

---

1 Account books of Dr. Thomas Williams, PVMA Library.

Caesar and Mesheck
Property of Ebenezer Hinsdale (1707-1763)

Caesar, like a number of other Deerfield slaves, served in the French and Indian War in the 1750s.[1] There is also evidence of Caesar's presence in the account books of Deerfield merchants. In 1750, for instance, Hinsdale[2] was charged by Ebenezer Arms for making shoes for Caesar.[3]

> 10 Dec 1750   Cor[ll] Hinsdell D[r] to making Cesars shoes   0-2-8

He also appears in Elijah Williams' account books, making a number of purchases of small items at the Williams store.[4] On October 31, 1753, for instance, we read in Williams' account book –

> Cesar   Col Hinsdells negro   a pair of Shoe Buckels

But beyond the mentions of his war service, his shoes, and his store purchases, there is no further record of Caesar's existence – no mention in a will, estate inventory, church record, or bill of sale.

Mesheck, also a slave of Hinsdale's in 1752, was frequently moved around town during his time in Deerfield, belonging to four different owners. First he belonged to Reverend John Williams, who acquired him sometime after returning from his own captivity among the French and Indians after the famous 1704 attack on Deerfield. When Williams died in 1729, "the molatto Boy Meseck" was listed in Williams' probate inventory, along with various household items.[5]

the molatto Boy Meseck	80-00-00
a Box 2[s] a trunk 7[s]	00-09-00
a chest 5[s] ditto 4[s]	00-09-00
a Small trunk at 2[s]	00-02-00
twelve pewter plates, & a brass Server	00-19-00
Hay, indian corn, peas, barley and flax	41-05-00

---

1 Sheldon (1895), p. 894.
2 Hinsdale, Hinsdell, and other variations. Ebenezer changed his name for business purposes from Hinsdell to Hinsdale in 1749. (Sheldon (1895), Genealogy Section, p. 204.)
3 Account book of Ebenezer Arms, PVMA Library. *Cor* [ll](*Cor..ll*) is an abbreviation for *Colonel*.
4 Account books of Elijah Williams, PVMA Library.
5 Hampshire County Registry of Probate.

Mesheck then became the property of Williams' daughter Sarah, who died at an early age in February, 1737. Town gossips said that she had expected to marry the new minister, Jonathan Ashley, but "died of a broken heart" when he married someone else.[6] Doctor Crouch of Hadley treated Sarah on several occasions in the mid-1730s, though not explicitly for a broken heart. His records show charges for "hysteric pills", "accompanied purging mixture", "Blister salve, &c", and treatment for a "Bleeding foot".[7]

There is a curious note, apparently referring to Mesheck, at the end of Sarah's estate inventory.[8]

Mem there is a molatto fellow belonged to the S^d Dec^d or Something Else in Lieu of him.

Mesheck then passed into the possession of another Williams daughter, Abigail, who had married Ebenezer Hinsdale a few years earlier, and thus Mesheck became Hinsdale's property. (When a woman married, all her property – slaves included – automatically became that of her husband.) Abigail, who outlived three husbands, returned to Deerfield many years later as Mrs. Silliman, owning further slaves in her own right and freeing her slave Chloe at the time of her death in 1787. Mrs. Silliman's will, written in 1785, will be discussed in the Addendum to this chapter.

Hinsdale had business affairs at two places, not only in Deerfield but also just over the border in southern New Hampshire, in the town now called Hinsdale. Mesheck was entrusted with significant responsibilities by his owner. Sheldon reports that when Hinsdale was occupied at one location, Mesheck was in charge of Hinsdale's business at the other. And Mesheck, like so many other Deerfield slaves, made occasional purchases at Elijah Williams' store in Deerfield.[9]

Mesheck was baptized by Reverend Ashley in January, 1747/48,

Janry 31. 1747   Baptized Mesheck Servant to Mr Ebenezer Hinsdell

---

6 Sheldon (1895), Genealogy Section, p. 378; Miller (1962), p. 12. Reverend Ashley married another Williams, Dorothy Williams, daughter of William Williams, Hatfield's longtime minister, and Sarah's second cousin. Williamses, almost all related to one another, were ubiquitous in the valley.
7 Judd Manuscripts, Forbes Library. (Judd's notes on Dr. Crouch's accounts.)
8 Hampshire County Registry of Probate.
9 Sheldon (1895), p. 891.

and on the same day "Admitted to Full Communion" in the church.[10]

A year later, Mesheck was summoned into court to answer the charge by Peter Evans of Northfield that he had stolen a mare belonging to Evans and, by mistreatment, had caused the horse's death. Mesheck was represented by an attorney, Mr. Joseph Hawley. Whether any witnesses were called in the case of *Evans v. Mesheck* is not clear from the record.[11]

> At a Court of General Sessions of the Peace and Inferiour Court of Common Pleas begun and held at Northampton within and for the County of Hampshire on the second Tuesday of February being the 14th day of Said Month, Anno Domini 1748 ... Peter Evans Jun[r] of Northfield in y[e] County of hamsphire husbandman pl[tf] vs Mesheck a Molatto Servant of Ebenezer Hinsdells Esq of Deerfield which said Mesheck commonly dwells at the fort called Hinsdells Fort at y[e] place called the Cellars in y[e] Province of New Hampshire & is Employed in husbandry. De[ft] in a plea of Trespass upon y[e] Case and Whereupon y[e] pl[tf] says that on or about y[e] 15th day of July last past at a place called Hinsdells Fort at y[e] Cellars in Northfield afores[d] y[e] p[tf] was possessed of a large Bay mare 14 hands high about ten years old ... worth £23 money as of his proper Estate & y[e] Def[t] then and there without leave from y[e] pl[tf] took y[e] said mare knowing her to belong to y[e] pl[tf] and did put a halter upon her & put her into a Stable & with disign to injure y[e] p[tf] then tied her with a halter up to a bar of y[e] Stable in such manner that by frighting and beating & other ways vexing said Mare y[e] Def[t] caused her to break her Neck by means whereof y[e] said Mare died immediately and y[e] p[tf] hath Entirely lost y[e] Said mare by y[e] malefeasance of y[e] Def[t] ...

Neither Mesheck's plea of not guilty nor his attorney's arguments were persuasive to the jury, who found him guilty and ordered him assessed damages of £15 new tenor and costs. It seems likely that the assessed damages and costs, as well as the fee charged by attorney Joseph Hawley, were eventually paid by Mesheck's owner, Ebenezer Hinsdale.

---

10 Deerfield minister's record book, PVMA Library. The minister's records treated the new year as beginning on March 25, so a date of "January 31, 1747" is one that we can write in dual-year notation as "January 31, 1747/48" (a Sunday).

11 Hampshire County, Massachusetts Courts. Common Pleas/General Sessions. Court records, too, generally treated March 25 as the beginning of a new year, so the date of the court case could also be written as "February 14, 1748/49" (a Tuesday).

Ishmael
Property of Samuel Hinsdell (1708-1786)

Samuel Hinsdell, who lived at the north end of the street, just beyond his older brother Ebenezer Hinsdale (owner of Caesar and Mesheck) and across the street from Reverend Ashley, had an account with Dr. Thomas Williams, who charged him 4 shillings on May 27, 1749 for bloodletting a slave.[1]

To Phleb. Your Negroe 4/

On several occasions during 1751 Ebenezer Arms charged Hinsdell for repairing or making Ishmael's shoes.[2]

August 1751	Samuel Hinsdell D[r] To Soleing y[r] Negros Shoes 0 – 0 – 8
September 1751	Samuel Hinsdell D[r] To making y[r] negro Shoes 0 – 2 – 8
November 1751	Samuel Hinsdell D[r] To y[r] Wifes Shoes & y[r] negros Shoes 0 - 12 -0

Ishmael also made purchases at Elijah Williams' store, for instance buying "vest buttons" in December, 1751.[3]

Ishmael Negro Sam[el] Hinsdells Servant D[r] to 20 vest Buttons [?] 5/

No other information about Ishmael is known to have survived.

---

1 Account books of Dr. Thomas Williams, PVMA Library.
2 Account book of Ebenezer Arms, PVMA Library.
3 Account books of Elijah Williams, PVMA Library.

Jenny (ca.1722-1808), Cato (1738-1825), and Titus (1725-)
Property of Jonathan Ashley (1712-1780)

Now Historic Deerfield's "Ashley House", this house was home to Jenny and Cato for much of the 18th century and to Titus during the 1750s. Originally built in 1734 and remodeled in the late 1700s, the house was moved to another site and converted into a barn in 1869 but returned to its original site and restored in the 1940s. (Author's photograph.)

It seems appropriate to treat these three Deerfield slaves together. Jenny was Cato's mother, and a great deal of what we know about Titus comes from his appearances together with Cato in their owner's account book. Jenny, according to Sheldon, was born in Africa ("a native of Guinea") about 1722.[1] "By the tale she always told, she was daughter of a king in Congo, and when about twelve years old, she was one day

---

[1] All references to Sheldon in this section, unless otherwise noted, are to the "Negro Slavery" section of his book. (Sheldon (1895), pp. 888-905.) "Guinea" was sometimes used as a generic reference to Africa, sometimes it had a more specific meaning. ("Guineaman" was a common term for a slave ship.)

playing with other children about a well, when they were pounced upon by a gang of white villains, and the whole party were seized and hurried on board a slave ship, 'and we nebber see our mudders any more'." "Three or four years after being kidnapped," she was bought at Boston by Reverend Ashley and brought to Deerfield "with a baby [Cato] in her arms".

Think about that quotation – "We nebber see our mudders any more." This is oral tradition, not a document, just words passed down from one person to another in Deerfield and eventually to historian George Sheldon who wrote them down a century later. "Just words." Who can tell how accurately the words represent what Jenny actually said, whether "nebber" and "mudders" correspond to her pronunciation? But even with those reservations, this is Jenny, speaking to us from over two hundred years ago!

When Sheldon was a young boy, he actually knew Cato, who lived next door.

> Cato was the one Deerfield slave of whom I have a personal recollection, although he died when I was six years old. I recall seeing him when "dunging out", use his hands instead of a shovel.[2] It was probably the oddity of it that made this lasting impression, or it may have been his feeble tottering footsteps. I remember seeing him often sitting on a bench in an outhouse, where he would spend hours singing in a gruff voice the famous ballad of Captain Kidd, drumming an accompaniment with both hands on the board at either side; his finger nails were long and thick and each one gave a blow which sounded like the stroke of a tack hammer. Solomon, son of Parson Ashley, was a fine dancer, and Cato a fervent admirer of his skill, tried to imitate his steps. His practice was usually on the barn floor, and sometimes he was seen with a switch whipping his legs, "to make um go like Massa Solomon's." Cato was very fond of horses, and was a furious rider when he could indulge his passion unobserved. If caught, he would protest that the horse ran away with him. "Couldn't stop um nohow, Massa." Another favorite seat of Cato's was in the kitchen chimney corner, where he could get the full benefit of the blazing fire, which he would enjoy like a salamander. Col. T. W. Ashley, his latest "Massa," was one of the earliest to substitute a cooking stove for the fireplace. Cato was disgusted with this change and was always cold after it. The big, black pile of iron yielded no warmth or comfort to *him*. He would hug the stove and sweat and shiver, and shiver and sweat, till he could

---

2 "Dunging out" – Spreading ground with dung (manure).

stand it no longer; then he would go into the room of Madam Ashley, widow of the doctor, to warm himself at her blazing fire. Seeing was believing with him.[3]

We do not know from whom Ashley bought Jenny and Cato. No bill of sale survives, and my own inquiries in Boston have not been successful. The fact that Jenny – like Lucy Terry – was purchased in Boston is interesting, because surviving bills of sale suggest that it was more likely for western Massachusetts slaves to be purchased from farther down the Connecticut River – from Middletown or Windsor, Connecticut, for instance. Perhaps it was in response to an advertisement of the following sort in a Boston newspaper that Ashley found the young woman and child he decided to purchase.[4]

> To be Sold at publick Vendue by Ephraim Baker on Thursday the 9th of March, at 3'o Clock Afternoon at the House in which Mr. John Darvill lately dwelt in Union Street, at the Head of the Town Dock, Boston, viz. One large Iron Grate, seven 8 Garlixs, Nuns Hollands, Holland Tapes, Sheeting Hollands, Cutlery Ware, Brushes of all Sorts. Mens White and Colour'd Gloves, Figs, Raisons Saddles, Looking Glasses, Broad Cloths, Druggets, Callimancoes, Silk Stuffs, Earthen Ware, Hungary, Anchoves, diverse sorts of Men's Wearing Apparel with other sorts of Goods, also a very valuable Collection of Books; all which are to be seen at the Place abovementioned, where Attendance is constantly given to shew the same.
>
> N.B. Any Person that wants to purchase a fine likely Negro Wench about 22 Years old, and a Child about Four Years old, may hear of them by enquiring of the abovesaid Ephraim Baker
>
> *New-England Weekly Journal*   March 7, 1738

Could this perhaps be the very advertisement that led to the arrival of Jenny and Cato in Deerfield? Sheldon writes that Jenny was purchased in Boston at about the time of the death of the Ashleys' firstborn child, who died on March 17, 1737/38[5], just about the time that

---

3 Jonathan Ashley died in 1780, and his son Elihu (1750-1817), "the doctor", moved into the house and became responsible for Jonathan's slaves, Jenny and Cato. After Elihu's death, it was Elihu's son, Thomas W. Ashley (1776-1848), a "Colonel of Cavalry in the Massachusetts Militia", who lived in the house and was Cato's "Massa" until Cato's death in 1825. (Sheldon (1895), Genealogy Section, p. 49.)

4 Most newspapers, including the *New-England Weekly Journal*, treated January 1 as the date of New Year's Day. In dual-year notation, the date of publication would have been written as "March 7, 1737/38".

5 Sheldon (1895), Genealogy Section, p. 48.

this advertisement appeared in the *New-England Weekly Journal*. With minor modifications in some obviously approximate statements made by Sheldon and by the auctioneer, Ephraim Baker, this advertisement fits the facts rather well.[6] But, interesting though it is to speculate, in the absence of evidence such as a bill of sale or the account books of auctioneer Ephraim Baker, it is impossible to definitively tie this particular advertisement to Ashley's purchase of Jenny and Cato.

Whether as a one-year old or possibly at age four or five, Cato was baptized by Reverend Ashley in 1739. In the list of baptisms in the minister's record book, we read[7] –

> 1739   Aug 19   Cato Serv. Jona Ashley Rev

The fact that Cato was baptized in 1739 does not by itself tell us anything about his age – many Deerfield slaves were baptized as adults. Jenny was never baptized, at least not in Deerfield – she may very well have been baptized by a previous owner in Boston.

There are only three surviving documents from Jenny's time that refer to her. One is Ashley's 1780 will, which includes this memorable sentence.[8]

> I give, devise, & bequeath to my beloved Wife Dorothy Ashley; my Riding Chair, my Grey Mare, two Cows & ten Sheep, also my Easy Chair, all the Silver Utensils which She brought with her at our Marriage, my

---

6 My estimate of a birth date of "about 1722" for Jenny is based on Sheldon's statements that Jenny was "about twelve" when kidnapped in Africa and that Ashley bought her "three or four years" after the time she was captured, together with the statement that the purchase date was 1738. Those statements ("about twelve" and "three or four years") are obviously estimates. And attributing a birth date of 1738 to Cato is based on Sheldon's description of Jenny arriving in Deerfield "with a baby in her arms". When Jenny died in 1808, her age was estimated at ninety, implying approximately 1718 as her date of birth. We need only change Jenny's date of birth from "about 1722" to "about 1718" and suppose that Cato was not a newborn baby but a little boy of three or four to make it quite plausible that it was this advertisement that led to the purchase of Jenny and Cato. (Sheldon used the phrase "with a baby in her arms", but he really had no precise information about Cato's age.) Remember, too, that auctioneer Ephraim Baker was only estimating the ages of the "fine likely Negro Wench" and her child when he composed that advertisement. (Piersen assigns to Jenny a birth date of 1703. He gives no reason for this choice, and that date would make Jenny 105 at the time of her death in 1808. He also gives an incorrect date, 1828, for the death of Cato, who actually died in 1825. (Piersen (1988), pp. 75-76.))

7 Deerfield minister's record book, PVMA Library.

8 Hampshire County Registry of Probate.

Part of Jonathan Ashley's 1780 will, including the sentence by which Jenny was left to his wife, Dorothy. (Hampshire County Registry of Probate.)

Negro Woman Servant Jenny - and also one half of all my Household Furniture to be to my said Wife to her Use & Behoof forever, excepting however the Beds and Linnen, which my Daughters, Elisabeth and Charissa have made, which Beds and Linnen I do hereby give & bequeath to my said Daughters to be equally divided between them.

The second is the record of the accounts of Zadock Hawks, a Deerfield shoemaker, showing that on several occasions Jonathan Ashley and later Elihu, Jonathan's son, paid to have Jenny's shoes repaired.

(Hawks apparently could never make up his mind about the spelling of Jenny's name.)[9]

Feb 1763	To mending Gins shoes	$0 - 6 - 6$
Nov 1763	To a pair of shoes for Jeni	$1 - 10 - 0$
Oct[r] 1788	D[r] Elihu Ashley To mending Jins Shoes	$- 1 -$

And last is an item from the death records. In the 1700s, deaths of Deerfield slaves were not even recorded, but by 1800 deaths of black residents, *former* slaves, did receive official mention. When Jenny died in 1808, her death was listed as[10] –

Jenny   Negro   90

Sheldon refers to Jenny variously as Jenny, Jinny, or Jin.[11] Since the two most "official" of the surviving documents, the will and the death record, call her "Jenny", I consider that to be her "real name". Or rather, since we will never know the name given to her by her parents, Jenny is now the most appropriate name by which to refer to her. "Jinny" is simply a variation, as is "Jeni", and "Jin" and "Gin" I consider to be abbreviations or nicknames. I have heard the claim that "Jin" was actually Jenny's birth name, her African given name – in the absence of evidence, this can only be regarded as speculation.

One mystery associated with Jenny and Cato is the surname that Sheldon gives them – Jenny *Cole* and Cato *Cole*.[12] None of the contemporary documents use *Cole*. Who was Cole? Who was Cato's father? And who was Jenny's previous owner? Perhaps Jenny's previous owner was Mr. Cole, and possibly Mr. Cole was *also* Cato's father. Sheldon provides no explanation of the name *Cole*, though it may be that among the many boxes of Sheldon notes and correspondence in the Deerfield library there is an answer to be found. The printed volume of Deerfield vital records lists Jenny and Cato with that surname, but the compilers

---

9 Hawks often charged Reverend Ashley for repairing shoes for Cato and Titus as well as for Jenny, not to mention those of Ashley family members. Shoemakers Ebenezer Arms and Joseph Stebbins did a variety of shoe repair work for Cato, Titus, and members of the Ashley family, but not – apparently – for Jenny. (Account books of Zadock Hawks, Ebenezer Arms, and Joseph Stebbins – PVMA Library.)

10 Deerfield minister's record book, PVMA Library. In the church records, this appears as – "Jenny a black woman   killed by a fall 90".

11 Sheldon (1895), p. 896 and Genealogy Section, p. 129.

12 Ibid.

of those records, published in 1920, many years after the publication of Sheldon's history, had access to his book, and they give no indication of any other source for that information.[13]

Jonathan Ashley died in 1780, and both his widow, Dorothy Ashley, and Jenny lived on in Deerfield for twenty-eight years, Jonathan's son Elihu now being head of the household. (Jonathan, I think, was not an easy person to live with.[14] I suspect that for both Dorothy and Jenny, those were the happiest twenty-eight years of their lives.) Slavery had surely come to an end in Massachusetts by 1800. Did anyone ever tell Jenny that she was now free? Would she have cared? Sheldon writes that only a few weeks before Jenny and Dorothy died, a neighbor found them "sitting together busily engaged in sewing, and chatting merrily over their work like children making dresses for their dolls". Jenny died in 1808, followed only a few weeks later by Dorothy. Dorothy Ashley has a gravestone in the old Deerfield burying ground, right next to Jonathan's.[15] But where Jenny was buried, whether her grave was marked with an impermanent wooden marker or not marked at all, no one knows.[16]

Even for information about Jenny's life in Deerfield we must depend primarily on speculation. The Ashleys had six children who survived beyond infancy (born between 1739 and 1757), so Jenny almost certainly helped to take care of the children. But we are left to wonder about the nature of her interaction with Reverend Ashley and the other members of the family, with the other slaves in Deerfield. Did Jenny, for example, have a love life during her long years in Deerfield?

Sheldon writes that Jenny "fully expected at death, or before, to be transported back to Guinea; and all her long life she was gathering, as treasures to take back to her motherland, all kinds of odds and ends,

---

13 *Vital Records of Deerfield* (1920).

14 Whether Jonathan was even partially to blame or not, Dorothy Ashley was subject to severe depression during her later life and apparently made at least two suicide attempts during the 1770s. See Miller (1962), pp. 29-30; Sheldon (1895), p. 743; Miller and Riggs (2007), pp. 5, 23, 298.

15 Look for it next to that of Jonathan, the tallest surviving gravestone in the entire burying ground.

16 A gravestone was something of a luxury item, and many less affluent whites were buried without a stone to mark the site. There are no gravestones for slaves in the Deerfield burying ground. There are almost certainly more graves than gravestones, and slaves and others may have been buried there, perhaps in the northeast corner of the burying ground where there are few gravestones. There may be gravestones for slaves in the Connecticut Valley but very few.

colored rags, bits of finery, peculiar shaped stones, shells, buttons, beads, *anything* she could *string"*. Apparently Jenny passed on this tradition to her son, for Cato, as well as Jenny, writes Sheldon, "gathered trinkets to provide for his translation,[17] his most valued possessions being brass or copper buttons". Cato, too, lived on with the Ashley family, dying in 1825, his death – like that of his mother – being entered in the town records.[18]

There was a third Ashley slave, Titus, bought as a young man in 1750 from Samuel Kendall, minister at New Salem.[19]

> Know all men by these presents that I Samuel Kendall of New Salem So called in the County of Hampshire & province of the Massachusetts Bay in New England clerk[20] for and in Consideration of the Sum of fifty three pounds Six Shillings and Eight pence to me in hand paid by M[r] Jonathan Ashley of Deerfield in the County & Province aforesaid have Sold assigned Set over & Delivered to him the Said Ashley a Certain Negro Man Named Titus aged about twenty five years of a Sound Constitution to have & to hold to him the Said Ashley his heirs & assigns During the term of his Natural life and I do hereby oblige my Self my heirs & do warrant Secure & Defend to him the Said Ashley his heirs & Assigns the Said Negro against the Claims & Demands of any person or persons what Soever. In witness whereof I have hereunto Set my hand & Seal this twenty ninth Day of May Annoque Domini 1750
>
> Signed Sealed & Delivered,
>
> Sam[l] Kendall

And a note at the bottom of this bill of sale records Ashley's sale of Titus ten years later, in 1760.

> This may Certify that I the Subscriber Do assign & Deliver the above mentioned Negro man Titus to be his property During the term of his Natural life to M[r] Elijah Williams of Stockbridge as witness my hand this Third day of January 1760.
>
> Jonathan Ashley

---

17 "His translation", i.e., his eventual journey to his ancestral home in Africa.

18 Deerfield minister's record book, PVMA Library.

19 Dwight Collection, Norman Rockwell Museum, Stockbridge, Massachusetts (Hampshire/Franklin County Papers #22).

20 *Clerk* or *clerc* – "A man ordained to the ministry or service of the Christian Church; a churchman, clergyman, or ecclesiastic. For greater distinction, cleric is now often substituted." (*Oxford English Dictionary*.)

Cato spent virtually his entire life in Deerfield, while Titus only belonged to Ashley for a decade. About the daily lives of Cato and Titus during the 1750s, we do know quite a bit, thanks to the preservation of Jonathan Ashley's account book.[21] Ashley was a farmer as well as a minister and surely Cato and Titus did farm work for Ashley, but what we learn from the account book is that Ashley frequently rented Cato and Titus to other Deerfield men – and that he received a fairly steady income from these rentals. One of the many Deerfield residents to whom Ashley rented Cato and Titus was Deerfield's one free black, who appears in Ashley's account book sometimes as "Abijah Prince" but sometimes as "Abijah Negro".[22]

Ashley rented Cato and Titus to many others besides Abijah Prince. From the entries in Ashley's account book, we can learn about the variety of agricultural work that Cato and Titus did. Sometimes the notations are simply "1 Days work" or "½ Day", but often the kind of work done is shown, including thrashing, milking cows, husking, mowing, mowing bushes, dressing flax, pulling flax, spreading flax, ploughing, cutting wood, sugaring, hoeing, harrowing, killing hogs, planting, reaping oats, picking corn, and clearing land.

Ashley also occasionally used the labor of Cato and Titus to settle some of his own debts. In the account books of Dr. Williams we find various Ashley "payments" of this sort.[23]

September 20, 1758	Titus's Mowing
April 4, 1759	Titus & Cato ½ Day Cutting Wood
November 28, 1759	Cato Fetching a Load of Pine from Cheapside
July 21, 1766	Catos reaping 1 Day

In December, 1759, according to a paragraph in Ashley's account book – "I agreed to find my own firewood for one year ... & that I may know what it cost I propose to keep an account of work done." There follows a long list of the days on which Cato and Titus brought in wood,

---

21 Account book of Jonathan Ashley, PVMA Library. Unfortunately, Ashley's account book contains no mention of the purchase of Jenny and Cato or of the purchase and sale of Titus.

22 Jonathan Ashley was not the only one who referred to Abijah Prince as if his surname were "Negro". In June, 1756, for instance, "Abijah Negrow" bought a "Drum Rim" at Elijah Williams' store. (Account books of Elijah Williams, PVMA Library.)

23 Account books of Dr. Thomas Williams, PVMA Library.

A page of Reverend Ashley's account book, showing some of the
times that he rented Cato and Titus to "Abijah Negro".
(PVMA Library, Deerfield, Massachusetts.)

the number of loads, and the value put on their time, a list that runs from mid-December, 1759 until early February of the following year. In this long list of dates, Sundays are conspicuously absent, but Titus and Cato did bring in firewood on December 25 and January 1 – both days were ordinary work days. (Between 1659 and 1681, it had actually been illegal to celebrate Christmas, "either by forbearing of labour, feasting, or any other way".[24]) By the terms of Ashley's contract with the town, the town was supposed to furnish his firewood. When he agreed to get his own firewood for one year, it is not clear whether he was accepting, in effect, a temporary salary reduction or whether he expected to be reimbursed by the town for the value of his slaves' work.

Sheldon reports that both Cato and Titus saw military service. "In 1754-7 'Titus, se^{r}vant to Rev. Mr. Ashley' was serving as a soldier in the last French War", and "Cato served at least one campaign in the Last French War".

Both Cato and Titus had small accounts at Elijah Williams' store. A sampling of the entries in Elijah Williams' account books indicates the various ways in which the identities of slaves were recorded at the store, the nature of some of their purchases, and some of the ways in which they squared their accounts.[25]

Titus is listed variously as "Titus Negro", "Titus Ashley", "Titus Mr Ashley^s", "Mr Ashleys Titus", "Titus Ashley Negro", "Titus Mr Ashley^s Negro", and even simply as "Titus". Cato appears on various dates as "Cato Ashley", "Cato Mr Ashley", and "Cato Mr Ashley^s Negrow".

Among Titus' purchases were the following –

April 1, 1752	1 wosted cap
December 21, 1752	1 Pint Rhum

---

24 Nissenbaum (1996), p. 3. It was not until the 19th century that a significant number of New Englanders began to celebrate either Christmas or New Year's Day as holidays, whether religious or secular. The relevant passage in the 1659 law reads – "For pventing disorders arising in scucrall places wthin this jurisdiction, by reason of some still observing such ffestiualls as were superstitiously kept in other countrys, to the great dishonnor of God & offence of others, it is therefore ordered by this Court and the authority thereof, that whosoeuer shall be found observing any such day as Christmas or the like, either by forbearing of labour, feasting, or any other way, vpon any such accounts as aforesaid, euery such person so offending shall pay for euery such offence fiue shillings, as a fine to the county." The 1659 law lasted only twenty-two years. A brief 1681 note in the records of the colony reads – "The law against keeping Christmas to be left out." (*Massachusetts Records*, Vol. 4, Part 1 (1650-1660), p. 366 and Vol. 5 (1674-1686), p. 322.)

25 Account books of Elijah Williams, PVMA Library.

October 26, 1753	20 needels of Silk
June 24, 1754	1 q^t of Rhum
December 20, 1754	3 Square needels
June 17, 1755	3 y^{ds} of gartering
June 18, 1755	a Lining Handkerchief
September 15, 1755	1 Gill of Rhum
February 19, 1756	1 pt Rhum
March 31, 1756	1 pt Rhum, 5 Nedles
April 21, 1756	½ pt Rhum

And Cato is recorded as having purchased the following items, among others –

March 29, 1755	a p^r of Knee Buckels
April 15, 1756	a p^r Shoe Buckels
May 1, 1756	2 pipes
June 29, 1756	1 Knife
July 8, 1756	½ p^t Rhum
July 20, 1756	1 p^t Rhum
September 25, 1756	4 Buttons
January 17, 1757	a Small pamphlet
March 10, 1757	a Snuff Box
May 23, 1757	a Knife

Titus paid some of his debts with labor – making a broom, bottoming a chair, a day's husking – and at least once with cash. On several occasions Cato balanced his account with cash rather than with labor. Where did they obtain the cash? And Cato's 1757 purchase of a "small pamphlet" is intriguing. Can we infer that he could read?

On Tuesday evening, January 23, 1749/50, Ashley preached a special sermon to the Deerfield slaves – apparently intended to allay any doubts they might have about their enslaved status. Jenny was probably present, and perhaps Cato as well. Proper writes that the timing of this sermon was "no mere coincidence", that Ashley's decision to lecture to the town's slaves was prompted by the death just two weeks earlier of Reverend Benjamin Doolittle of Northfield and the consequent freeing of his slave, Abijah Prince.[26] Proper's suggestion was that the Deerfield slaves would surely have known about Abijah's presence as a free black in a nearby town, that his "unique situation" would surely have caused them to think about slavery and freedom, and that Ashley found it appropriate

---

26 Proper (1997), p. 21.

at this moment to deliver a sermon explaining not only the legitimacy of slavery but also some of the benefits. However, Ashley's sermon to the town's slaves was not delivered just two weeks after Doolittle's death, as Proper writes, but a year after his death.[27] In addition, it has recently been learned that Abijah did not gain his freedom until May, 1751, over two years after Doolittle's death.[28]

Abijah Prince aside, it is easy to imagine Ashley's giving such a sermon to quell restlessness among the Deerfield slaves. Other New England ministers probably gave sermons like this to the slaves of their towns. The notes to this particular sermon have been preserved, and Ashley's notes were printed in an 1867 journal and are included in this book as Appendix I. After first announcing that "there are none of the human race too low & despicable for God to bestow Salvation upon", he goes on to show that Christianity permits the existence of slavery ("allows of the relation of masters and Servants") and warns them against temptations from the Devil – "What a temptation of the Devil is it therefore to lead Servants into Sin, and provoke God; to insinuate into them they ought not to abide in y^r place of Servant, – and so either forsake their master or are uneasy, unfaithful, slothful Servants, to the damage of masters and the dishonor of religion – the reproach of Xtianity." He assures his listeners that "such as are by Divine providence placed in the State of Servants are not excluded from Salvation, but may become the Lord's freemen". Then he shows "what a privilege it is to be the Lord's freemen", that freemen are "Children of God, adopted into his family", that "Christ's freemen when they come to die enter into everlasting rest and glory. They go to be with the Lord." He then gives some "directions to you that you may become Christ's freemen ... You must be contented with your State & Condition in the world and not murmur and complain of what God orders for you."

---

27 Doolittle died on January 9, 1748/49, and Ashley's notes on his sermon to the slaves were marked January 23, 1749. Does this mean January 1748/49 or January 1749/50? The ambiguity can be resolved by looking at various surviving manuscripts of Ashley's sermon notes – notes on his regular Sunday sermons – and considering those dated in the January 1 - March 25 interval in various years. Knowing that nearly all of his sermons were delivered on Sundays allows one to determine that it was Ashley's custom to date his sermon notes according to the convention that the new year began on March 25. Thus Ashley's notation on this special sermon, January 23, 1749, must be interpreted as January 23, 1749/50, over a year after Doolittle's death.

28 Gerzina (2008), p. 46. See also Abijah Prince's manumission document, shown earlier in this chapter.

One can only speculate as to whether this sermon had the desired effect on those who heard it.

Did Jonathan Ashley castrate Cato? This was one of the allegations and rumors about Ashley that were circulating in town during the 1770s or perhaps earlier – as shown by the documents to be mentioned below.[29] Sometime in 1774 Samuel Barnard was "called to account before the church for slandering Mr. Ashley".[30] Nothing in the church records from that time reveals in what ways Barnard had slandered Reverend Ashley, but the castration charge was almost certainly one of the accusations that Barnard had been circulating. Although there is documentary evidence that the rumor was being circulated, there is no evidence that Ashley was in fact guilty of the alleged crime.

The explanation of the desire of Barnard and others to defame the minister may be found in the politics of the time. In the years leading up to the outbreak of the American Revolution, the town of Deerfield was becoming increasingly polarized between Whigs and Tories. There was dissension in the church, caused at least in large measure by the strong pro-Tory loyalist views and statements of Reverend Ashley and by the Whig sentiments and activities of Samuel Barnard and others who were increasingly favoring the revolutionary cause. Ashley was becoming increasingly unpopular with a significant number of the members of his congregation, primarily, it seems, because of his outspoken loyalty to the crown and his criticisms of Barnard and others who were beginning to advocate a loosening of England's control over the affairs of her American colonies. (It was only some years later that demands for less interference turned into calls for actual *independence* from England.)

After Barnard was "called to account", the church voted to withdraw communion from Barnard, at which point Barnard and other "dissenting brethren" withdrew from the church and from Ashley's ministry. From that time until the end of the Revolution the dissenters held their own services, and as the majority of the town swung back and forth between Whigs and Tories, on several occasions the town voted to withhold Ashley's salary and the firewood that was due to him by his contract with the town.

29 Neither I nor several other historians with whom I have discussed this case are aware of any reports or even accusations from elsewhere in New England that a slave was castrated by his owner.

30 Sheldon (1895), p. 711. See also McClellan (ca. 1955), Chapter 12.

There are only two known surviving documents that explicitly refer to the castration charge. One of these is a long letter (almost six closely written pages) dated October 22, 1779, signed by six Deerfield residents (including Ashley's son, Jonathan, Jr.), addressed to the "Com^tee of ye Absenting Brethren of ye Church of Christ in Deerfield".[31] The authors repeatedly accused Barnard of spreading the "scandalous story", charging that he had not only spread the "foul story" but had done so with a "mind equally foul". After many repetitions of such charges, the letter ended with expressions of hope for a just and amicable resolution and talk of "Harmony, Joy, and Love".

It is hardly surprising that Samuel Barnard and his fellow dissenters did not rush to confess all their sins in response to this letter. In the spring of 1780 an Ecclesiastical Council was called in an attempt to reconcile the differences between Ashley and the dissenters, each side choosing several members of the council, but after meeting for ten days in May they were still hopelessly divided and no resolution was achieved. As for the specific charges against Ashley, the matter became moot, as Ashley was already seriously ill and died in August of that year.

The minutes of the council's deliberations have not survived. Perhaps because the rumor of the castration of Cato was one of the items discussed, someone may have decided to destroy the records in order to protect the reputation of the deceased minister. The second relevant document, the only known document that pertains to their discussions that spring, is an item dated May, 1780 that is partially quoted by Sheldon,[32] who carefully avoided the explicit words "cut" and "castrated".

> One of the papers used before the Council was a "declaration" made by one of the church members, that some ten years before he had repeated "an ugly, false, abusive story about Mr. Ashley." "I did not receive it as truth," he says, and "I am heartily sorry I ever mentioned it, tho' not conscious of any evil design. I feel that this is not to do as I would be done by." He asks the forgiveness of "the Rev. Pastor and brethren of the church." This paper was endorsed "May 25, 1780. A true copy from the files. Attest: JAMES DANA, Scribe."

---

31 PVMA Library. Filed under "Meeting House and Church, First Church, Pastors and Ministers, Miscellaneous Pastors and Ministers".

32 Sheldon (1895), pp. 734-735.

The original – of which the document that Sheldon describes is a "true copy" – has not survived. It is not clear who, if anyone, signed this "declaration".[33] So all we have to go on are two documents, one an attack on Samuel Barnard for having spread this "scandalous story", the other a copy of an apology, probably unsigned, for having repeated the "ugly, false, abusive story".

Why did Barnard choose to promulgate such a terrible accusation? Was there anything in the town's history that might have made such a charge even remotely plausible? There was a 1760 case in the neighboring town of Greenfield, a case of which the Ashleys and everyone else in Deerfield must have been aware. On February 12, 1760, as described in the following court record, Lucy Billing, daughter of Greenfield's minister, Edward Billing,[34] and Caesar, the minister's slave, were brought into court on the charge of fornication.[35]

John Worthington Esq. Attorney for our Sovereign Lord the King in this Court hereby informs and gives this Court to understand that one Caesar a Negro man Servant for Life to Edward Billing of Greenfield in s^d County clerk[36] on the fifteenth day of February last past at said Greenfield – wickedly and willingly had carnal knowledge of the body of Lucy Billing an English woman an infant[37] and Daughter of said Edward and then and there committed the Crime of fornication with said Lucy and then and there begot a Child on her body by fornication and so the said John says the said Caesar a Negro man as aforesaid at Greenfield aforesaid on the fifteenth day of February aforesaid committed the Crime of fornication with the said Lucy an english woman as aforesaid contrary to the Law of this province in such cases provided the peace of our said Lord the King his crown and Dignity – And the said Caesar being now brot before the Court had the foregoing Information read to him and pleaded not guilty thereto which plea aforesaid by the Leave of the Court afterward the said Caesar withdrew and then plead guilty to said Complaint – Its hereupon Considered and Ordered by the

---

33 Martha Noblick (private communication) suggests that perhaps the "declaration" was prepared by James Dana, scribe to the council, and that someone who had been active in circulating the rumor, perhaps Samuel Barnard, was asked to sign it but declined to do so.
34 Reverend Billing sometimes appears in contemporary records as "Billing", sometimes as "Billings".
35 Hampshire County, Massachusetts Courts. Common Pleas/General Sessions, Feb. 12, 1760.
36 That is, referring to Reverend Billing, a "cleric", or minister.
37 Infant – "A person under (legal) age; a minor." (*Oxford English Dictionary*.)

Court that the said Caesar be severely whiped thirty Stripes on his naked body and that he be sold out of this province and be sent away accordingly within the Space of Six months from this time, and that he be continued in prison at his Masters charge till he be sent away & pay Cost and stand committed accordingly –

Lucy Billing an infant and Daughter of Edward Billing of Greenfield Clerk a Single woman came before this Court & Confessed She had been guilty of the Crime of Fornication with Caesar a negro man Servant to her said father – Its hereupon considered & ordered by the Court that the said Lucy be severely whiped fifteen Stripes on her naked body and that she maintain her bastard Child at her own Charge and pay Cost and stand committed &c –

Court record of the 1760 trial of Caesar (slave of Reverend Billing) and Lucy Billing.

Thanks to the existence of a newborn baby girl, Patience, the charge was obviously impossible to deny.[38]

At that time there were two teenage daughters in the Ashley family – Dorothy (17) and Elizabeth (15). In addition, they owned two male slaves – Cato (22) and Titus (35). The townspeople might readily believe that Jonathan and Dorothy Ashley feared that what had transpired between Lucy Billing and Caesar might occur in their own household. Moreover, it was in January, 1760 – immediately after the birth of Patience, probably born in November, 1759 – that Ashley concluded the sale of Titus to Elijah Williams of Stockbridge. Perhaps the close timing of these two events, the birth of Patience and the sale of Titus, was simply a coincidence, but it might have appeared to others that – in selling Titus – Ashley was dealing with problems in his own house, and this might have made the castration rumor more believable.

As interesting as these documents may be, they do not resolve the issue of castration. There is no evidence that Ashley castrated Cato.

---

38 A sad postscript to the preceding court record is the following brief entry from "An Account of the Deaths in Greenfield" in the records of Roger Newton, who himself became minister at Greenfield in 1761 – "April ye 22^d. 1762. Patience, Daughter of Lucy Billing." From the same document we learn that Lucy herself died on November 5, 1773. (Record book of Roger Newton, PVMA Library.)

Caesar
Property of Jonathan Hoyt (1688-1779)

As with several of the other "Caesars" who lived in Deerfield in 1752, very little is known about this slave who belonged to Lieutenant Jonathan Hoyt. Caesar was baptized[1] by Reverend Ashley in 1741 and served in the French and Indian War in the 1750s.[2] Hoyt had an account with Dr. Thomas Williams – in 1750, for instance, Williams charged Hoyt eight shillings for bloodletting Caesar.[3]

> To Phlebot Cesar   0/8

In the mid 1750s, Caesar had an account at Elijah Williams' store, where he made occasional purchases. In June,1755, for instance, "Cesser Jonnath Hoit's negro" was charged 1/3 for "powder", and at various times during the year 1756, "Cesar Lieut Hoits Negrow" purchased "Rhum", cider, and powder.[4]

---

1 Deerfield minister's record book, PVMA Library.
2 Sheldon (1895), p. 894.
3 Account books of Dr. Thomas Williams, PVMA Library.
4 Account books of Elijah Williams, PVMA Library.

Ishmael and Peter (1709-   )
Property of Thomas Dickinson (1718-1814)

Ishmael, a slave belonging to Thomas Dickinson, had an account at Elijah Williams' store. Williams' account books show a number of purchases by Ishmael.[1]

Ishmael Mr Thos Dickinsons Negro

November 2, 1753	A pair of Wosted Stockings
December 12, 1753	Three pints of Rhum
February, 1755	A Silk Handkerchief and a pair of Knee Buckels
April 2, 1756	A pair of Gloves
August 17, 1756	A pair of Garters
May 23, 1757	A hand kerchief and Rhum

On several occasions, Ishmael balanced his account with small amounts of cash or with unspecified work. On April 24, 1756, he reimbursed Williams by digging a grave for Job Tute, a Deerfield man who had died as a soldier in the French and Indian War.[2]

No other information about Ishmael seems to have survived, so we do not know how or when Dickinson acquired Ishmael or what happened to him after 1757.

Peter first appears in Deerfield history in the 1731 bill of sale that records his purchase by Thomas Wells (Thomas Dickinson's uncle) from John Cook of Windsor, Connecticut.[3]

Know all men by these Presents that I John Cook of the Town of Windsor in the County of Hartford and Coloney of Connecticutt, for and in Consideration of the Sum of One Hundred Pounds in Currant money, to me in hand, well and Truely paid, or in the Law Secured to be paid by Capt Thomas Wells of the Town of Deerfield in the County of Hampshier, in the Province of the Massachusets Bay in New England, Have therefore And Do by these presents, full, freely and Absolutely, Bargain, Sell & Dispose of my Negro man Peter, (aged about Twenty Two years,) to him the Said Thomas Wells, and to his Heirs and Assignes forever, To Have and to Hold as his & their proper Estate

---

1 Account books of Elijah Williams, PVMA Library.
2 Sheldon (1895), Genealogy Section, p. 348.
3 Hampden County Registry of Deeds.

in fee, to his and their proper use Benifit & Behoof forever, without Let, Sute, Claim Hinderance or Molestation, from me the Said John Cook, my Heirs, Executors, or Administrators, or any person from, by, or under me or them Warranting hereby for my Self my Heirs, Executors Administrators, to and with the Said Capt Thomas Wells his Heirs & Assignes, that at the time of the Ensealing and Delivery hereof, I am Lawfully and Sole Seized of Said Negro man, and that I have Good Right full power, and Lawfull authorety to Dispose of him as in and by these presents I have Done, and that therefore will forever warrant, Secure and Defend, the above Bargained Premises, to him the Said Wells, his Heirs &c, from all former, or other Gifts, or Bills of Sales, or whatever. In witness where of I have here unto Set my hand and Seal this fourth day of November, Anno Dom: One Thousand Seven Hundred & thirty one.

John Cook

Signed, Sealed and Delivered
in presence of us.
Samuel Allen
Tim° Loomis

Peter (together with Adam, another slave of Thomas Wells) next appears in the Deerfield record in 1735. On Sunday, June 15, 1735, Adam and Peter were baptized,[4] and we read in Reverend Ashley's record book that on the same day, during "Confessions in the Church", both Adam and Peter confessed to "Fornication & Drunkeness & Stealing". It is not clear whether the baptisms preceded or followed the confessions. The 1735 day of confession and baptism was not the only time that Adam and Peter were forced to stand before the congregation and acknowledge their guilt in public. On October 22, 1738, "Peter negro" confessed to "Drinking theft & Fornication" and on April 12, 1741 to "Lying Stealing Fornication". On August 2 of the same year "Adam Negro" con-

---

4 Deerfield minister's record book, PVMA Library. Lucy and Caesar, slaves of Ebenezer Wells, were also baptized on the same day, as was Pompey, a slave of "Justice Jonathan Wells". Of the fifteen slaves baptized in Deerfield during the entire time of Jonathan Ashley's ministry, five were baptized on that one day. This was a time of widespread religious revivals in New England, though several years before what is usually described as the "Great Awakening". (Wells was a common Deerfield name, and there were a number of Deerfield residents named Jonathan Wells in the early and mid-1700s. Pompey's owner was probably Jonathan Wells (1659-1739), Deerfield's first Justice of the Peace. (Sheldon (1895), Genealogy Section, p. 357.))

fessed to "lying", and earlier that summer "Pompey Negro" confessed to "Fornication".[5]

Confessions in the Church

1735 Jun 15	Adam Servt of Th^s Wells	Fornication & Drunkeness & Stealing
	also Peter do do do [ditto]	do do do
1738 Oct 22	Peter negro	Drinking theft & Fornication
1741 Apr 12	Peter Negro	Lying Stealing Fornication
1741 July 19	Pompey Negro	Fornication
1741 Aug 2	Adam Negro	lying

Most of the confessions recorded in Jonathan Ashley's record book were confessions to fornication by white members of the community, sometimes by a man, sometimes by a woman, and sometimes by a couple. (On one occasion in 1743, Amos Allen and Rebecca Nims must have enlivened the church service when they confessed to "Fornication & boasting of it".) Often it was a *married* white couple who confessed to fornication. Such an apparently anomalous confession can be understood by reference to the "seven month rule". Quite generally in colonial New England, if a couple had a child within seven months of marriage, that fact was taken as *prima facie* evidence of premarital intercourse.[6] Such a child could not be baptized and would therefore be condemned to spend eternity in hell unless the parents confessed – strong motivation indeed for parental admission of guilt.

Joseph and Hannah Bascom, for example, were married on August 3, 1737, produced a son on the following January 18 (only five

---

5 Deerfield minister's record book, PVMA Library. Sheldon describes the 1735 confessions of Adam and Peter and that of Peter in 1738 in somewhat different language than that used by Reverend Ashley – "Adam servant to Justice Thomas Wells confessed ye sin of *lewdness* and Peter, his servant confessed the sin of *lewdness* and drunkenness and stealing and they were received into charity with people" and (in 1738) "Peter, Negro confessed the sin of *lewdness*, of excessive drinking & stealing & was restored to charity". (Sheldon (1895), p. 893.) It is possible that Sheldon substituted *lewdness* for *fornication* to make the wording less jarring to his readers. It seems more likely, though, that Sheldon – who seems usually to have been scrupulously careful with his quotations – was copying from the church records rather than from the minister's book. The church and minister records are in most cases almost identical, but comparison here is impossible because the "Confessions" section of the church records was omitted when those records were microfilmed and are not now readily available. Sheldon also gives an incorrect date for the October, 1738 confession – Sheldon gives the date as October 2 (a Monday), rather than the correct date, October 22 (a Sunday).

6 Crawford (1914), p. 199; Thompson, Roger (1986), pp. 55, 211-212. See also Godbeer (2002), Chapter 7.

months later), and then – presumably seeking baptism for their child – confessed to fornication on February 5. Their son was baptized three weeks later. On June 14, 1741, Joseph Barnard (later the owner of Prince) and his wife Thankful confessed to fornication. Their son, born two months earlier – exactly seven months after their marriage in September, 1740 – was baptized on June 21, 1741, a week after their parents' confession.

White residents confessed not only to fornication but also to drunkenness, theft, swearing, and absence from communion. On July 15, 1750, for instance, Ebenezer Hinsdale (owner of Caesar and Mesheck) confessed to "hard drinking". And on one Sunday in 1739, Joseph Younglove confessed to "Abusing wife of the Pastor" – an interesting confession about which we would like to know more.

When Thomas Wells died in 1749 or 1750, he left his estate to his nephew, Thomas Dickinson of Hatfield, who soon moved to Deerfield.[7] Peter Negro was included in Wells' probate inventory, though no mention was made of Adam, who had perhaps died or been sold before 1750.[8]

> ... Turnips 18/8 twenty Eight y^d Cloath Serge 95/2 a flail 8^d. Peter Negro 160 / two Bagg & a Portmanteau 4/9 Cyder 21/8 ...

Peter was apparently at death's door in 1755, as we read in two entries in the diary of James Taylor.[9]

---

7 Sheldon (1895), Genealogy Section, p. 358. There is some uncertainty about just where Thomas Dickinson (and Peter and Ishmael) were living in 1752. Sheldon reports that Dickinson, having inherited his uncle's estate, moved to Deerfield in 1752 and, "about 1752", "built or extensively repaired" the house that now stands at 99 Old Main Street, which is what I show on my 1752 map. (Sheldon (1895), pp. 599-600.) McGowan and Miller, however, believe that when Dickinson first moved to Deerfield, he lived just to the north of that site and that it was not until sometime in the 1760s that he built the present house. (McGowan and Miller (1996), pp. 16-18.)

8 Hampshire County Registry of Probate.

9 Diary of James Taylor, PVMA Library. James Taylor kept this diary during 1755, when he was a schoolmaster in Deerfield. He studied theology with Jonathan Ashley and became minister at New Fairfield, Connecticut in 1758, a position from which he was soon dismissed as a result of a religious controversy that now seems obscure. On August 31, 1755, "Jas. Taylor and Mary Field" confessed to fornication in the Deerfield church. They were married the next day, their daughter was born in late October, baptized on October 27, 1755, and died shortly thereafter. Mary was thirteen years old at the time; James was twenty-six. In spite of this inauspicious beginning to their marriage, James and Mary had nine children who survived infancy and grew to adulthood, though Mary died of complications of childbirth in 1779, two days after giving birth to their last child. James was killed by a falling limb in 1785. (Sheldon (1895), Genealogy Section, p. 339.)

This day Peter a negro Fellow, who had been sick for some Days here was blooded & ye D^r determined he had ye malignant Pleurases & long[10] Fever, & looked upon his Case very dangerous. Thus I am brought to ye Close of another Day, praised be God for preserving Goodness.

And a few days later –

Mr Ashley ... taried some time, prayed with Peter, who is very ill & more dangerous than before. ... After prayers and sometime after twelve, having prepared all things necessary for my dear beloved wife, I retired to my bedroom ...

Though the outlook for Peter seemed bleak in 1755, apparently he recovered, for the account books of Elijah Williams[11] show that on April 22, 1756, "Peter Negrow" bought a tobacco box, for which he paid four days later "By Killing Cow & Cutting Colt".[12] And the account books of Dr. Thomas Williams shows several charges for pills and other medical supplies in February and March of 1756 and again in July, 1757 for "Pe-

Excerpts from the 1750 probate inventory of Thomas Wells, including "Peter Negro", valued at £160. (Hampshire County Registry of Probate.)

---

10 "Long" is probably an archaic form of "lung". "Lung fever" – pneumonia.
11 Account books of Elijah Williams, PVMA Library.
12 "By Killing Cow & Cutting Colt", i.e., killing a cow and castrating a colt.

ter Ladieu Negro".[13] Though this is the only instance I know of in which the name *Ladieu* is attached to Peter, it is probably the same Peter, for on the facing page of the doctor's account book, we see that these items were charged to the account of "Mr. Dickinson".

There is one mystery associated with Peter. According to 1751 court records from Hartford, Connecticut[14] –

> Whereas Peter Negro of Deerfield in the County of Hampshire in the Province of the Massachusetts Bay Recovered Judgment against Samuel Pettibone of Symsbury ... On the 2ᵈ Tuesday of Aprill 1751 for the Sum of £16.18.0 ... for Damage ... These are therefore in His Majesty's Name to Command you, That of the Goods, Chattels or Lands of the said Samuel Pettibone ... you cause to be Levied ... Paid, and Satisfied unto the said Peter Negro ... Dated at Hartford this 29ᵗʰ Day of Aprill Anno Domini, 1751. And in the 24ᵗʰ Year of His Majesty's Reign.

What had Pettibone done to cause so large an assessment of damages in favor of Peter? What was Peter doing in Simsbury? Simsbury is about fifty miles from Deerfield as the crow flies. Even today it would take over an hour to drive from Deerfield to Simsbury. Was Peter still the slave of Thomas Dickinson or had he somehow gained his freedom by 1751? The fact that he was involved in such a serious court case, at such a great distance from Deerfield, would perhaps suggest that he was free, though the fact that the court document refers to him as "Peter Negro" might suggest that he was still enslaved. That in itself is not compelling, though – recall that Jonathan Ashley (and other Deerfield residents, too) sometimes referred to Abijah Prince, a free black, as "Abijah Negro". The one fact that I find very hard to reconcile with the proposition that Peter was free in 1751 is that five years later Peter's medical treatment by Dr. Williams was charged to the account of Thomas Dickinson.

My guess is that Peter was still a slave of Thomas Dickinson at the time of his court case, but – whether he was enslaved or free in 1751 – questions remain.[15] What was "Peter Negro of Deerfield" doing in Simsbury? What was this court case about? And there is yet another possibility – that this was a different "Peter Negro of Deerfield" altogether.

---

13 Account books of Dr. Thomas Williams, PVMA Library.

14 Connecticut State Library. Hartford County Court, Executions, 1750-1759, L-Z, Drawer #478.

15 My attempts to find further court documents concerning this case at the Connecticut State Library have so far been unsuccessful.

"Our Poor Negro Girl" (-1757)
Property of Dr. Thomas Williams (1718-1775)

"Our Poor Negro Girl." There is no other way to identify this young woman, a slave of Dr. Thomas Williams. The only knowledge of her that we have comes from a 1757 exchange of letters between her owner – the town doctor – and his father-in-law, William Williams. On August 23, Dr. Williams wrote to his father-in-law, a minister in Weston, Massachusetts.[1]

Deerfield   Aug. 23. 1757

Hon.[d] S[r]

When Cous[n] Daniel Jones was here I was not able to write, which I desired him to inform you as also our circumstances & having this favourable oppertunity P B[r] Col[o] y[e] Bearer, would let you know them at this time. My Wife thro' y[e] goodness of God is restor'd to a considerable measure of health so as last Sabbath She was able to Attend upon the Publick Worship all day. – *our poor Negro Girl is yet living after 36 days confinement with y[e] Slow fever; her case Appears as yet very dubious, her blisters much canker'd, tumified, & threaten a Mortification, thro the Acrid, putred, & Alkaline State of her blood, & medicines have not (nor ever had in my practice) much sensible effect upon that Nation.* A Holy & Righteous God was pleased to take away our Babe after he had lent it to us Eleven days, I desire to be thankful it was so long & y[t] we had oppertunity to dedicate it to him in Baptism. I very much feared y[e] Affliction would have had Some bad Effect on my Dear Spouses mind, considering her case in a former lying in, but She Seems to bear up under the heavy Stroke with a truly Christian Spirit, neither despising the Chastening of y[e] Lord nor fainting when She is rebuked &c. Hon[d] S[r] I ask Your prayers y[t] God would Sanctify to us both Mercies & Afflictions for our Souls everlasting benefit & am with Duty to Mad[m] & hearty love & Service to B[r] & his Spouse & M[rs] Bettsey Stone.

Your Dutiful Son & Humb[l] Ser[t·]

Tho[s] Williams [Italics added.]

P.S. S[r] if your health will admit of sending a line it will be most gratefully rec'd.

---

1 Williams papers, PVMA Library. Dr. Williams and his father-in-law were also first cousins. (See Sheldon (1895), Genealogy Section, pp. 376-381.)

Deerfield augt. 23. 1757

Hon.d Sir

When Cous.n Daniel Jones was here I was not able to write, which I desired him to inform you, & having this favourable opportunity p Br. Col. & y.e Beans, would let you know my Wife thro' y.e goodness of God is restor'd to a considerable measure of health so as last Sabbath She was able to attend upon the Publick Worship all day. — our poor Negro Girl is yet living after 36 days confinement with y.e Slow feaver, her case appears as yet very dubious, her blisters much canker'd, tumefied, & threaten a Mortification, thro' the Acrid, putred, & Alkaline State of her blood, & Medicines have not (nor ever had in my practice) much sensible effect upon that Nation. A Holy & Righteous God was pleased to take away our Babe after he had lent it to us Eleven days, I desire to be thankful it was so long & y.t we had opportunity to dedicate it to him in Baptism, I very much feared y.e Affliction would have had some bad Effect on my Dear Spouse mind, considering her case in a former lying in, but She seems to bear up under the heavy Stroke with a truly Christian Spirit, neither despising the Chastening of y.e Lord nor fainting when She is rebuked &c. Hon.d S.r I ask your prayers y.t God would Sanctify to us both Mercies & Afflictions for our Souls everlasting benefit & am with Duty to Mad.m & hearty love & Service to Br. & his Spouse & Mrs. Bettsey Stone Your Dutiful Son & Humble Ser.t Tho.s Williams

P.! S.r if your health will admit of Sending a line it will be most gratefully rec.d —

Rev.d Mr. Williams

Letter of Dr. Thomas Williams about "Our Poor Negro Girl".
(PVMA Library, Deerfield, Massachusetts.)

When Williams wrote in August, the outlook for this (now nameless) woman was bleak. From a letter that he received from his father-in-law in November of that year, it is clear that "Our Poor Negro Girl" had died at some time in the intervening months.

Weston Novr 10th 1757

Dear Son –

It is but seldom that I hear from You, & Seldomer that I have opport^y to write to you. But understanding that Chandler is about to return gladly improve ye opp^{ty} to write tho' but a Line to let you know our State & to express my Concern relating to yours – I have heard of ye Kindness of God in giving my Daughter a Safe Delivery accompanied with his Frown in the Loss of y^r Child – *and also that you have lost y^r Servt Girl after long illness* – and adding to ye last, that you been visited with Sickness y^r Self – but that you & yours are now in a comfort^{ble} State of health, all which Dispensations, as others heretofore, must occasion you to reflect, that ye Providences of God are mix'd & checker'd in this present State, & call for ye Exercise of ye different Graces of Patience & Submission on ye one hand & Gratitude & Thankfullness on ye other. And if it pleases ye great & wise & just Disposer of all things, from whom all our fruit is found, together with his Corrections to give his efficacious Instruct^{ns} & to enable you so to behave your selves towards him, his Providences are then Sanctified, and you have ye happy occasion to apply that of ye Apostle – He for our Profit, that we might be Partakers of his Holiness. – O what Losses & Sufferings Should we not be willing to undergo, that we may reap this excellent Gain? – What greater Profit can we have than Holiness? – May you both as one seek earnestly to him for it who is ready to give ye Holy Spirit to them that ask him – that ask him humbly & earnestly Sensible of their need of his gracious Teaching. And I earnestly desire and hope that ye things which at present are not joyous but grievous may yield you ye peaceable fruits of Righteousness – and that ye many Mercys you enjoy may lead you to also Repent^{ce} & excite your Gratitude to ye inexhaust^{ble} Fountⁿ of all Good, & engage y^r constant care to obey & please Him. This is ye Return which he justly expects, – and this ye way, thro Faith in ye only Redeem^r to be crowned with everlast^g Mercy – This is ye Sincere & earnest wish of y^r affect^{te} Father.

Wm Williams [Italics added.]

It is certain that this young woman died in Deerfield, yet there is no way of knowing where she was buried. It is clear from these two letters that illness and death, the dangers of childbirth, and the very real possibility of the loss of a child in infancy were always present as an accompaniment to a precarious existence on the colonial frontier. Yet in spite of the fact that God was "pleased" to take away their newborn baby after "lending" it to them for eleven days, despite the death of their slave, Dr. Williams expresses continued confidence in God's righteousness and almost seems grateful for the afflictions he and his family have received.

These two letters are the only documents of this sort, family letters, that I have found that refer to Deerfield's slaves. All the others are bills of sale, estate inventories, account book entries, and the like. The nearly complete absence of such letters tells us something important about the attitudes of the owners toward their slaves.

Onesimus and Kedar
Property of Elijah Williams (1712-1771)

For many years, Elijah Williams ran an important store that was probably located somewhere on the land that is now the town common, in the midst of Deerfield Academy. A surviving tax valuation list dated 1769-70-71 shows Elijah as the owner of two slaves.[1] Most of the surviving tax lists from Deerfield simply list a total value of the property of each adult white male and do not give a breakdown that shows how much of that assessed value is due to cows, how much to real estate, how much to slaves, etc. The surviving tax lists from western Massachusetts that do break down the total by category generally have a column for "Servants", or "Servants for Life", or "Negro", or "Negro and Faculty".[2] The 1769-70-71 Deerfield tax list, which does provide a breakdown, is unusual in that the column in question is simply labeled "Slaves", of whom Elijah is listed as owning two.[3]

One of those slaves was probably called Onesimus (a fairly common name for black slaves in colonial times), for we read the following in Reverend Ashley's record book[4] –

Oct 19 1766   Baptized Onesimus Negro Servant to Major Williams

Elijah's father, Reverend John Williams (1664-1729), had owned at least five different black slaves during his time in Deerfield – Robert Tigo (who died in 1695), Frank and Parthena (both of whom were killed in the course of the famous 1704 attack on Deerfield), and Mesheck and Kedar, who were purchased by Reverend Williams after his return from captivity in Canada. Williams died in 1729, and Mesheck and Kedar (and

---

1 PVMA Library.

2 *Faculty* meant a taxable trade such as that of a licensed tavern operator or a skilled craftsman. Slaves and faculties were often lumped together on tax lists.

3 Elijah Williams ("Major Williams") died in 1771, and a state-wide valuation list, dated 1771, shows his son, John Williams, as the owner of two "Servants for life between 14 and 45 years of age". (Massachusetts State Archives. See also Pruitt (1978) for the collected results of the 1771 listing.) The law requiring such a state-wide valuation list in 1768 was quoted in Chapter Two. A similar law required another such census in 1771. John was only twenty years old in 1771. It was highly unusual for such a young man to be the owner of two slaves – it is almost certain that these were the same two individuals shown in the slightly earlier tax list as being owned by his father.

4 Deerfield minister's record book, PVMA Library.

Excerpts from the 1729 probate inventory of John Williams, including
"The molatto Boy Meseck" and "The Black Boy Kedar".
(Hampshire County Registry of Probate.)

Kedar's bed and blanket) are listed in his probate inventory.[5]

the molatto Boy Meseck	80-00-00
The Black Boy Kedar at Eighty pound	80-00-00
A Bed & Blanket of the Black Boy at 6ˢ	

Mesheck (or "Meseck") was owned by Ebenezer Hinsdale by 1737, as we saw earlier in this chapter. (Mesheck is consistently referred to as "molatto", so the blanket was probably Kedar's.[6]) Sheldon, commenting on Williams' inventory, says that "Kedar is not again heard of".[7] I suspect that just as Mesheck became the property of Reverend Williams' daughter Sarah (then of daughter Abigail and thus eventually the property of Ebenezer Hinsdale), Kedar became the slave of the reverend's son Elijah.

All of this – the fact that Elijah ran a busy store, that he owned two slaves in the late 1760s, that his father had owned quite a number of slaves at various times – strongly suggests that Elijah owned slaves in the year 1752, the focus of this chapter. On that basis, I put two slaves with Elijah as their owner on my 1752 map of the Deerfield street. That much seems quite solid – identifying them as Onesimus (baptized fourteen years later, in 1766) and Kedar (listed in Reverend Williams' inventory twenty-three years earlier, in 1729) is more conjectural.

---

5 Hampshire County Registry of Probate.

6 Curiously, in the typewritten transcript of this inventory (in the library of Historic Deerfield), the third item shown above was incorrectly written as "a bed & blanket of *Mesh* black boy" instead of "*the* black boy". But it is Kedar who is described here as "black", whereas Mesheck is referred to as "molatto", not only in this inventory but also in the record of his February, 1748/49 court appearance (*Evans v. Mesheck*) that was described earlier in this chapter.

7 Sheldon (1895), p. 890.

Humphrey and Phillis (1733-)
Property of Timothy Childs, Sr. (1686-1776)

Humphrey (or "Umphry") was baptized in 1762, on the same day as Daniel Arms' slave, Titus.[1]

Decem 5   1762   Baptized Humphry Servant to Timothy Childs &
                 Titus Servant to Daniel Arms

Humphrey appeared many years earlier, in Elijah Williams' account books, as a purchaser of small items. In July, 1745, for instance, he bought two pipes and then another one three months later.[2]

1745
July 19   Umphry D^r to 2 pipes   – – 4
Oct 9   to a pipe   – – 3

On at least one occasion, Humphrey settled his account with cash.

C^r by Cash   0 - 0 - 8

As early as 1746, Dr. Williams was treating Humphrey from time to time. On several occasions, Williams treated his hand and foot injuries and also subjected him, like most of his other patients, to phlebotomy, or bloodletting.

July 1749   To Dress Humphry & [?] foot
August 16th 1750   To Dress Humphry's hand 4 Times
Jan 23 1757   Phlebot Humph^{ry}
April 7th 1758   Dress Humphry's foot
June 16 1758   Phlebot Humphry

On one occasion in 1761, Humphrey paid Dr. Williams for his own or his owner's medical bills by "digging Pottatoes".[3] Humphrey's owner, by the way, was one of many who rented Cato and Titus from Reverend Ashley.

Phillis was one of several slaves owned by Nehemiah Bull, the minister at Westfield. Bull died in April, 1740, and though his will makes no mention of his slaves, his probate inventory, taken on June 22, 1740, lists three "Negro maids" by name.[4]

---

1 Deerfield minister's record book, PVMA Library.
2 Account books of Elijah Williams, PVMA Library.
3 Account books of Dr. Thomas Williams, PVMA Library.
4 Hampshire County Registry of Probate.

a Negro maid named Tanner 90 ditto named Phillis 65 ditto
named Dido 40 ....195 0 0

Excerpts from the 1740 probate inventory of Reverend Nehemiah Bull of
Westfield, including the "Negro maid named Phillis", then about seven years old
and valued at £65. (Hampshire County Registry of Probate.)

A year and a half later, in February, 1741/42, Phillis ("a Certain
Negro Girl named Phillis of about nine years of Age") was sold to Timothy Childs for £100 by Oliver Partridge and Elisabeth Bull, the executors
of Bull's estate.[5]

No further mention of Phillis is known to have survived. What
was her relationship to Reverend Bull's other two "Negro maids"? Tanner may have been her mother and Dido (who died[6] in June, 1741, seven
months before Phillis was sold) her younger sister.

---

5 Thomas Williams papers, New York Historical Society. The bill of sale is dated February 4, 1741 – February 4, 1741/42 in dual-year notation. A copy of the bill of sale is in the
PVMA Library. See Proper (1997), pp. 10, 42.
6 Carvalho (1984), p. 147.

Caesar
Property of Timothy Childs, Jr. (1720-1781)

In the 1730s Caesar belonged to Jonathan Wells, Jr., and when Wells died in 1735, Caesar became the property of his widow, Mary Hoyt Wells. Jonathan's probate inventory includes the line[1]–

A Negro Boy	£ 100 - 00 - 00

An excerpt from the 1735 probate inventory of Jonathan Wells, Jr., including "A Negro Boy", valued at £100. (Hampshire County Registry of Probate.)

As the slave of Widow Wells, Caesar was baptized in 1741 and taken into full communion in 1745.[2]

June 14 1741 Baptized Caesar Servant to the Widow Mary Wells
he Covinanting himself

April 28 1745 Caesar Servant to the Widow Mary Wells was admitted to the Communion of this chh

Mrs. Wells rented Caesar to other Deerfield residents – in 1741, for example, Joseph Barnard "p^d Wid° Wells for Cesar three days".[3]

Caesar occasionally bought small items from Deerfield merchants.[4]

---

1 Hampshire County Registry of Probate.
2 Deerfield minister's record book, PVMA Library.
3 Account books of Joseph Barnard, PVMA Library.
4 Account book of Elijah Williams and David Field, PVMA Library.

Cesar Wid° Wells D^r to a pair of knee buckels   0 – 4 – 0
Garlic   0 – 8 – 0

In December, 1745, two different Caesars, Caesar who belonged to Widow Wells and Caesar who belonged to Ebenezer Wells, paid some of their debts at Elijah Williams' store with fox skins at the same time.[5]

Cesar Wid° Wells and En^s Wells
C^r by 2 foxes

The Wells' daughter, Mary, married Timothy Childs, Jr. in 1744, and sometime during the next few years, Caesar became Timothy's property. (Mary's mother, "Widow Wells", died in 1750.) A document signed by Timothy Childs, Jr. in 1751 lists many items that came with the marriage.[6]

An Acco^t of Mrs Mary Childs has had of her fathers Personal Estate delivered her by her Mother at & after Marriage ... A platter 20/ Mustard pot 2/6 ½ pound of Indicoe 19/   To Cash her Husband had in part of Caesar the negro man 140 - 0 - 0   To Cash Rec^d of Mother Wells 93-3-4...

Apparently, in the years that had passed since 1735 the "Negro Boy" had become "Caesar the negro man", with an increase in value from £100 to £140.

In 1751 and 1752, Childs paid shoemaker Ebenezer Arms for repairing Caesar's shoes.[7]

Oct 29 1751   Leu^t Childs D^r To y^r Negroes Shoes   0 - 6 - 8
Dec 20 1751   Timothy Childs Junr D^r To y^r Negros Hi^{tp} Shoes 0 - 7 - 9
March 11 1752   Leut Childs D^r To mending y^r negros Shoes   0 - 1 - 9

Caesar continued to make purchases of small items at Elijah Williams' store after he became Timothy Childs' slave. The account books show, for instance, that Caesar, now "Cesar Tim° Childs Negro" rather than "Cesar Wid° Wells " made a number of purchases during the year 1753.[8]

Cesar Tim° Childs Negro
a Woosted cap
a pair of Shoe Buckels

---

5 Account books of Elijah Williams, PVMA Library.
6 Hampshire County Registry of Probate.
7 Account book of Ebenezer Arms, PVMA Library.
8 Account books of Elijah Williams, PVMA Library.

On at least one occasion, Caesar settled his account with "½ a fox".

Cesar   Cr by ½ a fox   £ 0 - 08 - 0

And Sheldon reports that " 'Cesar servant of Timothy Childs' is recorded several times as a soldier in the French and Indian wars".[9]

Mary and Timothy Childs, Jr. later moved to Turners Falls (a village in what is now the town of Montague, across the river from Greenfield). The following account by Sheldon probably refers to Caesar.[10]

> Friends from Deerfield visiting the Childses at the Falls found a negro slave whom they had taken with them from Deerfield sick unto death, and lying in a cold shed, on a rickety bedstead, with scanty covering, and not even a bed of straw under him, with nothing between his body and the bed-cords but an empty bed-tick.

---

9 Sheldon (1895), p. 894.
10 Ibid.

Conclusion

One of the major findings of my own study of slavery in colonial Deerfield is that in the mid-1700s many more slaves lived on Deerfield's main street than had previously been thought.[1] About twenty-five black slaves – according to my best estimate – in the year 1752, 8% of the total number of people (about 300) living on that street. The relatively large number of black slaves who lived there has very definite implications. Slaves were an important source of labor in the farming towns of the Connecticut Valley. In addition, the number of slaves was large enough to constitute a black community, though we know very little about the nature of that community.

Rather than list every known slave who lived in Deerfield from the late 17th century to the end of the 18th century, I focused on a particular moment in order to give a more meaningful idea of what life was like for a black slave living there at that time, something that is almost always ignored in descriptions of life in colonial New England. By presenting so much of the available detail about Deerfield's 1752 slaves, I have tried to move beyond statistics in order to tell as much as possible about the lives these people led.

Making this map, this snapshot of slavery on the main street of Deerfield in the year 1752, has helped to bring these slaves out of obscurity. When I walk or drive up that street, I now see not only handsome restored colonial houses, but also Titus, Humphrey, Phillis, Ishmael, Jenny, and Cato. And I cannot help thinking about the fact that some of those houses that have survived from the 18th century were probably built, in part, by slaves. This is not a thought that often crosses the mind of a 21st-century New Englander.

Consider the sources of our information about those who lived on that street in 1752. All of our knowledge is derived from writings by whites, almost all in the form of legal or official or semi-official documents – wills, probate inventories, bills of sale, church records, tax lists, account books, etc. Almost none of it comes from informal sources such as diaries or family letters. Elihu Ashley, Jonathan Ashley's son, kept a

---

1 As of 2009, for example, one could read the following statement on the website of the Pocumtuck Valley Memorial Association – "Deerfield never had a substantial black population – blacks comprised no more than 2% of the total population."

fascinating diary during the 1770s.[2] But even though his family owned at least two slaves during the whole time Elihu was growing up, though Cato was just twelve years older than Elihu and though Jenny probably prepared thousands of his meals, there is not a word in his diary about Jenny, Cato, or Titus, or about any other Deerfield slaves.

Of all the evidence cited in this chapter, there are only two letters (those that refer to Thomas Williams' "poor Negro girl") and one diary (James Taylor's diary with its description of the time that Ashley came to pray with Peter). I keep hoping to come across an Ashley letter, perhaps one that Jonathan or his wife wrote to a married daughter in which they might have passed on news about Jenny or Cato. Even though all the children grew up with Jenny and Cato in the same household, there are no such letters among the surviving documents.[3]

Jenny lived in Deerfield for seventy years. Cato came to Deerfield as an infant and lived in the Ashley house for almost ninety years. Yet no one even knows where they ate and slept. It is often said that Jenny, Cato, and Titus slept in the attic of the Ashley house. But I know of no *evidence* to support that statement. There is no record – anywhere in the valley – of anything like a row of slave cabins behind the "big house", cabins like those at Monticello or Mount Vernon, but slaves may well have slept in the barns or other outbuildings. From Ashley's account book, we know something about the kind of work that Cato and Titus did, at least on those days that they were rented out. But on other days? During winter storms? Cato and Titus often worked together. How did they get along? What did they talk about? What did the slaves do for recreation? For sex? Indeed, we are almost completely ignorant about the daily lives of all the Deerfield slaves. We do not even know where

---

2 Ashley, Elihu (1773-1775). The original manuscript of Elihu Ashley's diary is in the PVMA Library. An edited version has recently been published – Miller and Riggs (2007).

3 There are some surviving letters that Reverend Ashley wrote to his daughter Dorothy – none of which refer to Jenny or Cato – two that he wrote in 1760 when Dorothy, then seventeen, was attending school in Boston, one that he wrote in 1764 after her marriage, another that he wrote in March, 1765 when Dorothy was about seven months pregnant, and another (this one addressed to his daughter's husband) in May of 1765 just after the birth of Jonathan's first grandchild. (PVMA Library.) The last two of these letters in particular, with repeated talk of "trials and afflictions", descriptions of the imminent childbirth as Dorothy's "expected hours of sorrow", and general thoughts about the "uncertainty and fading of all worldly joys", contributed to the view I expressed earlier in this chapter, that Jonathan Ashley was not an easy person to live with. His sermons were generally no less gloomy than his letters to his daughter.

they were buried. Prince, Joseph Barnard's slave, dug graves for whites in the old Deerfield burying ground. Were he and his fellow slaves buried there or somewhere else?

It is a sad fact that our only physical descriptions of Deerfield's slaves come from "Runaway" (or "Freedom Seeker") notices.[4] There are only two known Deerfield runaway notices, the one quoted earlier in this chapter that Joseph Barnard placed when Prince ran away in 1749 and the one that will be quoted in the Addendum to this chapter, seeking the return of "Peter Pur (alias Pompey)" who ran away in 1728.

What have we learned about the attitudes of the white residents of Deerfield toward their slaves? Their almost complete absence from surviving letters and diaries speaks volumes. They were *property*, listed as such along with the livestock, the furniture, and the real estate. Almost never given the small dignity of a surname, they were often referred to with no names at all, such as the "Black Negro Wench & 2 Children" who appear in Samuel Dickinson, Jr.'s 1781 probate inventory, the "Negro Boy" in the inventory of Jonathan Wells, and David Field's "Negro Female" who was treated by Dr. Williams.[5]

There is no evidence that Connecticut Valley slave owners were reluctant to separate families by sale. Jenny and her son Cato came to Deerfield together,[6] but nine-year-old Phillis, one of three "Negro maids" owned by Westfield's minister, came to Deerfield alone. Whether Tanner, the more valuable slave listed together with Phillis in Reverend Bull's inventory, was her mother or not, it is unlikely that Phillis ever saw her again.

One document that is very revealing about the attitudes of Deerfield residents toward their slaves – though unintentionally so – is a 1751 "Computation of the Expenses of a family Consisting of a man a

---

4 Deerfield is hardly unique in this regard. Except for the occasional description that appears in a "For Sale" advertisement, this limitation is generally true for the whole of New England. Descriptive words in those advertisements, however, were typically terms such as *likely, choice, prime, young,* or *lusty,* positive-sounding words that might catch the attention of a prospective buyer but are actually not very informative.

5 One consequence of the lack of surnames and the fact that so many names such as *Caesar* and *Titus* and *Pompey* were overused is that it is extraordinarily difficult to learn where slaves went if and when they became free and to discover whether or not they have any descendants who might now be living somewhere in the United States. When even the assigned name is unknown, the task is hopeless.

6 Though the identity of Cato's father remains a mystery.

1751 Computation of the Expenses of a family Consisting of a man a woman 4 Children & a maid

Wheat 40 bushels at 22/6	45-0-0
Beef 500 ℔ at 12	25-0-0
pork 17 Score 9½ at 18	26-5-0
Mutton & Veal	10-0-0
fish	3-0-0
Indian Corn 12 bushels at 11/8	7-0-0
malt 11 Bushels	11-0-0
Cyder 12 Barrels	18-0-0
Rum wine metheglin &c	20-0-0
Sugar 100 ℔	25-0-0
Tea Corolate & Rice &c	12-0-0
Butter 200 ℔ at 3/6	35-0-0
milk 2 quarts per day	35-0-0
apples	4-0-0
Turnips	2-0-0
Spices raisins &c	6-0-0
Salt	4-0-0
peese	1-0-0
Chees 60 ℔ at 3/	9-0-0
Tallow 27 ℔ at 3/	4-1-0
Clothing for the family	125-0-0
Doctors Bill	20-0-0
Pocket Expenses	10-0-0
Blacksmiths bill	5-0-0
keeping a horse	15-0-0
pipes & tobacco	4-0-0
Books	15-0-0
paper ink & quils	2-0-0
Schooling girls	7-0-0
maids work	47-0-0
mans help	10-0-0
House repairs & wear of household goods	25-0-0
	587-1-0

A town committee's estimate of Reverend Ashley's annual expenses. (PVMA Library, Deerfield, Massachusetts.)

woman 4 Children & a maid".[7] This computation was made in response to one of several appeals for a salary increase made by Reverend Ashley. (It is not clear from the document itself whether the computation was made by Ashley or by a town committee; a subsequent letter from Ashley to the town makes it clear that it was the committee that drafted this document.[8])

When I first saw this document, I thought that the "maid" must be Jenny and that Cato, then in his teens, was one of the "4 children". (Titus was also an Ashley slave by 1751, a fact I did not know at the time.) Then I realized that in 1751, the Ashleys had four children of their own. That is, Cato was not included as one of the children in this cost-of-living calculation and – in all probability – the "maid" was a white servant girl. Thus neither Cato nor Jenny (nor Titus) were included. But surely the committee that drew up this list knew about Jenny, Cato, and Titus. And they must have known that at the very least food was needed for the slaves, even if they could be clothed with castoffs from members of the Ashley family. Was the cost of keeping two or three slaves simply understood as part of the normal cost of living for an important man such as the minister, a cost that did not even need to be mentioned in an itemized list such as this? What could the committee have been thinking when they omitted Jenny, Cato, and Titus? Even the cost of "keeping a horse" was included. And Ashley himself neglected to mention the expenses of keeping his slaves in his reply to the committee's computation. It is very hard to understand these omissions.[9] Anyone who thinks that slaves in western Massachusetts were "just members of the family" might have second thoughts if they were to consider the implications of this document, innocuous though it seems at first glance.

No census figures are ever exactly correct. This is true in the 21st century, and it is even more true when we are talking about colonial times and trying to count enslaved blacks. I do not want to assert that precisely twenty-five black slaves lived on this street in 1752. "About twenty-five" or "more than twenty" is a more accurate description of my findings. There are a number of reasons why the number "twenty-five" might be too low or too high. In order to emphasize the fact that I

---

7 PVMA Library. See also Sheldon (1895), pp. 538-539.

8 Sheldon (1895), p. 539.

9 Sheldon, too, comments on the fact that Jenny and Cato were not mentioned in this computation. (Sheldon (1895), p. 538.)

make no claim to an exact figure, I would prefer to cite the number as 25 ± 3. (Read that as "twenty-five plus-or-minus three".) By that I mean that if, somehow, the "truth" could miraculously be revealed to us, then if the correct number turned out to be as low as twenty-two or as high as twenty-eight, I would not be at all surprised. But if it turned out to be as low as eighteen, say, or greater than about thirty, then I would begin to wonder how I could have gone so far astray.

If one looks critically at the evidence presented in this chapter, one can easily see possible sources of error. Consider a few examples. My belief that in the year 1752 Daniel Arms owned a slave named Matthew is somewhat tenuous, based as it is on just a few entries from the late 1750s and early '60s in Arms' account book. He might well have bought Matthew sometime in the mid-1750s. Or consider Phillis, who was sold to Timothy Childs, Sr. in 1742. That Phillis came to Deerfield at that time seems quite certain. But illness and death were hardly unknown in this frontier town, and Phillis may have died sometime before 1752, no more notice being taken of her death in the town or church records than of the deaths of other Deerfield slaves. And think about Ishmael (who belonged to Samuel Hinsdell) and Ishmael (who belonged to Thomas Dickinson). The latest information I have found about Hinsdell's Ishmael is a store record from December, 1751, and the earliest record of Dickinson's Ishmael comes from November, 1753. It is therefore possible that these two "Ishmaels" were one and the same person, that Hinsdell sold Ishmael to Dickinson sometime in the interval.

In trying to learn who lived in this place at that time, one must be careful not to include slaves who belonged to non-Deerfield owners. "Cesar Billing", for instance, made some purchases at Elijah Williams' store in 1757.[10] But there was no Billing living in Deerfield at that time – Caesar Billing was almost certainly the property of Greenfield's Reverend Edward Billing.[11] And "Cato Johnson" bought several knives at the same store in 1747. Cato – a name never used for a white person, as far as I know – was probably the property of an owner named Johnson but, again, there was no Deerfield Johnson to whom he could have belonged.

Thus there are various ways in which one could arrive at a spuriously high 1752 figure. But the other side of the coin is that there may

---

10 Account books of Elijah Williams, PVMA Library.
11 See the discussion of Lucy Billing and Caesar, whose 1759 affair was described earlier in this chapter, as well as the Greenfield section in the next chapter.

well be Deerfield slaves of whom no record at all has survived (or no record that I myself have yet come across). Consider Caesar, property of Samuel Childs. The only thing we know about Caesar is that he served in the French and Indian War in the 1750s. Had he not seen service in the war or if George Sheldon had not found those war records, Caesar would be truly lost to history. There may well have been Deerfield slaves about whom no record, not a single scrap of paper, has survived to reveal their existence. My guess – and it is only a guess – is that if my figure, twenty-five, is wrong, it is more likely to be in error by being too low rather than too high. That is, I think it is more probable that there are still undiscovered "1752 slaves" than that one or more names on my 1752 map do not belong there.

An astute reader of my 1752 map will notice that of the twenty-five slaves on the map, nineteen can be identified as male and only six as female. Does the preponderance of males reflect the true proportion, perhaps because – with the need for farm workers – more male slaves than females were purchased? Or is there possibly a systematic bias that makes the appearance of a female slave in the surviving documents less likely? Some of our information about male slaves comes from their service in the French and Indian War; this is one fact that makes a male slave more likely to be known to us now. Many male slaves purchased items at Elijah Williams' store, but the only purchases at that store (or those of other Deerfield merchants) by a female slave that I have come across are those of Lucy Terry.[12] Phillis never made a store purchase, as far as I know. Neither did Thomas Williams' "Poor Negro Girl", or Samuel Dickinson's Phebe. And Jenny, during all her time in Deerfield, never made a store purchase. There is no surviving bill of sale to record her arrival in town. Had Jenny died in 1775, say, before the minister had a chance to mention her in his will, and if Zadock Hawks' account books showing the occasions on which he fixed her shoes had not survived, we would not know that Jenny had ever existed. Perhaps there were a number of female slaves who are now truly unknown.

Here are some examples of the sort of necessary *guesswork* that went into the construction of my 1752 map. The first thing I knew about Prince, Joseph Barnard's slave, was that he ran away in 1749. Neverthe-

---

12 From the account books of Deerfield store owners, it would be nearly impossible to discover that any women, black or white, lived in Deerfield. There was an occasional purchase by "Widow Wells", for instance, but very few others.

less I put him on my map, because I guessed that he had probably not succeeded in running away, that he had somehow been captured and returned to Deerfield. It was only later that my guess was confirmed, when I learned that Prince had again been rented out in the summer of 1750 and that Barnard had bought him a coffin in June, 1752.

Another example, where I made a different guess, is the case of "Amos", who may have been a slave belonging to Timothy Childs, Jr. In 1749, Dr. Williams twice charged Childs for tooth extractions.[13]

> Tim° Childs Jr D^r to Extract 1 Tooth for Amos 4/
> To Ext. 1 Dent. 5/ Amos

On several further occasions, in 1750 and then again in early 1753, Dr. Williams treated "Amos" and prescribed medicines. Amos was a name often used for slaves. And Childs had no children by that name. Amos may well have been a slave belonging to Timothy Childs, Jr., but in the absence of further evidence, such as an account book entry referring to "Amos Timothy Childs Negro" or even "Amos Negro", I decided not to put Amos on my 1752 map.

Another case in which I had to make a guess and – as with Amos – decided to omit someone from my 1752 map is that of a female slave who apparently belonged to Jonathan Wells in the 1730s. When Wells died in 1735, his probate inventory[14] included not only Caesar ("Negro Boy, £100"), who later belonged to Timothy Childs, Jr., but also "Negro Womans Cloathing 02 - 02 - 00". Strangely, the "Negro Woman" does not appear in Wells' inventory, only her clothing, but during the following years, on several occasions Dr. Crouch charged Mary Wells ("Widow Wells") for treating her "Negro woman".[15]

> visits ... Negro woman had some. 1738 to 1743 inclusive, £ 30.3.7

It is not clear from Judd's notes whether this rather large sum was exclusively due to treatments of Widow Wells' "Negro woman" or whether it included charges for visits to family members as well. Knowing nothing more about this woman, knowing that she had been ill and treated by Dr. Crouch (perhaps many times), I decided not to put her on my 1752 map.

---

13 Account books of Dr. Thomas Williams, PVMA Library.
14 Hampshire County Registry of Probate.
15 Judd Manuscripts, Forbes Library. (Judd's notes on Dr. Crouch's accounts.)

Another person who may very well have been a 1752 Deerfield slave owner was Colonel William Williams (1713-1785), a Harvard graduate in the class of 1729. "Colonel Bill" was the grandson of Reverend William Williams, longtime minister of Hatfield, both cousin and brother-in-law of Dr. Thomas Williams – owner of "Our Poor Negro Girl" – and also a cousin of Major Elijah Williams, the Deerfield store owner. Like his cousin[16] Elijah, Colonel Williams operated a store on the main street of Deerfield until about 1754 and in all probability was a slave owner like Elijah. In *Sibley's Harvard Graduates*, we read – "The Colonel lived elegantly, served by a Negro girl named Pendar and a Negro man named Hartford."[17] The author of this essay was not specific as to when Williams owned these two slaves, and though it seems probable that he owned Pendar and Hartford or other slaves in 1752, I decided – lacking further evidence – not to put him on my 1752 map.

In order to obtain a figure for the *percentage* of those living on this street in 1752 who were slaves, one of course needs a figure for the total population – men, women, and children, free and enslaved. My figure of 300 for the 1752 population is necessarily an estimate. There were some forty homesteads on the street at that time.[18] On average, there were perhaps seven or more people living at each of those sites.[19] Simple multiplication led me to the approximate result of 300 and thus about 8% (25 / 300) for the percentage who were enslaved.

What should one carry away from this lengthy discussion of slavery on the main street of Deerfield in 1752? First, I hope that if you have been on that street before, the information presented here will let

---

16 I use "cousin" in the generic sense – Col. William and Major Elijah were actually third cousins, once removed.

17 *Sibley's Harvard Graduates*, Vol. 8, pp. 638-657 (1951). See also Sheldon (1895), Genealogy Section, p. 382; McGowan and Miller (1996), p. 147.

18 McGowan and Miller's book is a priceless source for learning who lived where at various times. (McGowan and Miller (1996).) But they are primarily concerned with the owners, that is, almost exclusively with adult white males (but not with white servants or laborers who did not own property), so it is not possible to use their data directly to calculate the total population of the street. The genealogy section of Sheldon's book is also extremely useful and does include information about children.

19 There were nine people living in the Ashley house in 1752 – Jonathan Ashley, his wife, four children, and three slaves. In addition, they occasionally had a white live-in maid or a young man studying for the ministry. That figure of "nine plus" for the Ashley house is probably a bit higher than average, since the Ashleys had three slaves. As one can see from the map at the front of this book, by no means were all the residents of the street slave owners; there were no slaves at about two-thirds of the houses.

you see the street in a new way. And even if you have never set foot in the Connecticut Valley, you may now have a somewhat different view of what life was like here in colonial times than you had before. There were many enslaved blacks here in the 1750s. But these are people most visitors never hear about, of whom even most longtime residents are unaware. To borrow Ralph Ellison's term, the black slaves of the Connecticut Valley are the invisible men and women of our colonial past.[20]

Second, slavery was a central feature of life in the valley in colonial times. Slavery was perfectly acceptable here, with many community leaders such as Jonathan Ashley and Elijah Williams owning slaves. Slavery was important in various ways, though it did not dominate the scene the way it did in the South. To invoke a common distinction, this was not a "slave society" (like Mississippi or South Carolina in the decades before the Civil War), but it *was* a "society with slaves".

Third, slaves were not members of the family. They were property – bought and sold, taxed together with the cows and horses, passed on to descendants by will, subject to being sold away at the whim of the owner, sold away from their children or their parents. Look again at some of the "Slaves for Sale" advertisements in Chapter Three. Think about the chilling language in bills of sale, such as that by which Thomas Wells purchased Peter in 1731 – "I John Cook ... do freely and absolutely bargain, sell and dispose of my Negro man Peter to Thomas Wells and to his heirs and assigns forever ... And I have good right, full power and lawful authority to dispose of him." Standard legal language – "to his heirs and assigns *forever*", "good right to *dispose* of him" – the same language with which a piece of real estate might be sold.

Finally – many slaves lived in Deerfield in the mid-1700s, not just a few but about twenty-five, slaves who worked together, went to church together, and interacted with one another in ways about which we can only guess.

---

20 Ralph Ellison, author of *Invisible Man* (1952).

Addendum – Deerfield, Before and After 1752

In the preceding sections of this chapter we looked closely at the available information about those slaves who were living on the main street of Deerfield in the year 1752. My purpose was to reveal – using that place and that moment as an example – as much as possible about the lives of the slaves in the Connecticut Valley of Western Massachusetts in the mid-1700s. In this Addendum we will look, much more briefly, at the stories of a few other Deerfield slaves, not mentioned previously, who lived in Deerfield before and after 1752.

Deerfield's first settled minister, John Williams, began preaching in Deerfield in 1686 and was ordained in 1688. He may have brought with him one or two black slaves, though the earliest surviving mention of a Deerfield slave is the record of the 1695 death of Williams' slave, Robert Tigo.[1]

Robbert Tigo, Negro Servt to Mr Jno Williams died ye 11th day of May 1695

At least by 1703, Williams had purchased two new slaves, Frank and Parthena, who married – probably in June of that year.[2] On the morning of February 29, 1703 / 1704, there occurred the event for which Deerfield is now most famous – a devastating raid by the French and Indians. Some fifty Deerfield residents were killed during the course of the attack (out of a total population of about 260), and 112 others were taken captive and began the long march to captivity in Canada. Parthena and two of Williams' children were killed during the attack, while Frank, Reverend Williams, his wife, and five of his children were taken captive. Both Frank and Mrs. Williams were killed by the Indians early in the march.[3]

---

1 Sheldon (1895), p. 889. Kevin Sweeney suggests that "Robbert Tigo" may have spent some time in the West Indies and that he may previously have been known as "Roberto Santiago".

2 "Our next glimpse of slavery here is this record on the town book: – 'Frank and Parthena, Mr Jno Williams his negroes were joyned in Marriage by ye Reverend Mr Jno Williams, June 4: 170- .' The year of the century is gone. It was in the sunny month of June and probably 1703." Sheldon makes a point of the fact that this marriage is not recorded in the place where other marriages were listed – "This record is not on the page where marriages were regularly entered, but stands by itself on the fly leaf of the volume." (Sheldon (1895), p. 889.)

3 The story of the 1704 attack has been told many times, most recently and most thoroughly by Haefili and Sweeney (2003). John Williams and all but one of his captive children

Several years later Reverend Williams returned from captivity, wrote a bestseller about his experiences (*The Redeemed Captive Returning to Zion*[4] – still in print as of 2009), and in 1707 became minister at Deerfield again, where he acquired a new wife, five new children, and at least two new slaves. At the time of his death in 1729, his probate inventory listed Mesheck and Kedar among his possessions. Mesheck eventually became the property of Ebenezer Hinsdale, as we saw earlier in this chapter, while Kedar, I believe, became the property of Reverend Williams' son, store owner Elijah Williams.

In 1710 John Sheldon (1658-1733) bought "a negro lad Called Lundun" from the estate of Henry Wolcot, as described in the bill of sale quoted by his descendant, George Sheldon.[5]

> Whare as wee Abiah Wolcot adminstratricks, and Mathew Allyn, adminstrator on the estate of Mr. Henry Wolcot, Esq. late of Winsor in the County of Hertford and Collony of Connectycut in New England, have recieved of Capt. Timothy Thrall as agent for Mr. John Sheldon of Dearefeield in the County of Hamsheier forty five pounds in Province bills.
>
> Doee thare fore sell unto him the said John Sheldin a negro lad called Lundun of about fourteen years of age by the best account we can come at, which s[d] negro rode behind s[d] John Sheldin towards Dearefield on the last day in March in the year 1710 which negro did belonge to s[d] Mr. Henry Wolcot and was parte of his estate. We thare fore the above named adminstratricks and adminstrator doee here by sell and confirme to the said John Sheldin his heaires and assignes, our whole right and titill to said negro lad, and also the right that any other person shall Legally make out, from, by, or under s[d] Mr. Henry Wolcott, as witness ouer hands & sealls hereunto set this fifth day of Apriell 1710.
>
> her
Abiah x Wolcot Adminstratricks
mark
Math Allyn Admistrator

---

were ransomed and returned to New England within a few years, while his daughter Eunice, seven years old at the time of her capture, grew up in Canada, married an Indian, and declined to be ransomed. Her story has been told by John Demos (Demos (1994)). Eunice Williams was just one of more than twenty of the 1704 captives who remained in Canada. (Haefili and Sweeney (2003), Appendix D.)

4 Williams, John (1707).

5 Sheldon (1895), p. 891.

Shortly after 1710, John Sheldon (or "Sheldin") moved to Hartford, where at the time of his death in 1733 he owned seven slaves, who were listed with their values in his estate inventory – Coffee and his wife and child (£130), Boy George (£80), Boy Coffee (£80), Boy Robbin (£70), and Girl Sue (£60). Because of his ownership of seven slaves in 1733, he has sometimes been described as Deerfield's biggest slave owner. However, there is no evidence that he owned more than one slave during the time he lived in Deerfield.[6]

Mehuman Hinsdell owned a slave, "Peter Pur, alias Pompey", who ran away in 1728.

> Ran-away on the 13th. of Novemb. Instant, from their Master Mahuman Hinsdell of Deerfield, Two Men Servants. The one John Griffin, a White young Man, about 16 years of Age, something pock broken, short brown hair, had on a Castor Hat, a Kersey Coat, homespun Jacket with Pewter Buttons, leather Breeches, and gray yarn Stockings. The other a Pequot Indian, named Peter Pur, alias Pompey, of midling stature, hair about 3 Inches long, has a remarkable Scar on the midst of his Forehead, had on a blue Broadcloth Coat, Kersey Jacket with Pewter Buttons, and leather Breeches, speaks good English. They carried away with them 2 Guns, 2 Silver Spoons, & 2 Duffil Blankets. Whoever will take up and convey the said Runaways, or either of them, to their abovesaid Master at Deerfield, shall have Five Pounds Reward for each of them, and all necessary Charges paid.

> *New-England Weekly Journal*   December 9, 1728

John Griffin was probably an indentured servant, but Peter Pur (or Pompey) was almost surely a slave. Although his owner describes him as a Pequot Indian, the alias "Pompey", a common name for enslaved blacks, suggests that he was of mixed Indian and African ancestry.

Mehuman Hinsdell (1673-1736) was the father of Ebenezer Hinsdale, owner of Mesheck and Caesar, and of Samuel Hinsdell, owner of Ishmael, all of whom we met earlier in this chapter. Mehuman Hinsdell's gravestone bears an interesting epitaph.

---

6 Both Sheldon and Baker report that soon after Reverend Williams' return to Deerfield in 1707, John Sheldon moved to Hartford, but neither is specific as to the actual date. It must have been not long after 1710 when Lundun "rode behind said John Sheldin towards Dearefield". Baker gives 1734 as the date of Sheldon's death, while Sheldon gives both 1732 and "about 1733". (Sheldon (1895), p. 892 and Genealogy Section, p. 293; Baker (1878).)

HERE LYES BURIED THE BODY
OF LIEU^T MEHUMAN HINSDELL
DEC^d MAY Y^e 9th 1736.
IN THE 63^d YEAR OF HIS
AGE. WHO WAS THE FIRST
MALE CHILD BORN IN THIS
PLACE AND WAS TWICE CAPTIVATED
BY THE INDIAN SALVAGES
Math. 5. 7. Blessed are the mercifull
for they shall obtain mercy

It is perhaps not surprising that whoever wrote this epitaph did not stop to think that children had probably been born "in this place" before 1673 and that it would have been more accurate to describe Hinsdell as "the first *white* (or *English*) male child born in this place". The Indians do receive mention in this epitaph but not as possible former residents of Deerfield.

Mehuman Hinsdell was indeed, as his epitaph says, "twice captivated by the Indian salvages". The first time was during the famous attack of February 29, 1703/04, when Mehuman and his wife, Mary, were both captured and taken to Canada. Their son Samuel, age one, was killed during the attack. Mehuman and his wife returned from captivity in 1706, and their son Ebenezer (who eventually changed his name to Hinsdale and later became the owner of Mesheck and Caesar) was born during that return passage from Canada. Another Samuel (later the owner of Ishmael) was born in 1708. Then in 1709 Mehuman was captured in an isolated incident and taken to Canada for the second time, eventually returning to Deerfield in 1712 after a tortuous journey by way of France and England.[7]

Many Deerfield slaves were baptized. In addition to those mentioned earlier in this chapter, we find the following baptisms in the minister's record book.[8]

---

7 Demos (1994), pp. 88-91; Sheldon (1895), pp. 333, 367-368 and Genealogy Section, p. 203; Haefili and Sweeney (2003), pp. 173, 201-202, 257-260.

8 Deerfield minister's record book, PVMA Library. Two other slaves, already discussed in this chapter, were also baptized in 1741 – Caesar (property of Mary Wells and later the property of Timothy Childs, Jr.) and Caesar (property of Jonathan Hoyt). We will have more to say about Mrs. Silliman, whose "Servants" Patience and Lemuel were baptized in 1782 and 1786, later in this Addendum. At the time Patience and Lemuel were baptized, Jonathan Ashley had died and the baptisms were performed by Reverend David Parsons

1737   Titus Servt Jn Wells on his account
1741   Pompey Servt Eb^r Sheldon
1782   Patience Negro Servant of Mrs. Silliman by Mr. Parsons
1786   Lem^l Servant Mrs. Silliman

I originally decided to look at the baptism records while trying to identify more clearly the various slaves who lived in Deerfield. One of the difficulties is simply that there were so many slaves on the street with identical names – six "Caesars", for instance, in 1752. Because, I thought, no one is ever baptized more than once, the baptism records might give me some useful clues. Those records did not, as it turned out, help me in distinguishing the various "Caesars" and "Pompeys". They did, though, lead to the accidental discovery of the interesting "Confessions in the Church" section of the minister's record book.[9]

In addition, I came across two interesting exceptions to the "only one baptism" hypothesis. Ebenezer Nims, born in 1687, was captured by the Indians at age seventeen in the 1704 raid, and taken to Canada, where he married fellow captive Sarah Hoyt. Ebenezer and Sarah were "redeemed" in 1714 and returned to Deerfield together, together with their young son, Ebenezer, Jr., born in 1713 and baptized as a Catholic in Canada. In 1737, twenty-three years after their return, Ebenezer, Jr. – now a young man of twenty-four – decided to be baptized again.[10]

Eb. Nims Jun being dissatisfied with a baptism of the Papists Consented to the articles of xtian faith Entered into covenant was baptized & admitted into fellowship. 2 sermons were preached from Rev. 17-5 Showing the chh of Rome is the Mother of harlots spoken of by St John.

Another rebaptism, done for similar reasons, was that of John Victory, originally from Venice, Italy and baptized there as a Catholic, who had somehow ended up in Deerfield and whose first baptism was "corrected" on July 21, 1754.[11]

---

of Amherst. (The first Reverend David Parsons died in January, 1781; this was his son, the new minister of Amherst.) The date (1786) of Lemuel's baptism is interesting, because slavery was coming to an end in Massachusetts by that time. It is possible that Lemuel was not a slave but a white servant; the absence of a surname, though, suggests his status as a slave.

9 See the discussion of Peter (slave of Thomas Wells and then of Thomas Dickinson) earlier in this chapter.

10 Deerfield minister's record book, PVMA Library; Sheldon (1895), pp. 354-355 and Genealogy Section, p. 251.

11 Deerfield minister's record book, PVMA Library; Sheldon (1895), Genealogy Section, p. 350. Sheldon incorrectly gives 1764 as the date of Victory's rebaptism.

Baptized John Victory who had been baptized in the chh of Rome after he had publickly Renounced the Errors of the chh of Rome & professed his belief of the Doctrines of Christianity & had Entred into Covenant to walk agreeable to the Gospel.

These baptism records, with their citations of the passage from the book of *Revelation*, demonstrate the vigor with which the Calvinists of New England disliked Roman Catholics.[12]

In 1758, Matthew Talcott of Middletown, Connecticut sold his slave Hartford to Thomas Dickinson of Deerfield.[13]

Know all Men by these Presents that I Matthew Tallcott of Middletown in Hartford County have Sold unto Thomas Dickinson of Deerfeild in the province of the Masechusets bay one Certain Niegro Man Named Hartford of the age of about Twenty three years and do by these present Sell and Convey the S^d niegro unto the S^d Thomas Dickenson his heirs & assigns as a Slave for Life and do Contract and agree with the S^d Dickenson his heirs and assigns that ye S^d nigro is in a State of Sound body & helth and that I have Good Right to Sell and Convey the S^d Nigro & as aforesaid hearby acknowledging the Receit of Sixty pounds Lawfull Money p^d & Recorded To be paid To me in full Satisfaction for the Nigro in witness whereof I have heareunto Set my hand in presance off John Hall & Seth Wadsworth

Matthew Talcott

From the following brief document, we learn that Hartford appeared in court in 1761, to respond to unspecified charges.[14] What the outcome of this case was we do not know.

Hampshire S.S.   At a Court held in Deerfield Nov. 20, 1761 Before me Thomas Williams Esq. Elijah Williams Esq. Plaintiff & Hartford a Negro man slave to Thomas Dickinson of Deerfield aforesaid Yeoman, Defend^t.

---

12 *Revelation* 17: 3-6 reads – "I saw a woman sit upon a scarlet-coloured beast, full of names of blasphemy, having seven heads and ten horns. And the woman was arrayed in purple and scarlet-colour ... having a golden cup in her hand full of abominations and filthiness of her fornication. And upon her forehead was a name written, MYSTERY, BABYLON THE GREAT, THE MOTHER OF HARLOTS AND ABOMINATIONS OF THE EARTH. And I saw the woman drunken with the blood of the saints, and with the blood of the martyrs of Jesus ... "

13 Hampden County Registry of Deeds. In addition to the use of classical or biblical names for slaves, sometimes the names of cities were used, such as "Boston" or "Hartford".

14 Sheldon (1895), p. 904.

Upon considering y[e] proof made out against s[d] Negro recognize his s[d] master for his appearance at Court

Att. Thomas Williams.

Hartford had an account at John Russell's store in the early 1760s, where his most frequent purchases were rum (and molasses for making his own).[15]

5 Quarts of Molasses
2 Quarts and a point of molasses
Quart of Rhum
1 point of Molasses
1 Quart of Rum

And then in 1766 Hartford was sold again, this time to William Williams of Pittsfield.[16]

Deerfield December 16th 1766
Rec[d] of William Williams of Pittsfield Esq Fifty Pounds for my Negro Man named Hartford, which I acknoledge to be in full Consideration for him and hereby promise and oblige myself & my Heirs, to warrant, secure & Defend to him the said Williams his Heirs & Assignes against the Claims & Demands of all Persons whatsoever in Witness whereof I have hereunto set my Hand & Seal this 16th Day of December 1766

Tho[s] Dickinson

Lucy and Abijah Prince (and their children) are the only free blacks known for certain to have been living in Deerfield for any substantial period of time prior to the American Revolution. If there were others, their names do not appear in the church records. Names that may possibly be those of free blacks that occasionally appear in store account books are rarely accompanied by enough information to decide with certainty where they lived.

At least one free black who lived in Ashfield (then called "Huntstown"), ten miles west of Deerfield, makes an appearance in Deerfield account books. In 1750 Dr. Williams treated "Heber Negroe Honestman" by bloodletting, and Heber then settled his account with cash.[17]

---

15 Account books of John Russell, PVMA Library.
16 William Williams Collection, Document #219, Berkshire Athenaeum.
17 Account books of Dr. Thomas Williams, PVMA Library.

December 1750   Heber Negroe Honestman Huntstown
To Phleb   4
Contra – By Cash in full

On July 27, 1751 shoemaker Ebenezer Arms charged "Heber Negro" for a pair of shoes.[18]

Heber Negro D^r to a pair of Shoes   0-6-8

And in November, 1752 he sold "Ebor Negro" some leather.

Ebor Negro D^r To Leather for a Bridel   0 - 4 - 0

On July 8, 1755 "Hebar Negrow" purchased some items at Elijah Williams' store.[19] The next day "Hebar Honistman" bought a bushel of Indian corn and then at the end of the month one and a half bushels of wheat.

Hebar and his wife had been freed by their owner in Easton (south of Boston) in 1722 and moved to what is now the town of Ashfield. During the French and Indian War in the mid- and late-1750s, they, like many residents of Ashfield, moved temporarily to Deerfield for safety.[20]

There is an intriguing entry in the minister's record book for August 29, 1736 – "Pompey Negro & wife Rebecca" were "taken into Full Communion". Information about married slaves and slave marriages in Deerfield is exceedingly sparse. Who were Pompey and Rebecca? There were a number of slaves named Pompey in Deerfield at various times, but I have come across no other mention of "Rebecca". If Pompey and Rebecca were slaves, then this church record is unusual in that there is no mention of an owner or owners. It is possible that Pompey and Rebecca were free blacks who were living in Deerfield or in a neighboring town. Without further information, it is impossible to say.

The only Deerfield document I have found that contains a promise of manumission is the will of Abigail Silliman.[21] Signed in 1785 and

---

18 Account book of Ebenezer Arms, PVMA Library.
19 Account books of Elijah Williams, PVMA Library.
20 Gerzina (2008), pp. 82-83.
21 Hampshire County Registry of Probate. Lucy Terry was freed at or about the time of her marriage in 1756, but no document recording this fact has survived. A few slaves in other towns were freed before the time of the American Revolution. Abijah Prince, a Northfield slave (Lucy's husband) who was freed in 1751, is a notable example. A few slaves from other towns were, like Chloe, freed by will at the time of their owners' deaths, and occasionally slaves were able to purchase their freedom. Some examples will be mentioned in Chapter Five.

implemented after her death in 1787, this will led to the freeing of her slave Chloe.[22] Mrs. Silliman (1708-1787) – more fully Abigail Williams Hinsdale Hall Silliman – was one of the daughters of Reverend John Williams, and thus it was that Mesheck, a slave we met earlier in this chapter – originally the property of Reverend Williams – came into the possession of Abigail's first husband, Ebenezer Hinsdale, who died in 1763. Mesheck, too, was in all probability deceased by 1785 – his first appearance in the record was in Reverend Williams' 1729 estate inventory – but sometime in the ensuing decades Abigail had acquired one or more new slaves.

Abigail outlived not only Ebenezer Hinsdale but two more husbands as well and eventually moved back to Deerfield. After the usual preamble to her will and detailed distributions of money and possessions to a variety of nieces and nephews, Mrs. Silliman made provision for "the comfortable Support and Maintenance of my Servant William Clareck [probably a white servant, not a slave] during said William Clareck's natural Life". She then directed that one hundred acres of land that she owned in Westmoreland, New Hampshire be sold and went on to say that "the proceeds of such Sale I give to Jockton a Molatto formerly Servant of my said Husband Ebenezer Hindsdale".[23] There is a curious provision attached to this grant to Jockton – "... provided said Jockton shall within four years after my Decease be a Subject of either of the United States of America[24] and claim the Legacy aforesaid, but on Failure thereof I give the proceeds aforesaid of said Sale to my said Nephew John Williams ... "

But the most interesting feature of this will is that by its terms Mrs. Silliman gave her slave Chloe (or "Clo") her freedom. A particularly significant feature of the will is the date – 1785. Those who assert that slavery ended in Massachusetts in 1780 or perhaps in 1783 should

---

22 Sheldon accidentally gives two different dates, 1783 and 1787, for Mrs. Silliman's death. The 1783 date is obviously a mistake. (Sheldon (1895), Genealogy Section, pp. 204, 378.)

23 This is the only surviving reference to Jockton of which I am aware. When and where did Jockton belong to Hinsdale? Did Jockton live in Deerfield, or perhaps in Hinsdale, New Hampshire, where Ebenezer had another business. Jockton was *formerly* Hinsdale's slave. When and how did he become free?

24 The word *either* is interesting. (Surely "*any* of the United States of America" was what was intended.) At this time, "United States of America" was usually a plural noun, describing the collection of separate states, not the name of a nation. (Even today, in some formal situations, one will hear references to "these United States".)

consider the implications of wills such as this one.[25]

> My Will is That immediately upon my Decease my Negro Woman –
> Clo – shall be intituled to her Freedom and I do hereby give to the said
> Negro a Bible a cow – a Feather Bed and Bedstead 1 p^r of Sheets – my
> Brass Kittle – and Iron pot – 2 Trammels – a Chest with one Drawer –
> a p^r of Handirons – a Fire Shovel and Tongs – a Silver Table Spoon
> mark'd MT – 4 Black Chairs – 4 Large pewter Basons – 1 Quart D^o – 1
> pint D^o – 1 pewter Quart Cup – 4 pewter plates – and 2 pewter Dishes.
> ...
> ... In Witness whereof I have hereto set my Hand and Seal this Twenty
> Ninth Day of January in the Year of our Lord One Thousand Seven
> Hundred and Eighty Five.
>
>   Abigail Silliman

Excerpt from the 1785 will of Abigail Silliman, providing for the freedom of her
"Negro Woman Clo". (Hampshire County Registry of Probate.)

Mrs. Silliman wanted not only to give Chloe her freedom after her
own death but to give her some possessions (with a Bible and a cow at
the head of the list), to give her a chance to begin her new life as a free
person. And the effort apparently succeeded, for on September 27, 1794,

---

25 We will have more to say in Chapter Eight about when and how slavery came to an
end in Massachusetts.

Noble Spencer and "Chloe Syllaman" declared their intentions and were married a few weeks later.[26]

> Names of persons married by the pastor of Deerfield
> Oct 23 1794   Noble Spencer & Chloe Syllaman

What happened to Noble and Chloe Spencer after their marriage? There is a possible clue in the church records of the neighboring town of Shelburne, which show that on January 16, 1810 Samuel Thompson and Susannah Spencer, both of Shelburne and both identified as "Negro", were married.[27]

NEGRO MARRIAGES

> SPENCER, Susannah, and Samuel Thompson, both negroes, of S.,
> Jan. 16, 1810.

Although the date (1810) is less than sixteen years after the marriage of Noble and Chloe, it is possible – though I have not yet been able to confirm or disprove it – that Susannah was the daughter of Chloe and Noble Spencer.

And what about Mrs. Silliman's other slaves (or servants) whose baptisms were mentioned earlier in this chapter, Patience and Lemuel, baptized in 1782 and 1786 respectively? Neither is mentioned in the will nor do their names reappear in the Deerfield records.

---

26 Deerfield minister's record book, PVMA Library. See also *Vital Records of Deerfield* (1920), pp. 233, 237.
27 Church records of Shelburne. The information shown here is taken from the *Vital Records of Shelburne* (1931), p. 138.

CHAPTER FIVE

Other Towns in the Valley

Introduction

In the previous chapter, we took a close look at slavery in Deerfield, to show – using the main street of that town as an example – what we know, and what we do *not* know, about slavery and the lives of slaves in the Connecticut Valley. I chose Deerfield for this purpose because I happen to know more about Deerfield than about other valley towns, but in this chapter we will take a quick look at the institution of slavery elsewhere in the valley, giving enough information to show that slavery was pervasive throughout the area.[1] Slavery in some towns will be described very briefly, in others with more detail, but none of the towns will be treated with the thoroughness with which Deerfield was discussed in Chapter Four.

A striking feature of the history of slavery in the valley is the number of ministers who owned slaves. My own study of slavery here began with Jonathan Ashley, minister at Deerfield for almost half a century. After my initial surprise at learning that the minister was a slave owner, I soon learned of others. I began to collect slave-owning ministers from the valley. The table on the next page shows the twenty-four ministers for whom I have good evidence of slave ownership. Tax lists are of no help in finding slave-owning ministers, since ministers were exempt from taxation. One must depend on other sources such as wills, estate inventories, and account books. No doubt there were other ministers who owned slaves for whom I have not yet come across the evidence. Of the ministers in this table, the most well known is Jonathan Edwards of Northampton, who owned several slaves and whose name now calls to mind his famous 1741 sermon, "Sinners in the Hands of an Angry God".

---

1 Of course some information about other towns has already been mentioned in connection with Deerfield. Phillis, for instance, a slave of Timothy Childs, Sr. of Deerfield, was formerly a slave of Reverend Nehemiah Bull of Westfield.

Slave-owning ministers from the Connecticut Valley of western Massachusetts

Jonathan Ashley	Deerfield	1732-1780	Yale	1730	See Chapter Four.
Edward Billing	Greenfield	1754-1760	Harvard	1731	See Chapter Four.
Robert Breck	Springfield	1736-1784	Harvard	1730	Carvalho (1984).
Daniel Brewer	Springfield	1694-1733	Harvard	1687	Minkema (2002).
James Bridgham	Brimfield	1736-1776	Harvard	1726	Inventory.
Nehemiah Bull	Westfield	1726-1740	Yale	1723	See Chapter Four.
Isaac Chauncey	Hadley	1696-1740	Harvard	1693	Judd (1863/1905).
Ebenezer Devotion	Suffield	1710-1741	Harvard	1707	Inventory.
Benjamin Doolittle	Northfield	1718-1749	Yale	1716	See Chapter Four.
Jonathan Edwards	Northampton	1729-1750	Yale	1720	Marsden (2003).
Ebenezer Gay	Suffield	1742-1793	Harvard	1737	Ballantine (1737-1774).
Samuel Hopkins	W. Springfield	1720-1755	Yale	1718	Minkema (2002).
Samuel Hopkins, Jr.	Hadley	1755-1809	Yale	1749	By marriage.
Samuel Kendall	New Salem	1742-1776	Harvard	1731	See Chapter Four.
Noah Merrick	Wilbraham	1741-1776	Yale	1731	Will.
Roger Newton	Greenfield	1761-1816	Yale	1758	Newton's record book.
David Parsons	Amherst	1739-1781	Harvard	1729	Runaway notice.
John Russell	Hadley	1659-1692	Harvard	1645	Judd (1863/1905).
Jedediah Smith	Granville	1756-1776	Yale	1750	Carvalho (1984).
Ezra Thayer	Ware	1759-1775	Harvard	1754	Will.
Chester Williams	Hadley	1741-1753	Yale	1735	Will and inventory.
John Williams	Deerfield	1688-1729	Harvard	1683	See Chapter Four.
Stephen Williams	Longmeadow	1716-1782	Harvard	1713	Will and diary.
William Williams	Hatfield	1686-1741	Harvard	1683	Will and inventory

The dates given are the dates of their ministries (beginning with the year of their ordination) and the dates of their graduation from Harvard or Yale. The final column gives abbreviated information about some of the sources of evidence for slave ownership; the inventories and wills referred to here are kept at the Hampshire County Registry of Probate. (Suffield, now in Connecticut, was part of Massachusetts until 1749.)

By now, I am surprised when I find a minister who I can be fairly certain was *not* a slave owner. Several people have told me confidently that Solomon Stoddard, for instance, minister of Northampton for more than half a century, a leading citizen of the valley and Jonathan Edwards' predecessor (and grandfather), was a slave owner. But I have not discovered any evidence to support this claim. In fact, Stoddard's 1728 will

Number of Negro Slaves in the Province of the Massachusetts-Bay, Sixteen Years Old and Upward, Taken by Order of Government in the Last Month of the Year 1754, and the Beginning of the Year 1755.

	Males	Females	Total
Springfield	22	5	27
Hadley	13	5	18
Westfield	15	4	19
Hatfield	5	4	9
Deerfield			
Northampton			
Sunderland			
Brimfield			
Blandford			
Pelham			
Palmer	1	0	1
Southampton	0	0	0
South Hadley	0	0	0
Greenfield			
New Salem			
Montague	0	0	0
Granville	0	0	0
Greenwich			
Sheffield			
Stockbridge			

These are the results for Hampshire County. (Until 1761 when Berkshire County was formed, Hampshire County covered the entire western portion of the province, including the areas of the four modern counties – Hampden, Hampshire, Franklin, and Berkshire.) An important note accompanied the 1815 publication of these statistics – "Where there are blanks, the Returns have either been lost or were not made."

makes it clear that he had at least one servant who was an indentured servant, indentured for a specified period of time and not a slave – "I give to my Beloved wife, Esther, ... my Servant man *during the remainder of the time of his service.*"[2]

In 1754-1755 a census was taken of the number of slaves throughout the province, with the results shown above for Hampshire County

---

2 Hampshire County Registry of Probate.

towns;[3] for some towns, the data were either never collected or were lost before their publication in 1815. Some authors have published these numbers without taking into account the accompanying note calling attention to the missing data. Some have added the numbers to get a spuriously low total; others have used these data without pointing out the restriction to "sixteen years old and upward" or without noticing that this was a census of *slaves* and did not include free blacks.[4]

Springfield

William Pynchon came to the Springfield area in 1636, establishing a fur trading post and beginning to acquire land rights through negotiations with the Indians. William was not a slave owner,[5] but his son, John, was. In what is probably the earliest surviving mention of slavery in western Massachusetts, a 1657 entry in John Pynchon's account book shows that he owed John Leanord [*sic*] seven shillings and sixpence "for bringing up my negroes".[6] John Pynchon owned a number of slaves – Harry, Roco, Sue, Tom, and at least one other, a woman listed without a name in his probate inventory.[7] Roco is a rare example of a slave who owned a significant amount of property – by 1685 he owned sixty acres.[8] Roco and Sue were married by Pynchon in 1687 – "Roco and Sue my Negroes, Joined in Marriage".[9]

---

3 Collections of the Massachusetts Historical Society, Vol. 3 of the Second Series, pp. 96-98 (1815). The numbers of slaves shown for the towns at the head of the list (Springfield, Hadley, Westfield, and Hatfield) are very roughly similar to the actual numbers for Deerfield – one of the towns for which the data are missing – as fractions of the total population, though somewhat lower for Springfield and Hatfield than might have been expected. At the time of this census, several communities that later became separate towns were still subdivisions of larger towns. Amherst, for instance, was a precinct of Hadley, and Longmeadow, West Springfield, and Wilbraham were precincts within the town of Springfield.

4 For instance, Piersen (1988), p. 164; Minkema (2002), p. 50 (note 21); Greene (1942), p. 339; Proper (1997), p. 21.

5 Though Earle claims that he was. (Earle (1893), p. 92.)

6 That is, up the Connecticut River. (Account books of John Pynchon.)

7 Account books of John Pynchon; estate papers and probate inventory at the Hampshire County Registry of Probate; Trumbull, J. Hammond (1886), p. 406; Carvalho (1984), pp. 12, 158-161.

8 Carvalho (1984), p. 12.

9 *Pynchon Papers* (1982-1985), Vol. 2, pp. 236, 482. From "Records of the County Court of Hampshire".

Eight years later Roco and Sue purchased their freedom.[10]

Oct 20th 1695 Agreed with Roco Negroe ... That for his & his wifes freedoms which is to be absolute upon his paying to me as followeth which is to say He is to pvide & allow or pay me Twenty five Barrels of good cleane pure Turpentine of 40 gallons to a Barrel & Twenty one barrels of Good merchantable Tarr: where of he is to pay wt he can next yeare by this time 12 Mo & I give him for the Rest the yeare after so that within Two yeares he is to pay the whole & he is Intirely discharged from me upon the reading of this / Dick Negro came & desyred me to abate & he would Ingage with me & so I Doe as followeth & They & Each of them jointly & severally Bind themselves to pay for this [?] the Turpentine as aforesd that is to say five & Twenty Barrels & to be ful of Good pure Turpentine of 40 gallons to a Barrel al to be pd next summer & Roco is to deliver up to me al Implemts whatsoever he hath of mine

Hereunto each of them subscribe & Ingage by setting to their Hands this 20th of Octobr 1695 & each of them discharged

<blockquote>
The marke of Roco
The mke of Richard Blackleech the Negro Dick
</blockquote>

If the Summer be so cold that the Turpentine cant Run I pmise If they fal short then to stay for some of them til the next year after this coming doing their utmost Indeavors & following it Close

John Pynchon died in January, 1702/03,[11] and his probate inventory, taken three years later, on January 1, 1705/06, included –

A negrow Man Servant	10 - 00 - 00
A Negrow Maid Servant	30 - 00 - 00

The "negrow Man Servant" listed here was Tom. The name of the "Negrow Maid Servant" is not known, nor is the fate of Harry, another slave once owned by Pynchon.

Further papers show that the estate was not finally settled until the 1720s.[12] Estate papers dated from March, 1723/24 to October, 1726 list various further assets of the estate, including some of Tom's clothes – "a parcel of old Cloathing of Black Tom Negrow", for instance – and debts owed for purchasing some other items for Tom. A paper dated

---

10 *Pynchon Papers* (1982-1985), Vol. 2, pp. 482-483. From the account books of John Pynchon. (Sue died in 1711, but there is no record of Roco's death. (Carvalho (1984), p. 159.))

11 *Pynchon Papers* (1982-1985), Vol. 1, p. xxviii.

12 Hampshire County Registry of Probate.

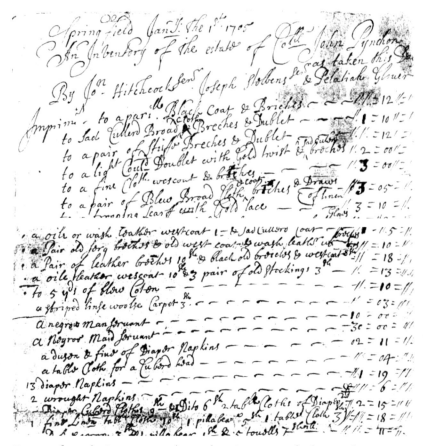

Excerpts from the January, 1705/06 probate inventory of John Pynchon. (Hampshire County Registry of Probate.)

November, 1723 shows that money was owed by Pynchon's estate for –

> Keeping Tom from ye 20th of March Last being a Charge to the Estate to the 27th Currtt being the day when he Dyed wth Extraordinary Trouble being Sick most all the Time & Not able to help Himself

Other charges were shown for "Digging Tom's Grave 3" and "A Coffin for Do 2/6", and another document shows "that the Sd Estate is Insolvent and not Sufficient to Discharge the Debts of Sd Deceasd". Was Tom still a slave when he died in 1723? If so, to whom did he belong after John Pynchon's death twenty years earlier? And why was Pynchon's estate still responsible, so long after Pynchon's death, for expenses related to Tom?

Many prominent Springfield citizens were slave owners, including Colonel William Pynchon, Dr. Charles Pynchon, Josiah Chapin, Deacon Jonathan Church, Colonel Josiah Dwight, Jonathan Dwight, Luke Bliss, Timothy Bliss, and Jedidiah Bliss, who owned "half a dozen or so of slaves, among them Prince and Peter, Pompey, Cambridge and Presence".[13] Springfield ministers were also slave owners. Reverend Breck, for example, owned quite a number of slaves at various times – Pompey, Ron, Rose, and Sylvia.[14]

Suffield

The Pynchons were also involved in the initial settling of Suffield, a bit down the river from Springfield, where Harry and Roco, John Pynchon's slaves, helped to build the first sawmill in 1672.[15] Two Suffield ministers are known to have been slave owners. Ebenezer Devotion's term as minister began in 1710, and sixteen years later the town voted money for the specific purpose of helping him purchase a slave – "£20 toward ye purchase of his negroes".[16] His probate inventory included "Phillip a Negro Man £30".[17] Devotion's successor, Ebenezer Gay, owned at least one slave, Sylva, who was frequently loaned to Reverend Gay's brother-in-law, John Ballantine, the minister at Westfield.[18]

Longmeadow

Stephen Williams, son of Reverend John Williams of Deerfield, was captured as a boy of ten in the 1704 raid on Deerfield and taken to Canada as a captive, together with his father and four of his brothers and sisters.[19] After his return from captivity he went to Harvard, graduating in 1713, and became minister at Longmeadow. Did his own experiences as a captive of the Indians or perhaps his Harvard education cause him to have doubts about the practice of enslaving others? Apparently not – at least not enough to keep him from acquiring slaves – for after beginning his

---

13 Morris (1879), pp. 211-212; Everts (1879), Vol. 2, p. 825.
14 Carvalho (1984), pp. 156-160.
15 Trumbull, J. Hammond (1886), Vol. 2, p. 406.
16 Ibid.
17 Hampshire County Registry of Probate.
18 Ballantine (1737-1774).
19 Haefeli and Sweeney (2003), p. 285; Haefeli and Sweeney (2006), p. 282.

Excerpts from the 1741 probate inventory of Reverend Ebenezer Devotion, including "Phillip a Negro man", valued at £30. (Hampshire County Registry of Probate.)

ministry at Longmeadow, Williams, like so many other ministers, purchased slaves. But in doing so, he was only following the example of Increase Mather, president of Harvard from 1685 to 1701.[20]

A personal note – Stephen Williams was the hero of *Boy Captive of Old Deerfield*, a book that I devoured as a child.[21] When I later became seriously involved with the study of colonial history, I remembered my childhood fascination with that book, and – now thinking about slavery – I was quite certain that his family's ownership of slaves was not

20 Hall (1988), pp. 291, 357.
21 Smith, Mary P. Wells (1904). See in particular pp. 7, 19, 45, 79.

mentioned in the book. I was wrong. Looking again at the book, I found that Frank and Parthena were very clearly described as slaves – "Parthena, the negro slave woman" and "Frank, his father's faithful slave". Had the author used the more common colonial term, *servant*, I might have been excused for not understanding what was meant. But even the unambiguous word *slave* was something that I, as a ten-year old, simply did not notice – what I focused on were exciting things like Indian raids, warfare, and scalping.

Stephen Williams owned quite a number of slaves during his long tenure as minister at Longmeadow – Cato, Peter, Phillis, Scipio, Stamford (or Stanford), Tobiah, and Tom.[22] Williams kept a detailed diary, in which he often pondered his proper duty toward his slaves.[23] He seemed quite proud of how "humble" he was. He was also confident that he treated his slaves very well, comparing himself favorably with other ministers. Perhaps that confidence was justified, but the fact is that two of his slaves committed suicide and one ran away. Many of his diary entries are given below.[24]

> March 26, 1719
> this day I bought me a Serv[t] man – Some of my neighbours think it may be for the better, others think not. I pray y – to help me to do my Duty towards him – & then I may be Easy – alltho he sh[d] not do as he ought to do for me.

> June 18, 1730
> M[r] H. & B & mySelf are projecting Something - concerning purchaseing of Slaves - y[e] L[d] grant we may not be immers[d] in O - & oh L[d] help us to do o[r] Duty - to all comitt[d] to our care -

In 1732, he visited several times with a black prisoner who was awaiting execution.

> October 29, 1732
> This day I preach[d] at y[e] town & endeavoured to adapt my discourse in Some measure to y[e] circumstances of y[e] poor condemn[d] negro – to w[m] I allso apply[d] – mySelf Pticularly – oh L[d] be pleas[d] – to pity & help him oh L[d] be pleas[d] to enlighten him by thy Spirit – & work in him, both to will & to do of thy own Good pleasure. – I have taken Some

---

22 Williams, Stephen (1715-1782); Carvalho (1984); Minkema (2002); Williams' will (Hampshire County Registry of Probate).
23 Williams, Stephen (1715-1782).
24 The entries quoted are taken from the typewritten transcript of his diary.

pains w^{th} & for this poor creature – more than Some others of ye ministers – I observe people are ready, to comen^d me for it – – I pray God
to make me humble & keep me humble. I have no reason to Boast – I
am a poor ignorant creature – & Slothfull – ye L^d have mercy upon me
o^h y^t I might be approv^d of God.

Again and again he wrote about the duties of owners toward their
slaves.

February 17, 1733/34
I have been discoursing of ye duties of masters & Serv^{ts}. ye L^d be pleas^d
to help – all in these relations to do y^r duty.

In the same entry he recorded the baptism of his own slave, Phillis.

I Baptiz^d Searg^t J. Cooley/negro & o^r Phillis – I pray God to pity &
own ye poor creatures and let y^e be made free by jX.

Phillis was apparently considering marriage in the late 1730s.
Stephen's wife, Abigail, was opposed to the idea, and Stephen found
himself "in a strait".

January 16, 1737/38.
I am in a Strait respecting Phillis – my wife is so averse to hr marrying

Phillis did indeed marry, but not until 1744, when she married Peter, a slave belonging to Captain George Colton.[25] It was probably Reverend Williams who performed the ceremony, but there are no surviving pages of his diary from this time.

Williams' slave Stamford became very ill in 1752 and died ten days
after the first mention of his illness in his owner's diary.

January 21, 1752
oh for patience & prudence – this day Stamford is taken wth the pleurisie
– & his Knee, leg – are Swel^d much – what ye Event will be, I know not
– ye L^d have mercy upon ye Soul of the poor creature. oh y^t G.d w^d
reveal himself – in his Love to the poor creature.

January 22, 1752
Stamford is very bad – ye L^d help us to do o^r Duty to ye poor creature –
& graciously prepare for thy pleasure oh Ld G.d.

January 26, 1752
Stamford is very bad – oh y^t G.d w^d reveal himSelf in his Son to ye poor
creature: oh y^t his Soul might be Sav^d.

---

25 Carvalho (1984), pp. 154-155.

January 28, 1752
Stamford is alive yet – & I hope – rather better – ye L^d be pleas^d to prepare for his holy will – w^{t}ever it may be if his life is prolong^d I hope it may be in mercy to him & us all –

January 31, 1752
in ye Evening Stanford dy^d – ye L^d be pleas^d to Sanctify his holy Hand – & Give us to learn ye lesson we Should – by this providence – & Enable Each one of us – to cary as we Should do.

February 1, 1752
this day Stanford is laid in dark Silent Grave ye place where ye Servant is free a^c his master – oh y^t G.d would help me, to remember – I have a master in Heaven – & oh y^t I might Serve him faithfully – obey him cheerfully – oh Ld Help me to do my Duty to all und^r my care –

Tom was the first of Williams' slaves to commit suicide, by drowning himself in the mill pond.

September 30, 1756
Davenport is return^d home – but hears nothing of poor Tom. I fear ye poor creature – has destroy^d – himself of living – I desire we may hear of him – oh for a Sutable frame of Spirit – under ye rebukes of Divine providence – upon one acc^t & another.

October 1, 1756
this day poor Tom was found Dead in ye mill pond; a most awefull case; oh for Grace – to be grant^d to us of this house, to cary as we sh^d under this providence & learn ye lessons we sh^d from it –

Abigail, the minister's wife, also kept a diary where she occasionally referred to the family's slaves. Here, for instance, she recorded her reaction to the news of Tom's death.[26]

Friday Oct 6 1756
Davenport found our negro man of (tom) 22 or 23 years of age drownd in ye mill pond at Longmeadow Brook after a fortnights absence ye last Tuesday. That such a sorrowful thing shod be amongst us a premeditated self Murder even ye poor creature tom our negro   O affect us suttably hierwith o al for X

In spite of Tom's suicide, Williams contemplated buying another

---

26 Abigail Williams' diary. Abigail did everything she could to save paper. Her minute handwriting and her use of every bit of marginal space provide a challenge to any would-be reader.

slave, but asked God for guidance.

July 4, 1757
we have had tho'ts of buying another Negro, but I am at a loss in my
own mind - I pray G.d to help me to do my Duty towards those und^r
my care.

A few years later Cato, another Williams slave, began behaving
strangely, asked to be sold, became concerned about death, "spoke out
loud" during church service, on one occasion "stripped himself naked"
and "ran after E.E. & flung her down", was "severely whipped" several
times, and finally drowned himself in a well.

January 13, 1759
this m- poor Cato came to me in my Study & Seems desirous to be
Sold: I want wisdom to conduct, my family – oh Lord, Grant me wisdom & patience & prudence.

January 12, 1760
this day poor Cato asks what he Shall do w^n I am dead – who he Shall
live with – an intimation of my own dissolution – & I wish I may duly
improve it – –

March 30, 1761.
this morning Cato moveingly advertis^d me of my mortality by asking
what he Shall do w^n I am dead – which he Says will be by & by. ye Lord
help me to realize this – & Give me, to wait in on my faith, repentance
& new obedience till my change may come & ye Lord be pleas^d to take
care of ye poor fellow, – and Enlighten him wth ye Knowledge of X &
bring him home to thySelf.

October 28, 1762
this Evening, Cato came to me, very much affect^d (Even to weeping)
at the tho't of christ which he had lit of – in his Book (as he s^d) – I am
Glad to See him concern^d – but his want of Knowledge – is Such y^t I
am at Great loss how to conduct toward/ him – oh for grace & wisdom, to do my Duty to this poor creature – oh y^t G.d w^d be pleas^d to
reveal himSelf in his Son – to this poor Servant & Grant he may be
made free ye Son of G.d –

October 30, 1762
we had an uncomfortable night – poor Cato was in a piteous case –
had (I fear) drank too much cidr & his mind – turmoil^d – I apprehend
– we were oblig^d to Send for Mr Giles – who with my Som Sam^{ll} Sat up

the Greatest part of yᵉ night wᵗʰ him

October 31, 1762
Cato – more calm – but is not as he was wont to be – he went to the
publick worship – but Spoke out Loud – at yᵉ End of yᵉ afternⁿ Sermon
– I am at a loss yet as to his difficulty – I ask for prudence – to conduct
aright.

November 13, 1762
yᵉ Lᵈ be pleasᵈ to Show me my Duty wᵗʰ respect to poor Cato – who
behaves unusually – oh yᵗ G.d wᵈ teach him & restrain him – & bring
him to know yᵉ true G.d as j X wᵐ he has Sent – oh yᵗ his reason might
be continuᵈ to him.

November 15, 1762
this day poor Cato behavᵈ himself in a most Audacious manʳ – Stript
himself nakᵈ – ran after E. E. & flung her down – but help came Speed-
ily – I am at utmost loss wᵗ to do – dont Know whether yᵉ fell.w is crazᵈ
& deprivᵈ of his reason – or Given up to his own Hearts Lusts – I ask
of G.d to Give me & my family wisdom – to direct us: oh yᵗ G.d wᵈ
prevent any mischief.

November 16, 1762
this by yᵉ advice of my neighbours Cato was whipᵈ very Severely – &
I have put him into yᵉ Hands of my Sons John and Samˡˡ after his correction he appearᵈ Somewhat penitent. I wish – he may be truly so.

November 17, 1762
I returnᵈ home at night – and found my family in a russle & Pplexity
again by reason of Cato/ conduct – who had oposᵈ & resistᵈ my Son –
Severall neighbours were present & he was Severely correctᵈ again. –
oh yᵗ G.d would direct & help us – Show us oʳ Duty and Grant us
wisdom & prudence - and oh Lᵈ be pleasᵈ to pity & pardon the poor
creature.

November 22, 1762
my Sons been killing hogg/ – thus yᵉ creatures are put into Subjection
to man & we are allowᵈ to use yᵉ for oʳ comfort – oh yᵗ God – wᵈ –
preserve us aᶜ luxury – oh Lᵈ be pleasᵈ to give us, so to use O/ good
things, as not to abuse yᶜ.

December 14, 1762
I am in concern & Pplexity about wᵗ we shᵈ do wᵗʰ respect to Cato – I
pray to God to Show us oʳ Duty & visitt us wᵗʰ his mercy; I do beg we
may not do, wᵗ is displeasing to G.d.

December 20, 1762
my Sons are projecting ab^t Cato – what to do wth him – oh Ld G.d be pleas^d to Show ye w^t y^r Duty is.

December 23, 1762
ye L^d be pleas^d to Show us o^r Duty wth respect to Cato.

January 8, 1763
this m- my Son Reynolds – came in very Early & brot us an account y^t Cato – was missing – & twas Sopos^d was drown^d in the well: a most awefull & affecting affair – oh y^t we might be humbled – we of ye family be humbled – & be Enabled to cary it, as we sh^d – oh y^t we may not dishonour G.d – or reproach religion – Give us to consid^r o^r ways, o^r conduct – & behaviour toward o^r Servants & oh y^t G.d w^d graciously forgive, w^t has been Amiss. Sam^{ll} went out – & acct y^y had drawn Cato out of ye well. ye L^d be pleas^d to teach us, Guide us – & pardon us – & Show us thy mind & will.

A decade later, another slave, Peter, ran away, "ungratefully". Reverend Williams reports that he had been thinking of giving Peter his freedom but wanted to be careful not to do anything "dishonourable to religion".

August 12, 1773
this day my Son John send/ me word, that Peter Negro is run away ungratefully, left my Son – (now under difficulty) who has been Kind to him & very tender of him – I had been thinking of Setting him at liberty (if it could be done without injury to me, or the publick) – w^t measures to take now – I am at a loss – desire I may not do anything, that may be dishonourable – to religion.

It was only a few months later that Williams wrote his will – in March, 1774, almost a decade before he died.[27] Williams realized that Peter might not return and allowed for this possibility in his will. He also took care to provide for Phillis, whom he had baptized forty years earlier.

Item my mind, and will is, that my Son John, and Sam^{el} do take Care of, and provide for my Servant phillis negro, what is proper, needfull and comfortable for her so long as she lives, and this to be done by my said Sons, in Equall proportion; and in consideration of thier thus taking Care of phillis – I do Give to my said sons John & Sam^{el} my Negro

---

27 Hampshire County Registry of Probate.

Servant Peter, to be thiers – thier heirs, and assigns; but inasmuchas Peter is absconded – or run off, if they never recover him – and Phillis becomes entirely helpless & wholly a charge – I expect that they (i e John & Sam^el) be at Expenses Equally.

Excerpt from the 1774 will of Reverend Stephen Williams. (Hampshire County Registry of Probate.)

Phillis died, however, not long after Williams wrote his will, as Williams recorded in his diary.

May 28, 1774
this m- Dy^d (in a Sort of Applolectick fit) my Negro woman; an affecting providence – Death is come into our House –ye Lord Grant we may hearken to his voice – phillis had ye charactr of being Honest – & I hope had had Sight of X by faith. ye Lord be pleas^d to pardon my Defects of Duty – towards her, & to my other Servants Deceas^d, oh Lord be pleas^d to make me Sincere in thy Service – make me thy faithfull Servt

May 29, 1774
& Sabboth – aftr meeting at night – phillis was buri^d – considrable numbr of people attend^d ye funerall – ye Lord Grant we may find it Good to attend at ye Grave, ye house appoint^d for all liveing.

And Peter, too, Williams was informed, died a few months later, though where he had been in the year since he ran away is not clear.

September 10, 1774
this m, Serg^t David Burt came in – told me peter negro dy^d last night very Suddenly, & allmost alone – a call to us all to prepare for Death – Especially to those of us – who are old

Wilbraham

Noah Merrick of Wilbraham was another minister who owned several slaves – Lucy, Luke, Meneder, Oronoke, and Scipio.[28] In his 1776 will he carefully divided the use of his "Negro Boy, Named Scipio" between his wife and his son.[29]

> ... I give to my Beloved Wife, Abigail, the use & property of one half my Negro Boy, Named Scipio, in Conjunction with my Son, Chileab-Brainerd[30]; as also, my Clock, my Bible & Psalm Book ... I give to my Son, Chileab-Brainerd, yᵉ one half of my Negro Boy, named, Scipio, in Conjunction, with his Mother; – – my brown horse, my newest Saddle & Bridle; A Yoke of Oxen, Such as he Shall choose, out of my Stock of Cattle ...

Palmer

John Scott of Palmer (then known as the "Elbow Tract" or simply "The Elbows") was "an affluent school teacher preparing for the ministry" who died in 1737 at the age of twenty-seven while visiting friends in the part of Hadley that later became the town of Amherst.[31] (Though a Palmer resident, Scott was buried in Amherst, the first person buried in Amherst's newly created West Cemetery.[32]) The first item under "Personal Estate" in Scott's November, 1737 probate inventory was "A Negro Man".[33]

A Negro Man att ..... 120 - 00 - 00

Thomas Wilson, in an 1852 "Historical Address" about Palmer, wrote that "According to the negro census of 1755, there was but one colored person in this town, and he a *slave !* owned by William Scott".[34] [Italics in original.] Wilson apparently did not realize that the census to which he referred did not include free blacks but was instead a census of

---

28 Carvalho (1984), p. 152; Minkema (2002), p. 50 (note 23).

29 Hampshire County Registry of Probate.

30 Brainerd was the maiden name of Merrick's wife, Abigail.

31 Temple (1889), p. 545; Smith, James (1999), p. 1; Smith, James (1984), p. 640; *Vital Records of Palmer* (1905).

32 Carpenter and Morehouse (1896), p. 58.

33 Hampshire County Registry of Probate.

34 Wilson, Thomas (1855), p. 24. William Scott was the father of John Scott, whose 1737 estate inventory was just mentioned. (Temple (1889), p. 545.)

Excerpts from the 1776 will of Reverend Noah Merrick. In his will, Merrick divided the use of his "Negro Boy Named Scipio" between his wife and his son. (Hampshire County Registry of Probate.)

Excerpt from the 1737 probate inventory of John Scott, including "A Negro Man", valued at £120. (Hampshire County Registry of Probate.)

"Negro *Slaves* ... Sixteen Years Old and Upward".[35] So even if the 1755 census results for Palmer were accurate, it is quite possible that there were also free blacks in Palmer at that time and perhaps slaves younger than sixteen.

  Temple gives a list of soldiers enlisted by the town of Palmer toward the end of the American Revolution, including two slaves.[36]

| Primus Jackall | July 5, 1781 | 24 | black | 5 ft. 1 in. | Farmer |
| Pelatiah McGoldsmith | July 31, 1781 | 20 | black | 5 ft 6 in. | Farmer |

  Temple continues –

The bounties paid to these men were as follows: To Jackall (who was a slave), £100 14 silver money; to Goldsmith (also a slave), £92 10 silver money ...

  And then, in a footnote –

It appears that the owners of these slaves afterwards claimed compensation for their services. And the next year the town "voted £128 19 0 for to pay for the two Negroes that the town has sent into the Three Years service." In 1784 the case was before the court at Northampton. And a town meeting was called "To see what the town will do about

35 The Hampshire County results for the 1754-1755 slave census were given earlier in this chapter.
36 Temple (1889), p. 196. Both Jackall and McGoldsmith are listed in *Forgotten Patriots* (2008); Jackall is listed in *Massachusetts Soldiers and Sailors*.

the Negro man Primus, that Capt. Watson bought of Mr. Bardwell of Belchertown, to serve in the army: Also Pelatiah Goldsmith, bought of Maj. Aaron Graves, for the same purpose." Dea. John Smith was appointed agent to act for the town. The result is not recorded.

Westfield

There were many slave owners in Westfield. Reverend Nehemiah Bull died in April, 1740, and his probate inventory, made two months later, included three "Negro maids" – Tanner, Phillis, and Dido.[37] Phillis (who was discussed in Chapter Four) was sold to Timothy Childs, Sr. of Deerfield in February, 1741/42. Dido, probably Phillis' younger sister, had died the previous June at the age of four.[38] Tanner, on whom a higher value was placed in Bull's inventory than either Phillis or Dido, may well have been their mother, but no one knows what happened to her after Bull's death.

Reverend John Ballantine, Bull's successor, was apparently not himself a slave owner, but on many occasions he borrowed Sylva, a slave of his brother-in-law, Reverend Ebenezer Gay of Suffield. His diary includes frequent references to Westfield slaves.[39] A few excerpts are given below.

March 23, 1743	Sent f[r] in y[e] morning to pray wth D[r] Ashlys Negro boy, reckon'd a dying. died before I got there, prayed with them.
March 24, 1743	pray[d] at D[r] Ashlys Negros funeral.
July 10, 1743	preachd from Acts 8.27. to 39 to Negroes
January 19, 1754	4 negros whip[t] publickly
March 24, 1763	married Nero & Chloe – Servants Cap[t] Bancroft
January 21, 1764	A Negro Fellow was Severly whip[t] at the Whipping Post by his Master M[r] Smith of Southampton & Josiah Parks for abusing s[d] Parks Daughter about 10 y[r] old.
January 29, 1768	Jock, Serg[t] Fowlers Negro, whip[t] 29 lashes for Severly abusing C[t] Mosely, etc.
June 2, 1774	married Benhadad negro & Dolle, Molatto rec[d] 6/

37 Hampshire County Registry of Probate.
38 Carvalho (1984), p. 147.
39 Ballantine (1737-1774).

The 1774 marriage of Benhadad (slave of Thomas Ashley) and Dolle (slave of Azariah Mosely) was performed over the objection of Dolle's owner. Carvalho, quoting from the Westfield records, writes that "ye master of Dolle entered his desent and forbid ye bands of matrimony". The dissent was entered on the record of marriage intentions.[40]

Reverend Jonathan Ashley's grandfather was one of the first settlers of Westfield, moving there in the mid-1660s, and by the mid-1700s there were many Ashleys in Westfield. Jonathan and three first cousins graduated from Yale together in the class of 1730 – four Ashleys in a class of eighteen. In addition to Jonathan (who became the minister in Deerfield), there was Israel (who became a doctor in Westfield), Joseph (who became the minister in Sunderland), and John (who became an important political figure in the far western part of the province). Joseph was probably not a slave owner, but Jonathan, Israel,[41] and John all owned slaves. John Ashley moved to Sheffield, becoming a successful lawyer, a judge, a colonel in the militia, and a representative of the town in the General Court of Massachusetts. One of his slaves was Mumbett (later Elizabeth Freeman), whose suit for freedom may have played a part in the ending of slavery in Massachusetts. (See Chapter Eight.)

John Gunn was a major slave owner in Westfield, and in his will dated January 19, 1747/48 he left his four slaves to his wife, providing that his two male slaves, Primus and Prince, were to be freed after his wife's death.[42]

> In the Name of God Amen. This nineteenth Day of January one Thousand Seven Hundred and Forty Seven Eight. I John Gunn of Westfield ... I Give and Bequeath to Elizabeth My Dear and well Beloved Wife ... Moreover I give her two feather Beds, Bolsters and Pillows and all the new Linnen & Wollen Cloth Belonging to me all my flax & Pork & Beef, Syder and two fat Swine Eight Bushel Wheat Twenty Bush^el Rye ... and the Crop of wheat and Rye now on the ground and all the Hay in my Barn and Furthermore I give her My Negro woman Named Ginney and a Negro Girl Named Chloe That are Likewise given to her for her Dispose forever.
>
> Item I Give to My Negro man Named Primus a Small Bible a narrow ax a Broad hough a Syth and Tackling and a Syckle and after my wives

---

40 Carvalho (1984), p. 37.

41 See the March, 1743 entries from Ballantine's diary quoted above. See also Carvalho (1984), p. 154.

42 Hampshire County Registry of Probate.

Decease I Give him his Time or freedom Provided he Conduct himself as He ought to Do and Improves his time well So that he Maintains himself well. But if he fails in these Things and that in the Judgment of the Selectmen of Westfield for the time Being then he Shall be put to Service and the Selectmen are hereby Impowered and Desired to Bind him out and To Take Care that what he Earns may be Secured for him So that he may not be a Charge to my Estate nor the Town and I give Him moreover ten Pounds old Tenor.

Item I give to My Negro man Named Prince a Bible a Narrow ax a Broad Hough a Syth and Tackling and a Syckle and after my wives Decease I give him his time also if he Conducts himself as he ought to Do and Improves his time well. So that he maintains himself as he ought to Do but if he fails in these things and that in the Judgment of the Selectmen of Westfield for the time being then he Shall be put to Service and the Selectmen are hereby Impowered and Desired to Bind him out and To Take Care that what He Earns May be Secured for him So that he may not be a Charge to my Estate nor to the Town and if any Such Trouble Should Happen, for the Selectmen they Shall be Paid out of his Earnings that Causes the Trouble and Charge.

Excerpt from the 1748 will of John Gunn, showing the provisions he made for his slaves Primus and Prince. (Hampshire County Registry of Probate.)

Having given both Primus and Prince a Bible, an axe, a hoe, and other farm tools and the promise of freedom after his wife's death (and some money – ten pounds old tenor – to Primus but not to Prince), then in a codicil he gave his wife authority to sell Primus and Prince in case they did not behave themselves "well and orderly".

> ... and furthermore it is my will that In Case my Negro man Named Primus Do not behave himself well and orderly During my wives Life She is hereby impowered to Sell Said Negro and Convert the Money to her own use and Benefit ... and also in Case my Negro man Named Prince Do not Behave himself well and orderly ...

John Gunn died shortly thereafter and his inventory included the four slaves, with their values in pounds.

A Negro man Named Primus 350   another Named Prince 350
A Negro woman Named Ginney 200   a Negro girl Named Chloe 100

Excerpts from the probate inventory of John Gunn, including his slaves Primus, Prince, Ginney, and Chloe. (Hampshire County Registry of Probate.)

Though Primus never married, he had a child by a white woman, Agnes Brown – who was later divorced by her husband. Primus confessed and "was forgiven before the church assembly" in September, 1750.[43] Unlike the 1760 case in Greenfield in which the minister's slave, Caesar, fathered a child by his owner's daughter, apparently neither

---

43 Carvalho (1984), pp. 156-157. See also Greene (1942), p. 206.

Primus nor Agnes were sentenced to be whipped nor was Primus ordered to be "sold out of the province".

Primus died in June, 1761, as Reverend Ballantine noted in his diary.

> June 17, 1761. Attended Primus' Funeral. Ætat 40. He was one on whom an Aged afflicted widow much depended for her Support.

In her will (signed less than a month after Primus' death), Gunn's widow, Elizabeth, gave Prince, who became free by the terms of her husband's will, a gun, gave Chloe to a Westfield neighbor – to become free at age twenty-five – and gave her "servant girl Jana" her freedom. ("Jana" is probably a variant spelling of Ginney, the older and more valuable of the two female slaves left to Elizabeth by her husband.) Elizabeth also gave various items to Jana and Chloe.[44]

Excerpts from the 1761 will of Elizabeth Gunn.
(Hampshire County Registry of Probate.)

---

44 Hampshire County Registry of Probate.

Item. I give unto Doct^r Samuel Mather of Westfield one Pound Six Shillings & Eight Pence in Money & also my Servt girl named Chloe untill she arrives at the Age of twenty five years & then to have her freedom.

Item. I give my Servt Girl named Jana her Time at my decease.

Item. I give to Prince my Husband's Gun.

Item. I give my two Servant Girls Jana & Chloe my Every Day cloths both linnen & Wollen & my two poorest Feather Beds & to Jana I give a Cover Lid Blanket & a Pair of Sheets & to Chloe a Cover Lid & Blanket, Chloe to Use her bed while she may live with Doct^r Mather.

Apparently Elizabeth had bought a young male slave, Seba, sometime after her husband's death, for she specified that Seba should be taught to read and write and then become free.

Item. It is my Will that Seba shall be put out to a Trade after my decease & to be taught to read & Write well To be left discretionary with my Executors where they shall think best & then to have his Time.

Northampton

Reverend Jonathan Edwards of Northampton was a slave owner. He traveled to Newport, Rhode Island in 1731 to purchase Venus,[45] bought further slaves during the next two decades, and after his dismissal from the ministry of Northampton in 1750, he and his family moved to Stockbridge, thirty-five miles west of Northampton, where he served as minister and missionary to the Indians, taking with them a slave, Rose. Edwards moved to Princeton in 1758, where – shortly after beginning his duties as president of the College of New Jersey (now Princeton University) – he died as the result of a smallpox inoculation. His 1758 estate inventory included "a negro boy named Titus", probably Rose's son, as part of his "quick stock".[46] There were many other slave owners in Northampton. Though Reverend Solomon Stoddard, Edwards' predecessor, was probably not a slave owner, his son, Colonel John Stoddard, was one of many important politicians, merchants, and militia officers who owned slaves – including Joseph Bartlett, Jonathan

---

45 Minkema (2002); Marsden (2003). At some time during the next few years, Edwards apparently gave Venus a new name, *Leah*. For a discussion of his decision to change her name and his probable motivation, see Bailey (2003).

46 Minkema (2002), pp. 43-44.

Clapp, Joseph Clapp, Captain Timothy Dwight, Nathaniel Edwards, Jonathan Hunt, Jr., Joseph Hunt, John Lankton, Major Ebenezer Pomeroy, Benjamin Stebbins, and Lieutenant Caleb Strong.[47]

There is a gravestone in Northampton's Bridge Street burying ground for a woman who probably had been a slave in the 1700s –

Sacred to the memory of
SYLVIA CHURCH,
A Colored woman, who for many years lived in
the family of N. Storrs, died 12 April, 1822, Æ 66.
Very few possessed more good qualities than she did. She was
for many years a member of Mr. Williams' Church, and
we trust lived agreeable to her profession, and is
now inheriting the promises.

Hatfield

Just north of Northampton is Hatfield, another very early settlement. Hatfield, on the west side of the river, was originally part of Hadley but was set off as a separate town in 1669, only ten years after the founding of Hadley, primarily because of the difficulties of crossing the river to attend church services on the east side of the river. In a 1667 petition[48] to the General Court from those living in what is now Hatfield, the petitioners pointed out that they had lived on the west side for six years and had –

> attended on God's ordinances on the other side of the river ... the passing being very difficult and dangerous, both in summer and winter. ... Sometimes we come in considerable numbers in rainy weather, and are forced to stay till we can empty our canoes that are half full of water. ... In winter seasons, we are forced to cut and work them out of the ice. ... At other times, the winds are high and waters rough, the current strong and the waves ready to swallow us – our vessels tossed up and down so that our women and children do screech, and are so affrighted that they are made unfit for ordinances, and cannot hear so as to profit by them, by reason of their anguish of spirit; and when

---

47 Minkema (2002), p. 51 (note 24); Trumbull, James (1898-1902), Vol. 2, p. 328. Caleb Strong was listed as the owner of one "servant for life" in the province-wide valuation list of 1771. (Massachusetts State Archives; Pruitt (1978).) Rozwenc writes that Caleb Strong owned a slave, who was "an accomplished fiddler who was taken along on picnics and parties". (Rozwenc (1954), p. 57.)
48 Judd (1863/1905), p. 79.

they return, some of them are more fit for their beds than for family duties and God's services, which they ought to attend. ... Our difficulties and dangers that we undergo are to us extreme and intolerable; oftentimes some of us have fallen into the river through the ice. ... That none hitherto hath been lost, their lives are to be attributed to the care and mercy of God. ... When we do go over the river, we leave our relatives and estates lying on the outside of the colony, joining to the wilderness, to be a prey to the heathen. ... Yet, not withstanding, our greatest anxiety and pressure of spirit is that the Sabbath, which should be kept by us holy to the Lord, is spent with such unavoidable distractions, both of the mind and of the body. And for the removing of this, we unanimously have made our address to our brethren and friends on the other side of the river, by a petition that they would be pleased to grant us liberty to be a society of ourselves, and that we might call a minister to dispense the word of God to us ...

This petition accomplished its purpose, and Hatfield indeed became a separate town in 1669. What is probably the earliest mention of slavery in the area that became Hatfield dates from 1664, while it was still part of Hadley, when the county court ruled on the estate of Richard Fellowes, making "an allowance of three pounds on account of a slave appraised for more than he could be sold for".[49]

William Williams, minister of Hatfield from 1686 to 1741and one of the most influential citizens of the valley, was one of many Hatfield slave owners. From his 1739 will[50] –

I give to my Son Israel whom I constitute the Executor of this my will all my Lands and Buildings in Hatfield, my Servant man Peter .. my Team and all my utensils for husbandry ...

And from his 1742 inventory –

An Inventory of the real & Personal Estate of the Rev[d] W[m] Williams of Hatfield dec[d] –
1 house & Lot of Land in Hatf[d] Cont[g] 16 acres
In the South field in D[o] 14 ½ acres
In y[e] Great Meadow 5 ½ acres ...
2 horses 2 oxen – 1 Negro – given to I Williams by will ...
Sundry Books & waring Apparels ...

Reverend Williams' son Israel was involved in numerous purchases of slaves. Several years before he inherited Peter from his father, he had

---

49 Morris (1879), p. 209.
50 Hampshire County Registry of Probate.

bought a young girl named Kate ("aged about eight or nine years") from an owner in Suffield.[51]

> May 22, 1734   then I Samuel Kent of Suffield Innholder, for the consideration £89 in cash in hand paid to me, have sold, set over and Delivered to Capt. Israel Williams of Hatfield a Certain Negro Girl named Kate, aged about 8 or 9 years, which I hereby engage for me my hiers, executors and adminstrators to warrant to him, his hiers executors and administrators against the Lawful Claim, Chalenge or Demand of any person or persons whatever, as witness my hand and Seal ye day aboves^d
>
> Samuel Kent

And in 1753, he purchased Blossom ("aged about sixteen years") from a Connecticut owner.[52]

> Know all men by these Presents, that I, Hezekiah Whitmore in Middleboro in the county of Hartford, for & in consideration, the sum of forty pounds Lawful money, to me in hand paid by Israel Williams of Hatfield in the county of Hampshire; do hereby sell, set over, & convey to him a certain negro Girl, named Blossom, aged about sixteen years. To serve him, his hiers & assigns for and During ye full term of her natural life hereby covenanting & engaging for myself & my hiers ex^ts & adm^rs to warrant to him his hiers & assigns to be sound & well & against the Lawful claims of any person whatsoever, as witness my hand & seal this 20th day of May 1753.
>
> HEZEKIAH WETMORE

In 1750 Ephraim Williams of Hatfield sold "a Certain Negro Boy Named Prince aged about nine years" to his cousin Israel.[53]

> For and in Consideration of the Sum of Two hundred and twentyfive pounds, old Ten^r to me Ephraim Williams j^r, well and truly paid by Israel Williams of Hatf^l Esqr I do hereby Assign Sell & Convey to him a Certain Negro Boy Named Prince aged about nine years, a Servant for life to hold to him his heirs ag^t ye Claims of any Person whatsoever as Witness my hand this 25th day of Septem^br Anno Dom^i 1750.
>
> Eph Williams jun^r

---

51 Sheldon (1895), p. 892.
52 Sheldon (1895), p. 903.
53 PVMA Library. (Sheldon gives a slightly different reading of the same bill of sale. (Sheldon (1895), p. 903.))

Bill of sale for "A Certain Negro Boy Named Prince".
(PVMA Library, Deerfield, Massachusetts.)

That was not the only time that Ephraim Williams was involved in the purchase or sale of a slave. In 1755, not long before he died, he purchased Romanoo from John Charles of Brimfield.[54]

> I John Charles Jr. of Brimfield in the Co. of Hampshire in consideration of the sum of fifty-three pounds six shillings & eight pence to me in hand paid by Maj. Ephraim Williams of Hatfield in the county aforesaid, the rec't whereof I do hereby acknowledge & myself fully satisfied and paid Do hereby sell, assign, set over, and convey to the s^d Ephraim Williams his hiers & assigns my Negro Boy Named J Romanoo aged about sixteen years to be the sole Property of s^d Ephraim his hiers and assigns to his and their use, Benifit and Behoof, as his & their Slave, during the natural life of the s^d J romanoo, and I do hereby covenant, Promise and agree, that before the ensealing hereof, I am the Rightful and Lawful owner of the s^d slave, and have good and Lawful Right to sell and Dispose of him in manner as aforesaid, and that I will by these presents, for myself & my hiers Exec^rs & Adm^rs shall always be held to warrant and secure the s^d Negro from this Day, During his Natural Life as aforesaid as the sole property of the s^d Ephraim, his hiers & assigns, to his and their use & Behoof, against the claim and chalange of any other person, and *all Rightful Pretentions of his own, to Freedom, by any Law or right whatsoever.* Witness my hand & seal this thirteenth day of February Anno Domini 1755 [Italics added.]

JOHN CHARLES JR.

Ephraim Williams is still a familiar name in western Massachu setts. Williams died in 1755 at the Battle of Lake George (the "Bloody Morning Scout"),[55] and on his way to Lake George, he wrote his will,

---

54 Sheldon (1895), pp. 903-904.
55 The Battle of Lake George (in what is now the state of New York) was a military disaster for the English in the French and Indian War.

leaving some money that eventually led to the founding of Williams College. In that same document, he left his homestead and his slaves to his brothers. Romanoo, purchased only a few months earlier, was presumably among the "Stocks of Cattle and Negro Servants now upon the place" that his brothers inherited.[56]

> In the name of God Amen. I Ephraim Williams of Hatfield in the County of Hampshire in New England, now at Albany in the Province of New York, on my march in the Expedition agains Crown-point, being of Sound & perfect mind and memory (blessed be God therefor) But not knowing how God in his Providence may dispose of my life, and remembring the uncertainty of it at All times, I do therefore make and publish this my last will and Testament in the following manner ... I give and bequeath unto my beloved brothers, Josiah Williams, and Elijah Williams, and the heirs of their bodies my homestead at Stockbridge, with all the Buildings and Apperterances therunto belonging, with all the Stocks of Cattle and Negro Servants now upon the place, to be Equally Divided between them ...

In a case similar to the 1760 Greenfield case of Lucy Billing and Caesar discussed in Chapter Four, "Ben Negro", slave of John Dickinson of Hatfield, was brought into court in 1737, accused of fathering "a Mollatto bastard Child" with Elisabeth Chamberlain, "an English Singlewoman". Specific reference was made to the 1705 law ("An Act for the Better Preventing of a Spurious and Mixt Issue") that was quoted in Chapter Two. Like Caesar in the Greenfield case, Ben was sentenced to "whipping on his Naked body fifteen Stripes well Laid on" and it was ordered that he be "sold out of the province". In contrast to the case of Lucy and Caesar, the child's mother was not sentenced to a whipping.[57]

> The Grandjurors of our Sovereign Lord the King for the body of the County of Hampshire Do on their oths present Ben Negro man Servant to John Dickinson of Hatfield In Said County yeoman for the Crime of fornication Comitted by the Said ben Negro In S^d Hatfield with Elisabeth Chamberlain an English Singlewoman of S^d Hatfield

---

56 The fact that Williams was a slave owner is not prominently displayed in the college's publicity brochures, but neither is it a secret. To the credit of the college, the complete text of his will is on the "Archives and Special Collections" page of the Williams College website – http://archives.williams.edu. The original copy of the will is at Williams College, a copy is in the PVMA Library, and the text of the will is also printed in Wright's biography. (Wright (1970).)

57 Hampshire County Court of Common Pleas/General Sessions, 1735-1741.

Sometime In the Latter End of feb^y or Begining of March Last the Said Chamberlain having been Delivered of a Mollatto bastard Child on the Second Day of November Last which Said Crime of S^d Negro is Contrary to an Act of the Province of the Massachusetts bay Intitled an act for the better preventing a Spurious and mixt Issue ... which presentments made at the general Sessions of the peace holden at Northampton on the first Tuesday of December 1737 ... Said ben Negro being brought before S^d Court pleads not guilty of Said presentments ... In this Case the Evidence being heard and Sworn ... it was Comitted to the Jury ... who being Sworn to try the Same returned their verdict that they finde the S^d Ben Guilty of Said presentments, the Court upon Consideration ... adjudge and Say that the S^d Ben Negro be Corporally punished by whipping on his Naked body fifteen Stripes well Laid on and Stand Comitted till Sentence be performed and pay Cost of prossiqution taxed at three pounds Nineteen Shillings and after he has rec^d Said punishment is to be Sold out of the Province and be accordingly Sent away within the Space of Six months and be Continued in prison at his master Mr John Dickinson of Hatfield yeoman [?] Cost & Charges till he be Sent away.

Amos Newport, probably born in Africa, belonged to Joseph Billing (or Billings) of Hatfield, who had bought him from David Ingersoll of Springfield in 1729. (Whether Ingersoll regularly bought and sold slaves is not known.) In 1766, when Newport had been Billing's slave for nearly forty years, Newport took the extraordinary step of going to court to seek his freedom and then, after losing in the lower court, pursuing an appeal, unfortunately an unsuccessful appeal, to the highest court in the province. There were a number of "freedom suits" by Massachusetts slaves at about this time, but this is the only such case from the Connecticut Valley.[58]

Billing, the owner and thus the defendant, was represented in court by Simeon Strong, a prominent Amherst lawyer, while Newport was represented by Moses Bliss, a Springfield lawyer. Perhaps Newport had accumulated enough money to hire Bliss, perhaps Bliss worked *pro bono*, or possibly the court costs were supported by Hatfield residents challenging the very existence of slavery.

---

58 For more information on freedom suits, see in particular Blanck (2002). John Adams, future president, served as counsel for the owner in several of these cases, including Newport's appeal to the Supreme Court of Judicature in 1768. (*Legal Papers of John Adams* (1968), Vol. 2, pp. 48-67.) There is also a very brief note about the Newport case in Adams' *Autobiography*. (*Diary and Autobiography of John Adams* (1961), Vol. 3, p. 289.)

The first court session, in the fall of 1766, resulted in postponement, as Billing and his lawyer requested time to prepare their defense.

Newport vs Billing   Inferior Court of Common Pleas
November Term, 1766

Amos Newport of Hatfield in ye County of Hampshire Labourer Pl^f vs Joseph Billings of Hatfield in ye same County Gentleman def^t in a plea of Trespass wheron ye said Amos Complains & says that s^d Joseph at s^d Hatfield on ye first day of December last past with force and Arms an Assault made on him ye s^d Amos he then and there being in our Peace & him the s^d Amos he ye said Joseph then and there with force & Arms falsely imprisoned and restrained of his Lawfull Liberty continuing the aforesaid Trespass as to the false imprisonment and restraining him ye s^d Amos of his Liberty for ye space of six months then next following & many other wrong injuries to him the s^d Amos he then & there did contrary to Law & against our peace & To the Damage of ye s^d Amos One Hundred pounds – The Pl^f appears by Moses Bliss Gent^n his attorney - And the said Joseph Billing by Simeon Strong Gent^n his attorney comes into Court and humbly prays the leave of this Honble Court to impart to the next Term of ye Court that he may have opportunity to make his defence &c and it is granted him. And the said parties accordingly have a day before the Lord the King here until the Second Tuesday of February next ensuing.

When the parties returned to court the following winter, Billing produced a bill of sale showing that he had purchased Newport quite properly from David Ingersoll in 1729.[59]

These presents witness that I David Ingersoll of Springfield in the County of Hampshire in the Province of ye Massachusetts Bay in New England, shopkeeper, have sold, set over & delivered in Plain St Green Market a certain young Negro Boy named Teo [or perhaps Leo?] alias Newport for consideration of fifty pounds to Joseph Billing of Hatfield in s^d County & Province aforesaid, yeoman. I ye vendor will forever warrant ag^t ye lawful claims challenges or demands of any person or persons whosoever. In witness whereof I have hereunto set my hand this 15th of March Anno Domini 1728/9.

David Ingersoll

Signed & delivered in the presence of
Christopher Jacob Lawford [signature]
Jerusha Smith [signed by mark]

---

59 Transcribed by Eric Weber from records of the Massachusetts Superior Court of Judicature at the Massachusetts State Archives.

Everything was in order. Newport had been the property of Ingersoll in 1729, he had been sold to Billing in an ordinary business transaction, there was no defect in the title or anything else that would indicate that Newport was not the property of Joseph Billing. Newport simply claimed that he was "a free man and not the proper slave of the said Joseph". The jurors, following applicable statutes, had no choice but to deny Newport's claim and to conclude that Amos Newport was indeed the proper slave of Joseph Billing.

Newport vs Billing   Inferior Court of Common Pleas
                      February Term, 1767

Amos Newport of Hatfield in y^e County of Hampshire Labourer vs. Joseph Billing of Hatfield in the Same county $Gent^n$ def^t in a plea of trespass as at large on record of the preceeding term the Plt^f appears by Moses Bliss Gentleman his Att^y And the said Joseph Billing by Simeon Strong $Gent^n$ his Attorney comes and defends the force & injury and says y^t the said Amos Newport to his writ ought not to be answered because he says the s^d Amos is y^e proper Negro Slave of y^e S^d Joseph & that one David Ingersoll at Springfield in y^e S^d county on y^e fifteenth day of March A.D. 1729 was possessed of ye s^d Amos as of his own proper Negro Slave & being so thereof possessed ye said David then & there in consideration of fifty pounds sold bargained & delivered to s^d Joseph ye s^d Amos Newport by ye name of [?] alias Newport to hold to said Joseph forever as his property whereby s^d Joseph became possessed of s^d Amos Newport, as of his own proper negro Slave & by virtue of ye Sale & delivery aforesaid has ever since held & still holds ye s^d Amos as his own proper Negro Slave all which ye s^d Joseph is ready to verify, wherefore he prays judgment of y^e s^d Amos Newport to his writ aforesaid ought to be answered. And the Said Amos replying by his Attorney aforesaid says that not withstanding anything y^e s^d Joseph in his plea aforesaid alledged he y^e s^d Joseph ought to answer to his y^e s^d Amos' writ $afores^d$ because he says that he y^e s^d Amos is a freeman & not y^e proper Slave of y^e s^d joseph and this he prays may be inquired of by the Country and y^e s^d Joseph likewise

Thereupon the jurors, at this time according to y^e [?] & effect of y^e statutes in this case provided returned and impanelled being demanded likewise come here. Who to say ye truth concerning the premises being duly sworn by Mr Elisha Cook their foreman declare upon their Oath that they find for the Said Joseph Billing the def^t his Costs of Court.

Therefore it is considered by the Court that the Said joseph Billing do recover against the Said Amos Newport Sixteen Shillings of Lawfull money for his costs in defending the writ of the Said Amos & thereof he may have his Law.

The said Amos in his proper person appeals from the judgment of this Court to the Superior Court of judicature to be holden at Springfield within and for the County of Hampshire on the fourth Tuesday of September next And Silas Graves of Hatfield aforesaid yeoman as next friend to said Amos recognizes as principal to the Said joseph with surities as the Law directs for the Said Amos presenting the appeal with effect as by said recognizance as on file it appears.

Newport was not easily deterred, though, and – as indicated at the end of the preceding report – determined to appeal the case to the highest court in Massachusetts, the Superior Court of Judicature. The case did not reach the Superior Court until September, 1768. It was at this point that John Adams, future president (and opponent of slavery) joined the legal defense team of the owner – though not in a major role. The defense argued that not only was the 1729 bill of sale properly executed, that testimony showed that it had been written in the hand of the Springfield owner, David Ingersoll, but also that a black should be presumed to be a slave. (John Adams' notes on the case, notes that record arguments made by another lawyer for the defense, not necessarily his own opinions, include the remark – "Presumption here is that an African black is a slave."[60])

The decision of the jury in the Superior Court case simply affirmed the decision in the Inferior Court – that "the said Amos was not a freeman as he alledged but the proper Slave of the said Joseph and therefore find for the said Joseph costs".[61]

Amos Newport is an unsung hero of the colonial era in the Connecticut Valley. Though he lost his appeal for freedom, he had made a valiant effort, exhausting every legal remedy then available. There is no evidence that Amos Newport ever gained his freedom. Smith writes that Amos did become free and eventually had a small farm in Whately.[62] Eric Weber, however, has been unable to find evidence that Amos ever became free.[63] He has also found evidence that the farm in question was actually in Williamsburg, that it was probably Amos' son Peter who

---

60 *Legal Papers of John Adams* (1968), Vol. 2, p. 56.
61 From a transcript made by Emily Blanck (private communication).
62 Smith, James (1999), p. 101.
63 Eric Weber, private communication.

owned that farm, and that Peter, while still a slave, became the legal owner of a piece of real estate – another unusual case, like that of Roco, slave of John Pynchon, who, still a slave, owned sixty acres in 1685, as discussed earlier in this chapter.

There is a modern reminder of Amos Newport and his unsuccessful attempt to gain his freedom. In 1984 Amherst College abolished its fraternities and assigned to the former fraternity houses, now dormitories, names of people who had previously been connected with those fraternities. The "Phi Delta Sigma House" was given a new name, "Newport House", chosen to honor two men who had had long affiliations with the college and the fraternity[64] – F. Dwight Newport (1859-1937), an athletic trainer and boxing instructor at the college, was Amos Newport's great-great-grandson,[65] and his son, Edward Foster Newport (1883-1968), an Amherst College student in the class of 1909,[66] was an athletic trainer like his father and also a custodian at the fraternity. Both Newports, father and son, were members of Hope Congregational Church in Amherst.

Hadley

On the east side of the river, opposite Northampton, is Hadley, a town similar to Deerfield but settled somewhat earlier. If we could construct a 1752 snapshot of slavery on the old main street of Hadley (a beautifully preserved double street bordering the common, now called West Street), we would probably find it very similar to that of Deerfield. The chances of learning about the details of Hadley history, though, were seriously diminished by a 1766 fire that destroyed the church records.

---

64 Phi Delta Sigma was a local fraternity. Many years earlier the Amherst fraternity had been a chapter of Phi Delta Theta, a national fraternity with restrictive rules excluding Jewish students – and, of course, black students. When the college trustees insisted, after World War II, that no Amherst fraternity could have such restrictions, the members of the Amherst chapter withdrew from the national organization and formed a new *local* fraternity, Phi Delta Sigma.

65 Smith, James (1999), pp. 101-105; Eric Weber, private communication. (Smith accidentally gives an incorrect date (1776) for Amos Newport's 1766 freedom suit.)

66 Edward Foster Newport attended Amherst College from 1905 to 1907 as a member of the class of 1909 and later attended the University of Maine from 1909 to 1911. (Amherst College Biographical Record, 1951.) Alumni files and catalogs at the University of Maine show that he was listed as a member of the class of 1913, attending the university in the years 1909-1910. (Brenda Steeves, private communication.) The 1912 University of Maine yearbook lists him as a second-year student in a "short course" in pharmacology.

"Newport House", an Amherst College dormitory, named in honor of descendants of Amos Newport, a Hatfield slave who sued for his freedom in 1766. (Author's photograph.)

A very early reference to slavery in Hadley dates from 1667, when Robert Boltwood filed a suit against Benjamin Wait, attempting to recover from Wait twenty pounds for selling Boltwood's slave without authority.[67]

The first four ministers of Hadley were all slave owners. John Russell,[68] Hadley's first minister, who led his fellow dissidents from Wethersfield, Connecticut to Hadley in 1659,[69] owned Margaret and Cyrus and at least one other slave, for Russell's 1693 probate inventory[70] included "a man, woman and child, valued at 60£". Margaret had an illegitimate child and appeared in court in March, 1670, as Judd reports[71] –

---

67 Morris (1879), p. 209.

68 Russell is famous for harboring the two "regicides", William Goffe and Edward Whalley, two of the English judges who had sentenced Charles I to death in 1649. When Cromwell's Puritan regime ended and Charles II became king of England in 1660, Goffe and Whalley fled to America to hide from royal authorities.

69 Judd (1863/1905), Chapter 2.

70 Judd (1863/1905), p. 46. Judd comments – "Mr. Russell and some other good men were interested in the detestable system of slavery, in an age when its injustice and wickedness had not been properly considered."

71 Judd (1863/1905), p. 89.

"Mr. Russell's negro servant, Margaret, had a child, and was to be whipped 15 stripes; and the father, John Garret [presumably a white man], was to be whipped 24 stripes, and pay to Mr. Russell £7, 10s." Although the illegitimate child born in 1670 was in her early twenties by the time Russell died, perhaps she was the "child" listed in Russell's 1693 inventory.

Not long afterward "Mr. Russell's negro wench", presumably Margaret, was involved with Thomas Wells, also probably a white man, appearing in court in September, 1670.[72]

> Thomas Wells Jr. of Hadley bound over by Hadley Com'rs for "unclean actings" with the negro wench, servant of Mr Russel. He appeared & by his own confession & other circumstances it is evident there was sinful dalliance between them in the barn. She says he threw her down. He denies this & says she came & sat down by him & pulled up her clothes and lay bare before him, & that if God had not kept him he fears he should have committed uncleanness with her; both say Hannah Dewey came into the barn & prevented them. Court adjudge Wells to be whipped by his father in presence of the constables or pay a fine of 20/. He paid fine. Her master had whipped her, & no more was done.

And in 1686 Cyrus also appeared in court – "Cyrus, Mr. Russell's negro, for fraudulent dealings with the Indians and violent carriages in his master's house, was to be whipped 15 stripes at Hadley, on the next lecture day, or pay 50s. to satisfy the Indians, &c."[73]

Russell's successor, Isaac Chauncey, owned Arthur Prutt and his wife Joan, who had at least seven children, including Caesar (born in 1727) and Zebulon (born in 1731).[74] We will hear more below about Caesar (inherited by Reverend Chauncey's son, Josiah) and Zebulon (sold to Moses Porter at age fourteen).

Chester Williams, Hadley's third minister, owned slaves and left Phillis to his wife Sarah in his 1753 will.[75]

> To my beloved Wife Sarah Williams I give and devise the use and Improvement of one Third of my real Estate during her Natural Life and also all my houshold Goods and within Door moveables (except my Silver Tankard) also my Negro Woman named Phillis my Cows and Sheep for her own use and Benefit for Ever.

---

72 Judd Manuscripts (*Selected Papers*, 1976), p. 132.
73 Judd (1863/1905), p. 90.
74 Judd (1863/1905), Genealogy Section, pp. 115-116.
75 Hampshire County Registry of Probate.

Excerpt from the 1753 will of Reverend Chester Williams, in which he left his "Negro Woman named Phillis" to his wife. (Hampshire County Registry of Probate.)

Though Phillis is included by name in his will, she appears simply as "A Negro Girl", valued at £40, in his probate inventory, immediately after "2 Hoggs, 4 Cows, & 22 Sheep".

Then in 1756, when Samuel Hopkins, Jr., the fourth Hadley minister, married Sarah Williams, the widow of Chester Williams, he became owner of Phillis. And thus Hadley has the distinction of having as slave owners every one of its four pre-revolutionary ministers.[76]

Ezekiel Kellogg (a prominent Hadley merchant and real-estate speculator) was a dealer in slaves, writes Judd[77] – "Ezekiel Kellogg was a trafficker in many things and used to buy and sell negroes for gain. There is a tradition that he used to shave off their hair to make them look young."

Several miles north of the village center of Hadley, still standing, is the imposing home built by Moses Porter in 1752 for his wife Elizabeth and their daughter, also named Elizabeth. By the time of Moses' death in 1755 at the Battle of Lake George,[78] he owned two slaves – Zebulon Prutt, born in 1731, purchased[79] as a fourteen-year old boy for one hundred and fifty pounds old tenor in 1745 from Jerusha Chauncey (whose father, Reverend Isaac Chauncey, had died a few months earlier), and Peg, a girl probably purchased about 1754.[80] Upon Moses' death his widow became owner of Zebulon and Peg, listed in Moses' 1756 probate inventory as "A

76 Remarking on the fact that Hadley's first three ministers were slave owners, Judd writes – "Mr. Chauncey, as well as his predecessor and successor, offended against right, by holding persons in bondage." (Judd (1863/1905), p. 320.)
77 Judd Manuscripts, Forbes Library – *Hadley*, Vol. 3, p. 19 and *Selected Papers* (1976), p. 376.
78 The same fight that took the life of Ephraim Williams.
79 Bill of sale, Porter-Phelps-Huntington Papers, Box 3, Folder 4.
80 See the 1772 diary entry below.

Excerpts from the probate inventory of Chester Williams, including "A Negro Girl", valued at £40. (Hampshire County Registry of Probate.)

Negro man" (valued at £53-6-8) and "Negro girl" (valued at £33-6-8).[81]

Zebulon ran away in 1766, and a notice seeking his return was placed in a Hartford newspaper.

Hadley, August 28, 1766.

Run away from the Widow Elizabeth Porter of Hadley, a Negro Man named Zebulon Prut, about 30 years old, about five Feet high, a whitish Complexion, suppos'd to have a Squaw in Company: Carried away with him, a light brown Camblet Coat, lin'd and trimm'd with the same Colour – a blue plain Cloth Coat, with Metal Buttons, without Lining – a new redish brown plain Cloth Coat, with Plate Buttons, no Lining – a light brown Waistcoat, and a dark brown ditto, both without Sleves – a Pair of Check'd, and a Pair of Tow Trowsers – a Pair of

---

81 Hampshire County Registry of Probate.

blue Yarn Stockings, and a Pair of Thread ditto – two Pair of Shoes –
two Hats – an old red Duffel Great Coat. – Whoever will take up said
Negro, and bring him to Mrs Porter, or to Oliver Warner, of said Hadley,
shall have Ten Dollars Reward, and all necessary Charges paid, by

OLIVER WARNER

Connecticut Courant   September 8, 1766

Like most slaves who ran away, Zebulon took quite an array of
clothes with him. Where he went and how he was recaptured and returned we do not know. When he did return to Hadley, over a year later,
he learned that "Widow Porter" had already sold him to Oliver Warner.[82]
The information about the sale comes from a diary kept by Moses' daughter Elizabeth, begun in 1763 when she was sixteen, a diary that contains

Excerpts from the 1756 probate inventory of Moses Porter, including "A Negro
Man" and "Negro Girl". (Hampshire County Register of Probate.)

---

82 A prominent Hadley citizen, who was a Hadley selectman at the time Zebulon ran
away. (Judd (1863/1905), p. 450.) See also Smith, James (1984), p. 750 for information about
Oliver Warner.

almost daily reports of the activities in the house, the comings and go-ings of visitors, and the lives, illnesses, and deaths of the many slaves and others who lived there.[83] As Elizabeth wrote in her diary –

> February 7, 1768 - this day a Negro man that was my fathers who ran away from my mother the which she sold to Mr. Oliver Warner for fifty dollars as soon as he went away was brought back to him - his name was Zebulon Prutt.

Zebulon died in 1802, having gained his freedom sometime in the final decades of the 18th century.[84]

From Elizabeth's diary we learn of the 1772 sale of Peg to Captain Fay of Bennington, in the area that later became the state of Vermont.

> March 28, 1772 – this Day our Peg who has Lived with us near 18 years of her own Choice Left us and two Children and was sold to One Capt. Fay of Benington with a Negro man from this town all for the sake of being his wife.

In 1770 Elizabeth had married Charles Phelps, who repurchased Peg from Captain Fay in 1778 for twenty pounds.[85] And, according to Elizabeth's diary, in 1782 Peg became free, though exactly how this oc-curred is not clear.

> June 9, 1782 - our Peg Left us most a fortnight ago, gone off free.

In 1770 Charles Phelps had purchased another slave, Caesar, from William Williams of New Marlborough, not far from Bennington, for sixty-six pounds and thirteen shillings.[86] Caesar went to war in 1776, and while at Fort Ticonderoga, he apparently became worried that Phelps might be planning to sell him to "Captain Cranston", whereupon he sent a poignant letter to his owner.[87]

> Camp At Ticontoroga   Sept the 30 ye 1776
> Sir I take this oppertunity to Enform you that I dont Entend to Live

---

83 Phelps, Elizabeth Porter (1763-1817).
84 Judd (1863/1905), Genealogy Section, pp. 115-116.
85 Bill of sale, Porter-Phelps-Huntington Papers, Box 4, Folder 17.
86 Bill of sale, Porter-Phelps-Huntington Papers, Box 4, Folder 15.
87 Porter-Phelps-Huntington Papers, Box 4, Folder 12. No one knows what happened to Sezor Phelps. There is no record of his returning to Hadley. Perhaps he *was* sold in spite of his letter, or perhaps he died at Ticonderoga. There is no listing of Sezor (or Caesar) Phelps in *Massachusetts Soldiers and Sailors* or in *Forgotten Patriots* (2008).

With Capt Cranston if I Can helpit and I Would Be glad if you Would
Send me a letter that I may git my Wagers for I have not got any of my
Wagers and I Want to know how all the Folks Do at home and I De-
sire yor Prayers for me While in the Sarves and if you Determin to Sel
me I Want you Shud Send me my Stock and Buckel. So no more at
Present But I Remain your Ever Faithful Slave

Sezor Phelps

This letter by Caesar (or Sezor) Phelps is a remarkable item. Of all
the documents quoted in this book (with the sole exception of a 1774
petition to the General Court of Massachusetts – see Chapter Eight),
this is the only one in the voice of a slave. The handwriting may not be
his own, he may have dictated the letter for someone else to write, but
this is *Sezor* speaking.[88]

The house where Caesar Phelps, Zebulon Prutt, and other slaves
lived with their owners in the 1700s has for many years been open to
visitors as the Porter-Phelps-Huntington House. Ever since tours of the
house were first offered in 1949, the fact that slaves lived in the house has
been mentioned to visitors, and more recently curators and staff have
prepared detailed information on what is known about the various
slaves.[89]

Dr. Richard Crouch was a well known doctor in Hadley, practicing
medicine from about 1730 until the time of his death in 1761. His account
books are replete with records of his treatments of valley residents, black
as well as white. Crouch often made house calls, not only in Hadley but
in towns as far away as Worcester. During the 1730s, he charged one
shilling to make a daytime visit in the Hadley village, twice that during
the night. Out of town visits were more expensive – Hatfield 2/6,
Deerfield 15/, Westfield 20/, Springfield 21/. Judd had a low opinion of
Crouch's treatments – "Doct. Crouch gave a great many medicines, bled
outrageously, and charged enormous prices for his medicines. Visits were
comparatively cheap. He blistered also extravagantly." Commenting on

---

88 Recall also the words of Ashley's slave, Jenny, that were quoted in Chapter Four, though
they do not appear in any documents from her time, words that were passed down in
Deerfield and finally written down by George Sheldon a century later – "And we nebber
see our mudders any more." In addition there is the famous poem about the 1746 "Bars
Fight" for which Lucy Terry Prince is so well known, though she herself – as far as we
know – never wrote down the words.
89 Susan Lisk, private communication. The story of the Porter-Phelps-Huntington House
has been told in detail by Elizabeth Carlisle. (Carlisle (2004).)

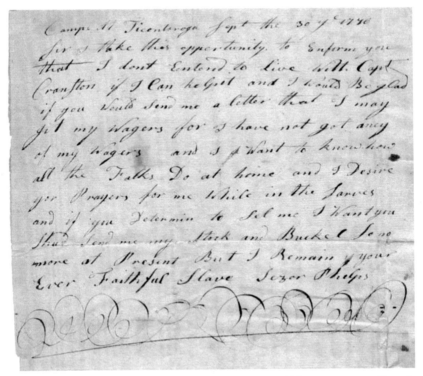

Letter from Sezor Phelps to his owner, 1776. (Porter-Phelps-Huntington Foundation, Inc., Hadley, Massachusetts. Porter-Phelps-Huntington Family Papers on deposit at Amherst College Archives and Special Collections, (Box 4, Folder 12.))

a case in which Crouch's patient died, Judd wrote – "I think he died of the doctor, & not of the disease."[90]

Moses Porter's uncle, Eleazar Porter (described by Judd as the "most wealthy man in Hadley"[91] and probably the largest slave owner in town) was just one of many Hadley residents whose families and slaves received medical attention from Dr. Crouch. Slaves of Eleazar Porter who appear in Dr. Crouch's account books include Scipio, Boston, Boston's son Joshua, Thankful, Simon, Tabitha, and Agnes.[92] Scipio probably died before his owner, for Eleazar's 1758 inventory[93] listed all the others (Boston, Thankfull, Simon, Tab, Josh, and Agnes), as well as Jeff, who did not appear in Dr. Crouch's records.

90 Judd Manuscripts (*Selected Papers*, 1976), pp. 411-412, 415.
91 Judd (1863/1905), p. 323.
92 Judd Manuscripts (*Selected Papers*, 1976), pp. 433, 436.
93 Hampshire County Registry of Probate.

Boston (probably the *Boston* who belonged to Eleazar Porter) played a role in another Hadley event. Records of slave marriages in colonial times are rare. Even more rare are reports of divorces. Judd writes that only one divorce – whether of a white or black couple – is known to have occurred in Hadley's early history, that of Ralph and Lois Way, a free black couple, who were divorced in 1751 because Lois, Ralph charged, had borne a bastard son by Boston.[94]

In addition to all those just mentioned, Eleazar Porter owned another slave, Adam, who apparently became free before the time of his owner's death. A 1767 land deed records the sale of a parcel of land in Sunderland from Joseph Hubbard of Hadley to "Adam, the Late Negro Servant of Eleazar Porter".[95] According to this deed, Adam had been freed by Porter (Adam does not appear in Porter's inventory), but I have not been able to find a manumission document.

> To all People, to whom these Presents shall come, GREETING, Know Y[e], That I Joseph Hubbard of Hadley in the County of Hampshire & Province of the Massachusets Bay in New England Gent[n] – For and in Consideration of the Sum of Twenty Six pounds thirteen Shillings & four pence – to me in Hand before the ensealing hereof, well and truly paid by Adam the Late Negro Servant of Eleaz[r] Porter Esq. who is now Manumitted & resides at Hadley affores[d] – the Receipt whereof I do hereby acknowledge, and my self – therewith fully satisfied and contented, and thereof, and of every Part and Parcel thereof, do exonerate, acquit and discharge the said Adam (his – Bondsman) Heirs, Executors, and Administrators, for ever by these Presents: HAVE given, granted, bargained, sold, aliened, conveyed and confirmed; and by these Presents, do freely, fully and absolutely give, grant, bargain, sell, aliene, convey and confirm, unto him the said Adam his – Heirs and Assigns for ever, A Certain tract or parcel of Land Situate in Sunderland ... TO HAVE and to HOLD, the said granted and bargained Premises, with all the Appurtenances, Priviledges and Commodities to the same belonging, or in any wise appertaining, to him the said Adam his – Heirs and Assigns for ever: To him and his only proper Use, Benefit and Behoof forever. And I the said Joseph Hubbard ... do covenant, promise and grant to and with the S[d] Adam his – Heirs and Assigns, that ... I am the true, sole and lawful Owner of the above-bargained Premises, and am lawfully seized and possessed of the same in my

---

94 Judd (1863/1905), p. 239; Greene (1942), p. 206.
95 Hampden County Registry of Deeds, Springfield.

own proper Right ... And have in my self good Right, full Power, and lawful Authority to grant, bargain, sell, convey and confirm said bargained Premises ... FURTHERMORE, I ... do covenant and engage the above demised Premises to him the said Adam his – Heirs and Assigns, against the lawful Claims or Demands of any Person or Persons whatsoever, for ever hereafter to Warrant, Secure and Defend by these Presents. In witness whereof ... this twentieth Day of Jan^ry Anno Dom. 1767 & Seventh Year of the Kings Reign ...

What is striking is the similarity between many of the words and phrases in this deed conveying a piece of real estate and those in many of the bills of sale for slaves that have been quoted earlier in this book – "well and truly paid", "fully and absolutely give, grant, bargain, sell", "unto him his heirs and assigns forever", "to his only proper use, benefit and behoof forever", "I am the true, sole and lawful owner", "I have good right, full power, and lawful authority to grant, bargain, sell, convey and confirm", "against the lawful claims or demands of any person or persons whatsoever, forever hereafter to warrant, secure and defend ... ".

Excerpt from the 1767 deed by which Joseph Hubbard sold a piece of land to former slave Adam of Hadley. (Hampden County Registry of Deeds.)

Amherst ("East Hadley")[96]

The earliest known document identifying an Amherst slave owner is the 1737/38 inventory of Zechariah Field of "Hadley third precinct".[97]

A Negro man ..... 130 - 00 - 00

Dr. Richard Crouch of Hadley reported his medical treatments of the slaves of several owners who lived in East Hadley.[98]

1731-1746	Ebenezer Kellogg	Negro Child
1735	Richard Chauncey	[?] for wife, your boy & negro. Blisters & bleeding & med.
1736-1742	John Ingram	Tully your negro
1751-1756	Daniel Kellogg	For wife, negro, self, child ...
1755	Ebenezer Kellogg	Negro kicked with a horse
ca. 1758	Ephraim Kellogg	[?] for his negro

John Ingram's son, Elisha, was listed on the Amherst tax list of 1759 – just after Amherst became a separate town – as the owner of one "negro".[99] Perhaps this was Tully, inherited by Elisha from his father.

David Parsons, minister in Amherst from 1739 to 1781,[100] owned a

---

96 In the early 1700s, the area that eventually became the town of Amherst was still part of Hadley – the East Precinct or Third Precinct. Often referred to as "East Hadley", it was renamed the Second Precinct when South Hadley became a separate town in 1753 and was finally "erected into a district" with the name Amherst in 1759. (Judd (1863/1905), Chapters 34-35.) In the early days, the Amherst area was also known variously as the "New Swamp", "Foote's Folly Swamp", "Hadley Farms", "East Farms", and "Hadley Outer Commons". (Carpenter and Morehouse (1896), p. 33.)

97 Hampshire County Registry of Probate; Smith, James (1999), p. 1; Smith, James (1984), p. 284; Judd (1863/1905), Genealogy Section, p. 51. Though the inventory gives the name of the deceased as *Zacariah Feild*, he appears most frequently in the town history as Zechariah Field (Carpenter and Morehouse (1896), pp. 18, 26, 33, 102, 607), though in one entry – apparently copied directly from the original records – on p. 1 of the Town Meeting Records Section of that history, he has the name *Mr. Zach' Feild*. Zechariah was a common given name in colonial times, subjected to a variety of creative spellings, and Field, too, was fairly often spelled *Feild*.

98 Judd Manuscripts, Forbes Library. (Judd's notes on Dr. Crouch's accounts.) In some cases, Judd's notes show only a range of dates for these visits and treatments. See also Smith, James (1984), pp. 109, 414, 437-438 for information on these owners.

99 Jones Library, Special Collections Department.

100 The years of Parsons' Amherst ministry (1739-1781) were nearly identical to those of Deerfield's Jonathan Ashley (1732-1780). Like Ashley, Parsons was an outspoken Tory at the time of the Revolution. (Carpenter and Morehouse (1896), pp. 86-87, 101-102, 108; Judd (1863/1905), pp. 410-411; Smith, James (1984), pp. 568-569.) At a town meeting on January 20, 1777, the town voted – "'That the conduct of the "Revd David Parsons is not friendly with regard to the Common Cause." (Carpenter and Morehouse (1896), Town Meeting Records Section, p. 76.)

Excerpt from the February, 1737/38 probate inventory of Zechariah Field, including "A Negro man", valued at £130. (Hampshire County Registry of Probate.)

family of three slaves – Pompey or "Pomp", who joined the Amherst church, transferring his membership from a church in Chicopee, his wife Rose, and their son Goffy, who was baptized in the Amherst church in January, 1748/49.[101] Family and church ties, though, were not enough to keep Pomp from running away in 1760, and Parsons offered a reward of three dollars for his return in a notice in the *Boston Post-Boy*.

> RAN away from his Master David Parsons of Amherst Hadley, A Negro Man Servant named Pomp, about 26 Years of Age; a Fel- of the tallest Stature, judged six Feet and half High, has been long in the Country, can Read and Write, speaks good English: Had on when he went away two Jackets, one of Leather, and under all a Flannel Jacket. Whoever takes up the said Runaway and will bring him to his said Master shall have THREE DOLLARS Reward, and all necessary Charges paid by me   David Parsons.
> N.B. All Masters of Vessels and others are hereby caution'd against harbouring, concealing, or carrying off said Servant as they would avoid the Penalty of the Law.

---

101 Smith, James (1999), pp. 6-7, 59. The minister's own child was baptized during the same service.

> **R**AN away from his Mafter
> David Parfons of *Amherft Hadley*, a Negro Man
> Servant named *Pomp*, about 26 Years of Age ; a Fel-
> of the talleft Stature, judged fix Feet and half High,
> has been long in the Country, can Read and Write,
> fpeaks good Englifh : Had on when he went away
> two Jackets, one of Leather, and under all a Flannel
> Jacket. Whoever takes up the faid Runaway and
> will bring him to his faid Mafter fhall have THREE
> DOLLARS Reward, and all neceffary Charges paid
> by me   *David Parfons.*
>   *N. B.* All Mafters of Veffels and others are here-
> by caution'd againft harbouring, concealing, or carry-
> ing off faid Servant as they would avoid the Penalty
> of the Law.   *Amherft Hadley, Feb.* 25. 1760.

Boston Post-Boy and Advertiser   March 17, 1760.
(Courtesy of the American Antiquarian Society.)

No further information about Pomp has survived, nor do we know whether his wife and son were still living and still the property of Reverend Parsons when Pomp ran away in 1760. We do not know whether he was recaptured and returned to his owner, but it seems unlikely that Pomp could have made good his escape – his unusual height, 6' 6", would have made it very difficult for him to remain inconspicuous.[102]

The Amherst meetinghouse, located on the site of what is now Amherst College's "Octagon", was the predecessor of what is today Amherst's First Congregational Church on Main Street.[103] (The Octagon is now home to Amherst College's Black Student Union.) The meeting house is shown on the 1772 map of Amherst on the next page, near

---

102 The other slaves whose heights have been mentioned in this book were all considerably shorter. Prince and Peter Pur (alias Pompey), described in the two runaway notices quoted in Chapter Four, were both "of middling stature"; a similar notice quoted in Chapter Three describes a runaway slave as about 5' 8" in height; Zebulon Prutt who ran away from the Widow Porter in Hadley is described as "about five feet high"; the two Palmer slaves mentioned earlier, Primus Jackall and Pelatiah McGoldsmith, were listed with heights of 5' 1" and 5' 6".

103 First Congregational Church of Amherst (1990). See also Carpenter and Morehouse (1896), p. 38.

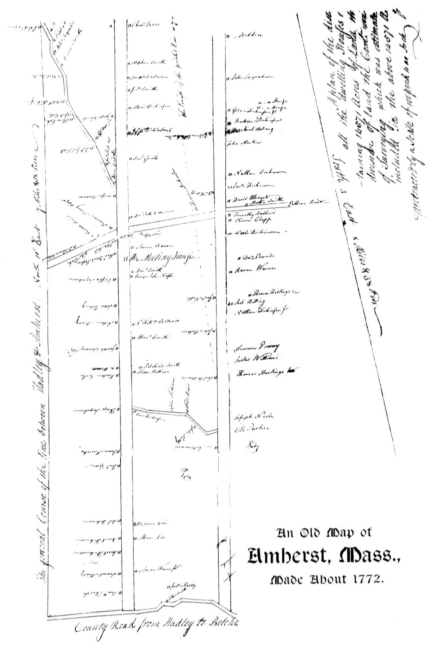

Map of Amherst, ca. 1772. (Carpenter and Morehouse (1896), facing p. 17; this map was not included in the 1959 reprint edition.)

the intersection of the streets that are now named College Street, Northampton Road, and South Pleasant Street.

Caesar Prutt, brother of Zebulon Prutt of Hadley, had a life that is as thoroughly documented as that of almost any slave in the valley. Caesar was born in 1727 as the slave of Hadley's second minister, Reverend Isaac Chauncey.[104] When Reverend Chauncey died in 1745, Caesar became the property of Isaac's son, Josiah Chauncey, who lived in East Hadley.[105] On the Amherst tax list of 1759, Josiah Chauncey (like Elisha Ingram, mentioned above) appears as the owner of one "negro", valued at £20.[106] Josiah Chauncey's house, home to Caesar Prutt for many years, is shown on the 1772 map of Amherst, on the west side of what is now South Pleasant Street, not far south of the meeting house. It was probably on the corner of the modern streets, South Pleasant Street and Hillcrest Place.[107] Elisha Ingram's house also appears on that map, almost directly across the road from the meeting house. (Turn the map upside down to read the names of Chauncey and Ingram.)

Caesar saw military service in the French and Indian War of the 1750s, joining a regiment raised in 1759 by Colonel Israel Williams of Hatfield to participate in the invasion of Canada.[108] Twelve years later, Caesar was in trouble with the law, caught dressing the carcass of a deer that he had shot, and was brought to court on a charge of poaching. He was not imprisoned or whipped but was sentenced to pay £6, a substantial sum of money.[109]

---

104 Judd (1863/1905), Genealogy Section, pp. 115-116.

105 Richard Chauncey – mentioned above in connection with Dr. Crouch's medical records – was another slave-owning son of Hadley's Reverend Isaac Chauncey, who, like his brother Josiah, lived in East Hadley. (Judd (1863/1905), Genealogy Section, p. 17; Smith, James (1984), p. 109.)

106 Jones Library, Special Collections Department.

107 The house now on this site is more recent; it bears a sign – "Horace Kellogg Homestead – c 1828". According to Carpenter and Morehouse, "[Chauncey] cultivated a large and excellent farm about half a mile south of the college now owned by Mr. Horace Kellogg." (Carpenter and Morehouse (1896), p. 102.)

108 Carpenter and Morehouse (1896), p. 63; Judd (1863/1905), p. 340; Judd Manuscripts (*Selected Papers*, 1976), pp. 547-549.

109 The fact that Caesar had the use of a musket is interesting – one of the few pieces of evidence that slaves were sometimes permitted use of guns, at least for hunting. Of course Caesar was breaking the law by shooting the deer – perhaps he also had borrowed a gun from his owner without permission. Judd makes a comment about another incident in Caesar's life, though he does not give the date – "Caesar was not always honest. Stole a sheep – restored the meat when suspected + left the town." (Judd Manuscripts, Forbes Library – *Hadley*, Vol. 3, p. 32. See also Judd Manuscripts (*Selected Papers*, 1976), p. 477.)

General Sessions of the Peace, Hampshire County, August term, 1771
John Worthington Esq Attorney to the said Lord the King in this be-
half here in Court complaining and gives your honours to be informed
that at Amherst in Said County of Hampshire on the last Day of July
last past one Cesar Prut a negro Servant for Life to Josiah Chauncey
Esq of said Amherst did with force and arms hurt and kill one wild
Deer and then and there had in his Possession the flesh and raw Skin
of one wild Deer kill'd since the twenty first Day of December last
contrary to one Law of this Province in that Case provided the peace
of the Said Lord the King his Crown and Dignity   Said John therefore
prays your Honours Cognizance of the premises and that said Cesar
may be dealt with according to Law in the Premises – Whereupon it
was commanded by ye Sheriff. And afterward now at this time comes
here the said Cesar in his proper Person & having had the hearing of
ye Complaint aforesaid he pleads guilty. Therefore it is Considered by
the Court that the said Cesar for the Trespass afores^d shall render and
pay a fine of Six pounds to be ye one moiety to ye Use of ye Lord y^e
King & disposed of in manner as the Statute in Such Cases provided
directs and the other moiety to ye use of Solomon Boltwood of
Amherst aforesaid yeoman the original informant & y^t he pay Costs
taxed at £ 0.18.11 standing Committed.

In the years leading up to the American Revolution, Caesar's owner,
Josiah Chauncey, was one of the leading Tories in Amherst. Nevertheless, Caesar became a soldier in the revolutionary army. His owner was
doubtless not in favor of Caesar's military service but apparently lacked
the influence to prevent it. Or perhaps Chauncey, in spite of his Tory
sympathies, was called up as part of the town's quota and sent Caesar as
a substitute. In May of 1775 Caesar (now forty-eight years old) joined a
company organized by Captain Reuben Dickinson (in which Daniel
Shays, leader of the Shays Rebellion in the 1780s, was a second lieutenant) and probably served at the Battle of Bunker Hill on June 17, 1775.
The following April, he was listed on the roster of a military hospital.
He did recover, joined the army again, and returned to Amherst after
the Revolution.[110] He is listed under the names *Caesar Prat* and *Caesar
Pratt* in *Massachusetts Soldiers and Sailors*[111] –

110 Carpenter and Morehouse (1896), pp. 80, 612; Smith, James (1999), pp. 7-8; *Forgotten
Patriots* (2008), p. 127; *Patriots of Color* (2004), pp. 184-185, 251.
111 *Massachusetts Soldiers and Sailors*, vol. 12, pp. 661, 670. Prospect Hill is in what is now
the town of Somerville.

This 1828 house on South Pleasant Street in Amherst is on the site where Josiah Chauncey and his slave, Caesar Prutt, lived in the 1700s. (Author's photograph.)

PRATT, CAESAR, Amherst. Capt. Reuben Dickinson's co., Col. Benjamin Ruggles Woodbridge's regt.; receipt for advance pay, signed by said Pratt and others, dated Charlestown, July 27, 1775; *also*, Private, same co. and regt.; muster roll dated Aug. 1, 1775; enlisted May 8, 1775; service, 3 mos. 1 day; *also*, company return dated Prospect Hill, Sept 28, 1775; *also*, order for bounty coat or its equivalent in money dated Prospect Hill, Oct. 26, 1775.

PRAT, Caesar, Amherst. List of men raised to serve in the Continental Army as returned by Capt. Eli Parker, agreeable to ordr of Council of Nov. 7, 1777; residence, Amherst; engaged for town of Amherst; joined Col. Sargent's regt.; term, 3 years or during war.

How and when Caesar became free is not clear. The confusion of revolutionary times and the Tory position of his owner probably facilitated his emancipation. On May 4, 1775, not long after the Battle of Lexington and Concord on April 19 and a month before Bunker Hill, according to the town meeting records[112] –

112 Carpenter and Morehouse (1896), Town Meeting Records Section, p. 72.

Voted. Upon the general clause in the Warrant Joseph Eastman Moderator. The Town enters into the examination of Mr Josiah Chauncey. Voted. Not satisfied with his answer to the charge laid against him. Voted. That s^d Chauncey should Burn all his Commissions he had ever received from the King, and also commit his Fire arms into the hands of the Select men of the District.

Judd writes that – "According to tradition, the whigs of Amherst burnt Capt. Chauncey's commissions under a tree, with some display."[113] Some time later (probably in 1777) it was decided at a meeting of citizens from Sunderland, Shutesbury, and Leverett, "by request of the Committee of Safety together with the Militia Officers of the Town of Amherst, to advise with and take into Consideration the Dangerous Situation of [Amherst] together with the State of America from a number of persons in [Amherst] who are suspected to be Enemies to the American States", that a number of persons, including Josiah Chauncey, "be confined ... all together at the house Mr John Field now Dwells in".[114] For the next few years Chauncey was surely not the influential voice in town that he had been. He had on many occasions before the Revolution been chosen as town moderator, had served several terms as a selectman, had been a Justice of the Peace for nearly twenty years, and had represented Hadley, South Hadley, Granby, and Amherst in the Massachusetts General Court in 1760 and 1762.[115] Somehow Chauncey escaped the revolutionary years unscathed, politically as well as physically, and once again became a force in town, serving as moderator once more in 1782 and being appointed to town committees in 1782 and 1783.[116] Chauncey moved to Schenectady County in New York about 1802 and died shortly thereafter.[117]

---

113 Judd (1863/1905), p. 411.

114 Carpenter and Morehouse (1896), p. 87. Among those confined with Chauncey were Simeon Strong (who had served as lawyer for the owner in Amos Newport's unsuccessful freedom suit in 1766) and Daniel and Ephraim Kellogg (listed as slave owners in Doctor Crouch's medical records cited above).

115 Carpenter and Morehouse (1896), pp. 60, 101-102, 585-588 and various entries in the Town Meeting Records Section; Judd (1863/1905), pp. 409-410, 445.

116 Carpenter and Morehouse (1896), Town Meeting Records Section, pp. 90-95.

117 Carpenter and Morehouse (1896), p. 102. There is some confusion, however, about Chauncey's post-revolutionary career and the date of his death. In an earlier passage, p. 26, Carpenter and Morehouse state that he moved to New York about 1781. Both Judd and Smith also write that he moved to New York about 1781 and died shortly thereafter. (Judd (1863/1905), Genealogy Section, p. 18; Smith, James (1984), p. 110.) In view of the town meeting records showing his service as moderator and committee member in the early 1780s, the 1781 date must be an error.

With his owner (or former owner) again a community leader in Amherst, perhaps Caesar Prutt lived with Chauncey again in the 1780s and '90s. If so, was he free or still enslaved? The next news we have of Caesar, by now presumably free, comes from Hadley, where he was "warned out" in 1796.[118] Then in April, 1801 – back in Amherst – Caesar (now seventy-four) was declared a town pauper, a town meeting of Amherst voting that his care for the coming year be auctioned off to the lowest bidder.[119]

> Voted that Ceasar Prut a Town Pauper, be Set up at vendue, to the Lowest bidder For Victualling and Beding and was Struck of to Ins Asa Smith for one year for one Doller per week.

This sort of auction (or "vendue"), used for white paupers as well as black, was a degrading spectacle in which any Amherst resident who was interested in providing room and board in return for a payment from the town could participate. Potential bidders presumably tried to estimate how cheaply they could provide for the pauper, how small a payment from the town they could accept and still make a profit, while also eyeing the pauper in question to gauge whether they might be able to use him for some work around the farm during the ensuing year. It all seems rather similar to a slave auction, though in reverse – in this case, the low bidder would of course be the winner. Every April for the next six years this scene was replayed, with Caesar Prutt in the central role. In 1802 Samuel Hastings won the right to house him for the next year with a bid of forty-four dollars. The next year it was yet another new "owner", John Ingram, for twenty-nine dollars and twenty-five cents. Then in 1804, Aaron Merrick was the winner with a bid of forty-one dollars and fifty cents, and in 1805 it was Daniel Moody with a bid of forty-eight dollars and twenty-five cents.

In April 1806, Caesar Prutt and Aaron Kellogg, a white pauper, were "set up" together.

> Voted to set up to the lowest bidder, Caesar Prutt and Aaron Kellogg, two of the town's poor, to be kept through the year insuing, with sufficient & suitable provision & necessaries, excepting for Physician or medicine, & to be returned at the end of the year as well clothed as

---

118 Judd Manuscripts, Forbes Library – *Hadley*, Vol. 3, p. 361.
119 All of the references to the auctioning of Caesar Prutt are from Carpenter and Morehouse (1896), p. 59 and Town Meeting Records Section, pp. 187-196.

they are now; accordingly, they were set-up, & struck off, on the conditions above expressed, for the sum severally following, that is to say; Caesar Prutt to Joel Kellogg for fifty one Dollars; and Aaron Kellogg to Lt. John Ingram for Sixty one Dollars & fifty cents.

Finally, in 1807, Caesar Prutt ("an aged negro", now eighty) was "struck off" for the last time, to an unrecorded bidder, for a payment from the town of sixty-five dollars for the year. Caesar was probably buried in Amherst's West Cemetery, the same cemetery where Emily Dickinson, her sister Lavinia, and their parents were buried.

It is not always a simple matter to determine the status of a black person, especially toward the end of the 18th century as slavery was gradually coming to an end in Massachusetts. An example of the difficulty is provided by the ambiguous case of Simeon Strong and the black woman, Phillis Finnemore.[120] Was Simeon Strong a slave owner? His name does not appear as an owner on surviving Amherst tax lists.[121] The enumeration sheet for the 1790 federal census includes a column headed "All other free Persons" and shows one such person, probably Phillis, in the household of Simeon Strong.[122] Phillis married Zacheus Finnemore, probably sometime in the 1790s, and a son, Augustus Caesar Finnemore, was born about 1800. Yet the 1800 census record,[123] like that of 1790, also shows one "other free person" in the Strong household, and in 1804, "Phillis" (without a surname), listed as "Mr. Strong's Negro Woman", was admitted into the First Congregational Church.[124] Does the expression "Mr. Strong's Negro Woman" suggest that at some date before 1790 Phillis had been a slave in the Strong household, that perhaps even after

---

120 Simeon Strong, another Tory, was a wealthy lawyer, a prominent citizen of Amherst who frequently held town offices. (Carpenter and Morehouse (1896), pp. 101-102 and various entries in the Town Meeting Records Section; Smith, James (1984), p. 711.) Strong represented the owner when Amos Newport of Hatfield sued for his freedom in 1766. The "Strong House" is now home to the Amherst Historical Society.

121 Jones Library, Special Collections Department. In Amherst's early years, the tax lists often had a column for "Negroes & Faculty". But the latest surviving tax list with such a column is one from 1777. Tax lists from subsequent years, which are in a quite different format, generally have a "Faculty" column but have no mention of "Negroes". Whether this change came about because there were no longer any slaves owned in town or for some other reason is not clear.

122 There are no entries in the column headed "Slaves".

123 This time the column was headed "All other free persons, except Indians not taxed".

124 Smith, James (1999), pp. 70-71. Surviving records of Amherst's First and Second Congregational Churches contain no references to blacks between 1758 and 1804; there are, however, significant gaps in these records. (Smith, James (1999), p. 7.)

1790 she had been a slave in fact if not in name? There is really no way of knowing.

Phillis died sometime in the late 1830s and, like Caesar Prutt, was probably buried in Amherst's West Cemetery. One of the Finnemores' grandsons, Charles, enlisted in the famous 54th Massachusetts Volunteer Infantry Regiment in 1863, fought in South Carolina, probably at Fort Wagner where many of his fellow soldiers died, was wounded in 1864 but survived the war and returned to Amherst.[125]

Greenfield

There were a number of slaves owned in Greenfield (a part of Deerfield until 1753), though probably not as many as in towns farther south in the valley. The 1759 affair of Caesar (slave of Greenfield minister Edward Billing) and Billing's daughter Lucy and the ensuing court case were discussed in Chapter Four. The fate of Caesar in the aftermath of that court case – sentenced to be "severely whiped thirty stripes on his naked body" and then sold out of the province – is unknown. Caesar was one of a number of slaves belonging to owners in various towns whose names appear from time to time in the account books of Deerfield store owners. In August, 1757, for instance, "Cezar M[r] Billings Negro" purchased a pair of garters at Elijah Williams' store. Then two weeks later "Cesar Billing" was in Deerfield again and purchased stockings at the Williams store.[126]

Billing's successor as minister, Roger Newton, was also a slave owner. In his record book,[127] he included information not only about the white residents but also about various slaves in town, recording, for instance the death of Umphry.[128]

Umphry, "Negro Serv[t], to Ensign Childs."   October 16, 1767

---

125 "Finnemore, Charles A. 27, mar.; farmer; Amherst. 10 Mch 63; 20 Aug 65. Wounded 20 Feb 64 Olustee, Fla." (Emilio (1891), p. 350.) See also Smith, James (1999), pp. 71-73.
126 Account books of Elijah Williams, PVMA Library.
127 Record book of Roger Newton, PVMA Library. Many of Newton's entries are included in Thompson, Francis (1904) and in *Vital Records of Greenfield* (1915). As mentioned in Chapter Four, Reverend Newton recorded in his book the death of Patience, infant daughter of Lucy Billing and Caesar, in 1762 as well as of Lucy herself eleven years later.
128 It is quite likely that "Umphry" is the "Humphrey" (or "Umphry") of Chapter Four, property of Timothy Childs, Sr.

He also recorded births, baptisms, and deaths of his own children and his own slaves.

Births & Baptisms –
Isaac, my Son & Tinner, my negro Girl – baptized September 20, 1767
Phillis, A Negro Child of Tinner, was born July 10ᵗʰ, 1774
Phillis, a negro Child, born in my House – baptized August 23, 1778
Violet, a negro Child of my family – baptized April 25, 1783

Deaths –
Phillis, "a negro Child," August 23, 1781
Violet, a Negro Child   April 27, 1783

In 1794, Dinah Freedom of Greenfield was married to John Rowley by Reverend John Taylor of Deerfield.[129] Both are listed as "Negroes" in the *Vital Records of Deerfield*. Dinah was probably a former slave, who chose her own surname on becoming free. Perhaps "Dinah, a Negro woman" who died in Greenfield in 1801[130] was really Dinah Freedom.

Thompson describes another female slave belonging to Reverend Newton, "Old Tenor" – "Old Tenor was a slave of Mr. Newton's and upon her death he preached a sermon saying among other things that she 'was no pilferer'."[131] Old Tenor may have been the same woman as "Tinner", baptized by Newton in 1767. And the name was used again, in various forms. In 1784, Mingo Proctor and "Tanor" of Greenfield were married.[132] "Tanor" was probably either "Tinner" who was baptized in 1767 or a daughter. Then in 1814, Tinner Proctor (or "Procter") of Greenfield – probably the daughter of the woman who had married Mingo Proctor in 1784 – married Peter Green, Jr. of Colrain.[133]

Peter Green, Sr. was born in Africa and was a slave in Colrain in the 1770s. He served as a private in the Revolution, gained his freedom, and returned to Colrain. His military service was discovered only recently, as a result of research carried out by the Mary Mattoon Chapter [of Amherst] of the Daughters of the American Revolution. It was also re-

129 Thompson, Francis (1904), Vol. 2, p. 716; *Vital Records of Deerfield* (1920), pp. 187, 224.
130 Thompson, Francis (1904), Vol. 2, p. 741; *Vital Records of Greenfield* (1915), p. 299.
131 Thompson, Francis (1904), Vol. 2, p. 980. The date of the death of Tinner (or "Old Tenor") is not given by Thompson, nor does it appear in the *Vital Records of Greenfield*.
132 *Vital Records of Greenfield* (1915), p. 209. Thompson, quoting from Reverend Newton's record book, writes in his list of Greenfield marriages – "Oct. 17, 1784. Mingo Proctor & 'Tenor' (Rev. Dr. Newton's servant)." (Thompson, Francis (1904), Vol. 2, p. 705.)
133 *Vital Records of Greenfield* (1915), pp. 178, 209; *Vital Records of Colrain* (1934), pp. 83, 115.

alized that although Peter Green, Sr. was probably buried in Colrain, there was no gravestone marking his burial place. Green's service was honored in 2005, in a ceremony organized by the D.A.R., dedicating a newly erected gravestone next to that of his son in Colrain's Brick Cemetery.[134]

Sunderland

Just south of Deerfield and on the east side of the Connecticut River is the town of Sunderland, where Joseph Ashley, cousin of Deerfield's Jonathan Ashley, was minister from 1747 to 1784. As far as can be determined, Joseph – in contrast to so many ministers in the valley – was not a slave owner. Indeed, there are few references to slave ownership in Sunderland. In an 1879 address to the annual meeting of the Pocumtuck Valley Memorial Association, Phinehas Field writes that Napthalo ("commonly called Naptha") was a slave belonging to Joseph Dickinson of Hatfield, who moved to Sunderland in 1720.[135] By 1783, Dickinson had died and none of his heirs lived in Sunderland. At some time before or shortly after Dickinson's death, Naptha acquired both freedom and a surname – Field, quoting from the town records, writes that in June, 1783, the town "voted that the Selectmen be directed to require the heirs of Joseph Dickinson, formerly of this town, deceased, to signify their minds to this town whether they are willing to give bonds or any other way oblige themselves to maintain Naptha *Freeman*, and report to this meeting". Ten years later, in March, 1793, the town voted that they "will not receive Napthalo Freeman in order to maintain him". One of Dickinson's heirs lived in Northfield, and in December, 1793, the town of Sunderland "Voted to pay Heman Farnam and Benj. Graves for transporting him to Northfield".

In his 1899 history of Sunderland, Smith quotes from Phinehas Field's discussion of Napthalo and then writes that "There is no record of the town of Sunderland having but one slave".[136] Though the number of slaves in Sunderland may have been fairly small, there were in fact other slaves besides Napthalo. The province-wide property valuation list of 1768 shows two "Servants for Life between 14 & 45 Years of Age"

---

134 Mary Mattoon Chapter, D.A.R. – Press release of June 1, 2005. See also *Forgotten Patriots* (2008), pp. 317, 333.

135 Field, Phinehas (1879).

136 Smith, John (1899), p. 161.

belonging to Joseph Skinner and one to Lt. Fellows Billing.[137] In the similar valuation list compiled three years later, Joseph Skinner's name no
longer appears at all, while Billing is still listed as the owner of one slave.[138]

Northfield

Ten miles north of Greenfield, close to the New Hampshire border, is Northfield. Most famous of Northfield's slaves is Abijah Prince,
for many years the slave of Reverend Benjamin Doolittle. As recounted
briefly in Chapter Four, Abijah won his freedom two years after
Doolittle's death in 1749 and moved to Deerfield a few years later, where
he married Lucy Terry.[139]

In his 1879 address,[140] Phinehas Field listed a number of Northfield
slaves of whom he had known, relying, as he wrote, on "tradition and
[his] own memory". Field mentioned Jack (property of merchant Aaron
Whitney), Tatnai and Mishap (property of Captain Samuel Hunt),
Meshach (property of Deacon Paul Field,[141] farmer), Caesar (property
of Ensign Ebenezer Field), and Ishmael Turner (property of Seth Field,
Esq., farmer). In a footnote, Field wrote that he later learned that Hunt's
slave, Tatnai, had been born in Deerfield in 1765. Samuel Hunt's Tatnai
was probably Tatnai *Prince*, son of Abijah and Lucy. If it was Tatnai Prince,
then he was free – not a slave, but rather an employee or perhaps an
apprentice or an indentured servant.

Conclusion

As this abbreviated discussion of Connecticut Valley towns from
Suffield and Springfield to Greenfield and Northfield demonstrates, black
slaves were present throughout the valley in colonial times. No account
of the history of western Massachusetts can ignore that fact.

---

137 Massachusetts State Archives. The 1768 act requiring such a list was quoted in Chapter Two.
138 Massachusetts State Archives; Pruitt (1978).
139 For the full story of Abijah and Lucy Prince, in Deerfield and later in Vermont, see
Gerzina (2008).
140 Field, Phinehas (1879).
141 In the 1771 valuation list, Paul Field is listed as the owner of one "servant for life".
(Massachusetts State Archives; Pruitt (1978).)

CHAPTER SIX

Why Did They Own Slaves?

Why did they own slaves? Why did so many of the leading citizens of the valley purchase and keep slaves? It was sometimes said, especially by the ministers, that selfless owners were really doing their slaves a great service by rescuing them from their heathen religions and turning them into good Christians. Perhaps the kindest label for this supposed motivation for slave ownership is "hypocrisy".

I have frequently heard it said that slave ownership was primarily a badge of importance in the community – a slave was a status symbol. Jonathan Ashley, for instance, as minister of Deerfield, was one of the most important men in town. Owning three black slaves not only added to his status within the town but also gave him reason to feel superior to his cousin Joseph, minister of Sunderland, just across the river, who owned none. Even as Connecticut Valley settlers were united in dealing with the possibility of attacks from hostile Indians, there was surely a constant, if perhaps covert, competition for status, not only between the residents of one town but also between residents of neighboring towns.

But life on the frontier of the English settlements was not easy. Even those who were relatively well off such as the ministers, as opposed to the common laborers, were often struggling to make ends meet, to feed their families, to deal with the ever-present hazards of Indian attacks, of illness and infant death. They were not so affluent that they could afford to own slaves simply for the sake of prestige.

Though at other times and in other places slaves may have been coveted primarily as status symbols, I think that the real reasons for slave ownership in the valley were different and a good deal simpler. First, a slave was a good investment. For Jonathan Ashley, rentals of Cato and Titus to other Deerfield men who needed labor provided a fairly steady stream of income. And in an agricultural community like Deerfield, a healthy male slave could always be sold if circumstances required. Moreover, Jonathan Ashley, a farmer as well as a minister, had fields to take care of. When he needed to have his crops harvested or his firewood cut, Cato and Titus were always available.

As for the role of Jenny, the Ashley household was crowded with people. The Ashleys had nine children, three of whom died in infancy. Sometimes a young man lived with them who was serving as schoolmaster or studying for the ministry. With Dorothy Ashley frequently pregnant, with as many as six children, they needed reliable household help. In addition to Jenny, there was often a young white girl living with them. Sarah Hawks, for instance, lived with the Ashleys at various times in the 1740s. The following entries from Ashley's account book indicate some of the problems associated with Sarah's employment.[1]

> Sarah Hawks came to live with us 1st of August 1745.
> Agreed to give her 9s per week.
> Whilst with us She Spun 46 run of worsted for other folks on act.
> She had two weeks & half to work for herself.
> Janry Beginning was Sick 1 week
> January 11 12, 13 was at Wappin
> April Begin, went Home 1 week & 2 days.
> May 14. She began to work for her Self in the mean time worked 4 days for us
> June 23 Began to work for us.
> July 2 Was taken Sick
> July 16 Began to work for us again
> August 12 . 1746. She went home was gone 4 days.
> Septem Was gone home 4 days.
> Octob 7 went home was at home 13 days.
> Nov. 9 went home was at home 3 weeks.
> January 23 was gone 3 days.
> March She was Sick one week
> April worked for her Self 3 days
> May beginning was gone home 1 week & 2 Days
> June 1 & 2 She was Sick
> June was sick & worked for her Self one week & 2 days
> July 9 Was taken sick
> 21 began to work again
> 1747 Sept. beg. Tended her Sister Mary 2 days
> August 17, 18, 19 worked for her Self
> Sept 12 taken Sick Came again Oct. 7

---

1 Account book of Jonathan Ashley, PVMA Library.

Nov begin Sick two days

No^v 14 went to tend her Sister Mary

Nov. At Thanksgiving time was gone a fortnight & one day to tend Mary

Feb. 29 She was taken Sick & went Home

April 12. came again & began to work for us.

July 11. 1748 Sarah Hawks began to work for us again at 15 S per week old tenor

Oct. 24 Came again to work for us at 15 S per week

Nov. Worked 4 days for her Self

Decem. 10 was Sick one week

Feb. Worked 2 Days for her Self

March was ill 4 days

March 20 taken Sick & went Home

August 1749 Was with us one week & a day

Oct 30th 1749 Came to Live with us again

Nov. 15 went away again

Decem 16 Came again to Live with us

Feb was Sick 4 days

Sarah came and went, sometimes worked for herself or left to take care of her sister. Jenny, by contrast, was always available. There were several motivations for slave ownership, but there is no question but that the availability of slave labor, in the fields and in the house, eased the burdens of frontier life.

CHAPTER SEVEN

18th-Century Doubts, Objections, and Protests Against Slavery

"Forasmuch as Liberty is in real value next unto Life: None ought to part with it themselves, or deprive others of it, but upon most mature Consideration."

Those are the stirring opening words of *The Selling of Joseph*, a striking antislavery tract written by Samuel Sewall in 1700.[1] Sewall went on –

> It is likewise most lamentable to think, how in taking Negros out of Africa, and Selling of them here, That which GOD has joyned together men do boldly rend asunder; Men from their Country, Husbands from their Wives, Parents from their Children. How horrible is the Uncleanness, Mortality, if not Murder, that the Ships are guilty of that bring great Crouds of these miserable Men, and Women. Methinks, when we are bemoaning the barbarous Usage of our Friends and Kinsfolk in Africa:[2] it might not be unseasonable to enquire whether we are not culpable in forcing the Africans to become Slaves amongst our selves.

Sewall was opposed to slavery, and in this he was far ahead of his time, though his opposition was based in part on practical considerations – "And all things considered, it would conduce more to the Welfare of the Province, to have White Servants for a Term of Years, than to have Slaves for Life. Few can endure to hear of a Negro's being made free; and indeed they can seldom use their freedom well; yet their continual aspiring after

---

1 Sewall (1700). Sewall is famous not only for his early and outspoken opposition to slavery but also for his leading role as a judge in the Salem witch trials in 1692 . On January 14, 1696/97, he made a public apology for his errors in having condemned to death the innocent "witches" of Salem, the only one of the Salem judges to apologize. (Sewall (1674-1729), Vol. 1, pp. 445-446. See also Francis (2005), pp. 181-183; LaPlante (2007), pp. 199-201.)

2 "Our friends and kinsfolk in Africa." – From the 1500s until well into the 1800s, Barbary pirates from the north coast of Africa raided European coasts for plunder and slaves and captured ships of all nations on the seas. They sailed as far west as Iceland, enslaving sailors and passengers, some of whom were ransomed but many simply sold in the slave markets of Algiers and other cities.

their forbidden Liberty, renders them Unwilling Servants." And he was hardly advocating social and political equality between blacks and whites, clearly believing in the inferiority of blacks – "And there is such a disparity in their Conditions, Colour & Hair, that they can never embody with us, and grow up into orderly Families, to the Peopling of the Land: but still remain in our Body Politick as a kind of extravasat Blood."

In may be that Sewall's goal was simply to stimulate others to think about the subject and begin to improve the ways in which slaves were treated. Nevertheless, *The Selling of Joseph* was a clear condemnation of the practice of slavery. A year later John Saffin responded with a forthright defense of slavery – *A Brief and Candid Answer to a late Printed Sheet, Entituled, The Selling of Joseph*.[3] Unimpressed though a modern reader would be by Saffin's arguments, general opinion at the time was that Saffin had the better of the argument, and it was a long time before anything remotely like *The Selling of Joseph* appeared in print.

Sewall continued his efforts to ameliorate the condition of the slaves, succeeding in inserting a provision in a 1705 law to keep owners from denying marriage to their slaves, trying unsuccessfully in 1716 "to prevent Indians and Negroes being Rated with Horses and Hogs" on the tax rolls.[4]

> December 1, 1705 – Deputies send in a Bill against fornication, or Marriage of White men with Negros or Indians; with extraordinary penalties; directing the Secretary to draw a Bill accordingly. If it be pass'd, I fear twill be an Opression to God, and that which will promote Murders and other Abominations. I have got the Indians out of the Bill, and some mitigation for them [the Negroes] left in it, and the clause about their Masters not denying their Marriage.[5]

> June 22, 1716 – I essay'd June, 22, to prevent Indians and Negros being Rated with Horses and Hogs; but could not prevail.

Is it possible that Sewall himself was a slave owner? Towner writes that Sewall "probably owned slaves", Greene lists him as one of the

---

3 Saffin (1701).

4 Sewall (1674-1729), Vol. 2, p. 143 and Vol. 3, p.87. (Diary entries of December 1, 1705 and June 22, 1716.)

5 The main purpose of the 1705 law ("An Act for the Better Preventing of a Spurious and Mixt Issue", discussed in Chapter Two) was to prohibit marriage between whites and blacks. The provision that Sewall succeeded in having inserted into the bill was this – "And no master shall unreasonably deny marriage to his negro with one of the same nation, any law, usage, or custom to the contrary not withstanding."

"leading" slave owners of Massachusetts, and Sweet asserts, though without giving reasons, that he was "probably a slaveholder".[6] But the entries in Sewall's diaries cited by Towner and Greene refer to Sewall's servant, Scipio, and to Boston, described by Greene as "his Negro, Boston". Though Scipio was a name frequently used for slaves, Kaplan convincingly demonstrates that Scipio was a free black engaged as a *servant* and not a slave and that Boston was a free black who sometimes worked for Sewall, pointing out that he was referred to as a "Negro Freeman" in an obituary published in a Boston newspaper.[7]

On at least eight occasions between 1714 and 1726, "Mr. Samuel Sewall, Merchant" placed advertisements in Boston newspapers, offering for sale "A Very likely young Negro Wench", "several likely Young Negro Men & Boys, Just Arrived", etc. The merchant offering slaves for sale was probably Judge Sewall's nephew.[8] It does seem odd, though, that in his lengthy and detailed diary, the author of *The Selling of Joseph* made no mention of the fact that his own nephew and namesake was a dealer in slaves.

Even in Boston, it was many decades after the 1700 publication of *The Selling of Joseph* before there were any significant public protests against slavery or even serious expressions of doubt. What about western Massachusetts, the Connecticut Valley?

"Surely the ministers must have been opposed to slavery." That is a view that I have heard many times from those who have heard me talk about slavery in the valley. But nothing could be further from the truth. As we saw in Chapter Five, a great many of the valley ministers were slave owners themselves. Ministers such as Jonathan Ashley gave special sermons to their towns' slaves, urging them to be "contented with [their] State & Condition in the world".[9] It may be that such sermons were intended simply to reinforce the control of white owners over their slaves – but perhaps the fact that ministers gave those sermons is an indication of their need to justify slavery to themselves as well as to their slaves, a hint that somehow they really knew that slavery was wrong.

---

6 Towner (1964), p. 41; Greene (1942), pp. 284-285, 354; Sweet (2003), p. 59.

7 Kaplan (1969), pp. 53, 60-63.

8 Towner (1964), p. 41; LaPlante (2007), p. 225.

9 We know that Ashley gave such a sermon on at least one occasion, because the text of his notes has survived. (See Appendix I.) Other ministers almost certainly gave similar sermons, but it is only for Ashley's 1750 sermon that I have seen the text of the minister's notes.

The few written observations about slavery that we do have, from the ministers or others in the Connecticut Valley, are for the most part either defenses of the institution or at best expressions of the view that slaves deserve compassion and that owners have a duty to treat their slaves decently.

Consider some of the entries from the diaries of Reverend Stephen Williams and his wife Abigail that were quoted in Chapter Five. Stephen prayed "God to help me to do my duty towards those under my care", a prayer that he repeated again and again. Williams was extraordinarily conscious of his responsibility to care for his slaves, to do his duty toward them. Over and over, the words are "duty" and "care". Only once in his diary did he allude to the possibility that he might free any of his slaves, and that was only after Peter had "ungratefully" run away in 1773. And Abigail, on Tom's suicide – "Even the poor creature Tom our Negro" is someone for whom we must have sympathy and concern.

John Ballantine, minister of Westfield, was not a slave owner, though he frequently borrowed a slave, Sylva, from his brother-in-law, Reverend Gay of Suffield. On one occasion, when both Gay and Sylva were in Westfield, Gay almost concluded a sale of Sylva to a fellow citizen of Suffield, Elnathan Bush, and Ballantine included some of his thoughts on the subject in his diary.[10]

February 9, 1768   Elnathan Bush of Suffield here to talk ab^t buying Sylva. wrote by him to Mr Gay –

February 10, 1768   Bush here – Mr Gay lodgd here –

February 11, 1768   Bush here treats with Mr Gay ab^t Sylva. They agreed, but Sylva so averse, takes on, puts an end to ye affair at present. Masters of Negros ought to be men of g^t humanity. They have an Arbitrary Power. may correct y^{em} at pleasure. may Separate y^{em} fro^m y^{eir} Children. may Send y^{em} out of ye Country.

Owners should be "men of great humanity", because they have arbitrary power, because they have the power to separate parents from their children. There is no sense here that such "arbitrary power" is wrong or that slaves such as Tom and Sylva are persons comparable in their humanity to their owners.

---

10 Ballantine (1737-1774).

Like Reverend Ballantine, Northampton's Jonathan Edwards at least had reservations about the power that owners had over their slaves, as described in two articles by Minkema.[11] About 1740, there was a dispute between some of the residents of Northfield and their minister, Benjamin Doolittle. For the most part the controversy concerned religious doctrine and practice, but – interestingly – among the criticisms made of Doolittle by his congregation (in addition to comments on the extra income that Doolittle derived from his medical practice, his extravagant lifestyle,[12] and objections to his salary and firewood demands) was the fact that he owned a slave.[13] Edwards became involved in responding to the charges against his fellow minister and wrote – though not for publication – on the issue of slavery. Although on theological points, Edwards was more in sympathy with the critics than with Doolittle, he defended slave *ownership*[14] (citing scripture, of course), while attacking the critics as hypocrites for not criticizing the slave *trade*[15] and for in fact themselves profiting from the availability of slave labor and using products derived from the transatlantic slave trade.[16]

Minkema also reports a marginal note that Edwards made in his Bible on a passage in *Job*, a note probably written several years before the Northfield controversy, in which Edwards seemed to be on the verge of condemning slavery.[17]

---

11 Minkema (1997); Minkema (2002).

12 As Edwards described it, his Northfield critics were "reproaching their Pastor as tho he lived in <notorous> iniquity & Indulgence of his Lusts". (Minkema (1997), p. 831.)

13 Abijah Prince, who became free several years after Doolittle's death, moved to Deerfield, and married Lucy Terry in 1756, as we saw in Chapter Four.

14 Edwards and Doolittle were just two of many slave-owning ministers in the valley. The valley ministers may have had theological differences but appeared to be in remarkable agreement about the acceptability of slave ownership.

15 "Partakers of a far more cruel slavery than that which they object against in those that have slaves here." (Minkema (1997), p. 831.)

16 He also claimed that most of their objections (about salary demands, firewood, and expensive lifestyle as well as slave ownership) were not sincerely meant but intended only to cause extra trouble for their minister with whom they had theological disagreements – "Let em own that their objections are not Conscientious but meerly to make difficulty & trouble for their Neighbours." (Minkema (1997), p. 832.)

17 Minkema (2002), pp. 40, 56. The passage from *Job* (31: 13-15) reads as follows – "If I did despise the cause of my man-servant or of my maid-servant, when they contended with me; What then shall I do when God riseth up? and when he visiteth, what shall I answer him? Did not he that made me in the womb make him? and did not one fashion us in the womb?"

If I despise the cause of my man or maidservant when they plead with me, and when they stand before me to be judged by me, what then shall I do when I come to stand before God to be judged by him? God may justly do by me as I do by my servant. If I despise my servant's cause, how much more may God despise my cause? I am God's servant as they are mine, and much more inferior to God than my servant is to me.

And then, in what could have been a strong antislavery statement, a call for abolition from the Connecticut Valley, Edwards went on.

We are made of the same human race, and [God] has given us the same human nature, which more clearly shows the why Job should not despise and abuse his servant. In these two things are contained the most forceable reasons against the master's abuse of his servant, viz. that both have one Maker, and that their Maker made 'em alike or with the same nature.

To a modern reader, it seems obvious that the fact that blacks and whites are "of the same human race, that both have one maker" is an argument against the whole institution of slavery, an argument for equality. But Edwards did not accept or apparently even think of such an implication – for him it was only an argument for treating slaves decently, for not abusing them. He had purchased his first slave in 1731 and continued to own slaves for the rest of his life.

And even those thoughts of Edwards were not expressed in public, only as a marginal note in his own Bible. Thus among the surviving documents from Connecticut Valley slave owners that I know of, we have at most an occasional note of sympathy for "the poor creature Tom our negro", a concern that the "arbitrary power" possessed by slave owners should be exercised with restraint, and never a hint that perhaps it was *wrong* for one human being to *own* another human being.

CHAPTER EIGHT

The End of Slavery in Massachusetts

When, how, and why did slavery come to an end in Massachusetts? The "why" part of this question is extremely difficult to answer. Even the seemingly straightforward queries, "when?" and "how?", are not easy ones to deal with, and historians continue to debate these surprisingly murky questions. Many authors have given straightforward (but incorrect) answers to these two questions. For example – "In Massachusetts slavery was outlawed in 1780", "The Bill of Rights of 1780 declared all slaves in Massachusetts free", or "Slavery ... ceased on the adoption of the constitution of 1780 which declares all men to be born free and equal, let the color of their skin be what it may".[1] Indeed, the Massachusetts Constitution of 1780 does declare all men free and equal (though it includes no mention of "skin color"), and a literal reading of Article I would lead one to believe that it prohibited slavery.

> Article I. All men are born free and equal, and have certain natural, essential, and unalienable rights; among which may be reckoned the right of enjoying and defending their lives and liberties; that of acquiring, possessing, and protecting property; in fine, that of seeking and obtaining their safety and happiness.

It is simply incorrect, however, to say that slavery ended in Massachusetts in 1780. There is no evidence to support the idea that those who wrote that article had any intention that it should apply to black slaves (or to women, for that matter). Massachusetts was the first of the colonies to legalize slavery, with the adoption in 1641 of its "Body of Liberties", and slavery was never *legislated* out of existence.[2]

---

1 Rosenthal, Bernard (1973), p. 79; Du Bois (1968), p. 62; Rantoul (1833), p.4. These are by no means the only authors who have seriously misunderstood the history of Article I of the Massachusetts Constitution and its interpretation. And there are a number of histories of Massachusetts – some of them quite recent – in which no mention at all is made of the fact that slavery ever existed in the state.

2 Except, one might say, by the state's ratification of the 13th Amendment to the United States Constitution in 1865. It took almost 200 years after the adoption of the

Somewhat closer to the truth is the frequently made statement that slavery was brought to an end by a decision of the Massachusetts Supreme Judicial Court[3] in 1783.[4] An important series of six cases began in 1781 when Quock Walker, a slave in Barre, brought a civil suit against his owner, Nathaniel Jennison, on a charge of assault. Walker had run away from Jennison and gone to work for John and Seth Caldwell (probably the children of his earlier owner, James Caldwell[5]). After Jennison attempted forcibly to bring Walker back, Walker filed suit. Walker not only accused Jennison of assault but also claimed that his previous owner, James Caldwell, had given him a promise of manumission. The fact that the initial court case (*Walker v. Jennison*) in the legal saga of Walker, Jennison, and Caldwell was based on a charge of assault (and not on the claimed promise of manumission nor on a claim that slavery was now unconstitutional) provides an immediate indication that untangling these cases and understanding their implications is not likely to be a simple matter.[6] The outcome of *Walker v. Jennison* was that Quock Walker was declared by the jury to be "a freeman, & not the proper negro slave of the Defendant". Jennison was found guilty of assault and assessed damages.[7]

> Issue being thus joined, the case after a full hearing was committed to
> a Jury sworn according to law to try the same, who returned their

---

1780 Massachusetts Constitution before finally, in 1976, Article I was amended to read – "All people are born free and equal and have certain natural, essential and unalienable rights; among which may be reckoned the right of enjoying and defending their lives and liberties; that of acquiring, possessing and protecting property; in fine, that of seeking and obtaining their safety and happiness. Equality under the law shall not be denied or abridged because of sex, race, color, creed or national origin."

3 Previously the "Superior Court of Judicature", Massachusetts' highest court had acquired a new name in 1780.

4 For example, "Massachusetts ... abolished slavery by judicial decision in 1783" – at best a gross oversimplification. (Blumrosen and Blumrosen (2005), p. 159.) Sometimes an author manages to get it totally wrong – "The Massachusetts constitution of 1783 abolished local slavery", for instance. (Piersen (1988), p. 33.)

5 The 1754 bill of sale by which Quock (or "Quaco"), then a nine-month-old child, was sold to James Caldwell is quoted by O'Brien (1960) – "Sold this day to Mr. James Caldwell ... a certain negro man named Mingo, about twenty Years of Age, and also one negro wench named Dinah, about nineteen years of age, with child Quaco, about nine months old – all sound & well for the Sum of One hundred and eight pounds, lawful money ... which Negroes, I ... do warrant & defend against all claims whatsoever ..."

6 There is a very large literature on the tortuous story of the Walker-Jennison-Caldwell cases. A sampling of these includes – O'Brien (1960); Cushing, John (1961); Zilversmit (1967); Zilversmit (1968); Spector (1968); MacEacheren (1970); McManus (1973); Blanck (2002).

7 O'Brien (1960), p. 226; Cushing, John (1961), p. 120.

Verdict therein upon Oath, that is to say, they find that the said Quork is a freeman, & not the proper negro slave of the Defendant and assess Damages for the Plaintiff in the sum of Fifty Pounds in lawful gold or silver, or bills of public Credit equivalent thereto.

Appeals were filed, Jennison sued the Caldwells for luring Walker away, and in 1783 the case finally reached the Supreme Judicial Court as *Commonwealth v. Jennison*. Once again, just as in the first of the Walker-Jennison-Caldwell cases, the charge against Jennison was one of assault. According to the report of the case[8] –

A Jury thereupon is impannelled & Sworn to try the Issue ... who after hearing all matters & things concerning the same, return their Verdict, and upon their oath do say, that the said Nathaniel Jennison is guilty: It is therefore considered by the Court that the said Nathaniel Jennison pay a fine to the Commonwealth of Forty shillings, pay cost of prosecution & stand committed till Sentence be performed.

At the conclusion of that 1783 case, the sixth and final case in the Walker-Jennison-Caldwell series, Quock Walker was undeniably free.

But there are many reasons for rejecting the conclusion that the 1783 case (or any of the five earlier cases) brought an end to slavery in the state. Chief Justice William Cushing's charge to the jury in *Commonwealth v. Jennison*, which included a reference to Article I of the 1780 Massachusetts Constitution, was indeed a sweeping condemnation of slavery.[9]

Sentiments more favorable to the natural rights of mankind, and to that innate desire for liberty which heaven, without regard to complexion or shape, has planted in the human breast – have prevailed since the glorious struggle for our rights began. And these sentiments led the framers of our constitution of government – by which the people of this commonwealth have solemnly bound themselves to each other – to declare – *that all men are born free and equal;* and that *every subject is entitled to liberty,* and to have it guarded by the laws as well as his life and property ... The court are therefore fully of the opinion that perpetual servitude can no longer be tolerated in our government.

---

8 "A brief, hand-written report of this trial, signed by Charles Cushing [a younger brother of the Chief Justice and clerk of the Supreme Judicial Court] on April 20, 1783." (O'Brien (1960), p. 236.)

9 This is a portion of Justice Cushing's charge. John Cushing describes this version as "what evidently was the final version". The italics here are as in Cushing's 1961 article. (Cushing, John (1961), pp. 132-133.)

As compelling as this statement was, it was only Cushing's charge to the jury. It was not a legally binding *decision* of the court, a dramatic decision that ended slavery in Massachusetts, though it has frequently been described in those terms.[10] Even at the highest level at this time, cases were actually decided by a jury, which simply rendered a brief verdict. There was no written decision with an explanation of the legal reasoning. We do not know what factors played a role in bringing the jury to its verdict, whether the wording of Article I of the state constitution had any influence at all in their thinking, whether Cushing's charge was important or not, whether Walker's claim of a promise of manumission was a significant factor. In any event, the lack of a written decision meant that no clear precedent was established.

There was another case in the early 1780s that may have helped to end slavery in Massachusetts. Mumbett (also known as Elizabeth Freeman, a name that she adopted after winning her freedom) was a slave belonging to John Ashley of Sheffield, in the southwestern corner of the state. (John Ashley was a cousin of Deerfield's minister Jonathan Ashley, one of four Ashley cousins in Yale's graduating class of 1730.) According to local folklore, during the previous decade Mumbett had frequently listened as John Ashley and other Sheffield men talked about the Declaration of Independence and the freedom that Americans were seeking from English oppression. (Unlike his Tory cousin Jonathan, Mumbett's owner, John Ashley, was a "patriot" and a strong advocate of independence.)

Mumbett did not get along well with Hannah Ashley, her owner's wife. One day Mumbett interceded as Hannah was about to strike Mumbett's younger sister, also a slave, with a heated shovel, and Mumbett received the blow herself, acquiring a scar that she carried for the rest of her life. Motivated by the conversations about freedom that she had overheard and reasoning that Article I of the new state constitution

---

10 For example, "Thus the court rendered one of the earliest decisions in the country applying a written constitution directly as law, and abolished slavery in Massachusetts as a legalized institution at a time when the legislature was afraid to act." (Hart (1927-1930), Vol. 4, pp. 37-38.) And Commager, reprinting an extract from "the original notebook of Chief Justice Cushing" that appeared in Hart, writes – "The court, however, speaking through Chief Justice Cushing, ruled that the first article of the Declaration of Rights [i.e., Article I of the 1780 Massachusetts Constitution] had abolished slavery in Massachusetts." (Commager (1949), Vol. 1, p. 110.) See also Cushing, John (1961), p. 132, note 20.

should apply to her as well as to whites,[11] soon after this incident Mumbett asked Stockbridge lawyer Theodore Sedgwick[12] for help in suing for her freedom. The case was tried in the Inferior Court of Common Pleas of Berkshire County in the summer of 1781 as *Brom & Bett v. J. Ashley, Esq.*,[13] and the jury ruled that "the said Brom & Bett are not and were not ... the legal Negro Servants of him the said John Ashley dureing life and Assess thirty shillings damages". Unlike other freedom suits such as that of Quock Walker, the Mumbett case was not complicated by any alleged promise of manumission nor by any claim that Ashley's title was defective (though the attack on Mumbett by Hannah Ashley may have been an issue). But the record provides no indication of the reasoning of the jury, of whether or not the recently adopted state constitution was important in their deliberations. Brom and Bett won the case and Mumbett, newly freed, went to work for her lawyer's family. No one seems to know what happened to Brom or whether Mumbett's younger sister also became free after the trial.

Colonel Ashley decided not to pursue an appeal of the verdict, and for that reason, because it never reached a higher court, this case never had the impact that the Walker-Jennison-Caldwell cases eventually had. Why did Ashley not appeal? Zilversmit[14] argues (unconvincingly, in my opinion) that "In all likelihood Ashley accepted the decision of the lower court ... because a few weeks earlier the Supreme Court had ruled in the case of *Caldwell v. Jennison*[15] that slavery was unconstitutional in Massachusetts". But *Caldwell v. Jennison* was just one of the series of six cases, and in neither that case nor any of the others did the court "rule" that slavery was unconstitutional. It seems unlikely that a jury verdict that

---

11 "She never heard but that all people were born free and equal, and she thought long about it, and resolved she would try whether she did not come among them." (Preiss (1976), p. 48.)

12 Sedgwick, later a United States senator from Massachusetts, was himself a slave owner, at least as of a decade earlier. In the 1771 valuation list, he was listed as owner of one "Servant for life". (Massachusetts State Archives; Pruitt (1978).)

13 Inferior Court of Common Pleas, Berkshire County, Great Barrington. Book 4A, page 55. Brom was a male slave who also belonged to Ashley, identified in the record as "Brom a Negro Man of Sheffield in our said County Labourer". Whether Brom had also been beaten by Hannah (or John) Ashley is not clear. Perhaps Brom was deliberately added as a second plaintiff with a view toward making the case a stronger test of the legality of slavery. The record of the case is printed in Rosenthal, James (1937).

14 Zilversmit (1968), p. 622.

15 The third of the series of six cases.

Quock Walker was free, unaccompanied by stated reasons, would almost instantly persuade another litigant to drop his appeal. My own speculation is that Colonel Ashley himself had reservations about the practice of slavery, and – perhaps more importantly – that he did not get on well with his wife, that he knew that she abused their slaves, and that he was just as happy not to have Mumbett, already a victim of at least one of Hannah's attacks, remain in his household.[16]

The Mumbett and Quock Walker cases were by no means the first or only freedom suits by slaves. Blanck lists twenty-eight such cases that went to court prior to 1783, most of them before 1780.[17] After 1763, in all but one of the cases that progressed to an appeal in the Superior Court of Judicature, the plaintiffs won their freedom. The sole exception was the suit of Amos Newport of Hatfield (see Chapter Five), a case that reached the Superior Court in 1768. Blanck observes, though – referring to all these freedom suits – that the Superior Court "had not been open to arguments, based on natural rights, that assailed the very foundation of slavery; instead, the court required a specific point of law [such as a claim of a promised manumission or a defective title] to decide in favor of the plaintiff".

After the middle of the century, a number of town meetings had passed resolutions protesting, first, the importation of slaves, and later – though less frequently – the institution of slavery itself. In 1755, for instance, the town of Salem[18] adopted a petition to the General Court protesting the importation of slaves, and a decade later the town of Worcester[19] instructed its representative to "use his influence to obtain a law to put an end to that unchristian and impolitic practice of making slaves of the human species". In 1767 an unsuccessful attempt was made in the General Court to adopt a bill "to prevent the unwarrantable and unusual Practice or Custom of inslaving Mankind in this Province, and the importation of slaves into the same".[20]

It has sometimes been claimed that slavery existed and continued in Massachusetts *only* because England insisted on it. Washburn, for instance, writes – "Whether Colony or Province, so far as it felt free to

---

16 Local folklore again – "He [John Ashley] was the gentlest, most benign of men and she was a shrew, untamable ..." (Quoted by Wilds (1999), p. 45.)
17 Blanck (2002), pp. 27-28.
18 Moore (1866), p. 109.
19 Moore (1866), p. 124.
20 Moore (1866), pp. 126-128.

follow its own inclinations, uncontrolled by the action of the mother country, Massachusetts was hostile to slavery as an institution."[21] And then – "Slavery never was in harmony with the public sentiment of the colony. It was sustained only by force of the policy and laws of the mother country and was abolished by the people by the very first clause in the organic law of the State."[22] To be sure, in the early 1770s the Great and General Court of Massachusetts considered various pieces of antislavery legislation that did not survive the scrutiny of the royal governor. In March, 1774, for instance, the General Court adopted "An Act to Prevent the Importation of Negroes or other Persons as Slaves into this Province; and the Purchasing Them within the Same". An earlier version of this bill had contained an extraordinarily strong antislavery section.[23]

> And be it further Enacted and declared that nothing in this act con-
> tained shall extend or be construed to extend for retaining or holding
> in perpetual servitude any Negro or other Person or Persons now
> inslaved within this Province ...

By the time the legislation was adopted, the bill had been amended by deleting this paragraph. Even the amended bill failed to receive the governor's approval, the only reason given being that "his Excellency had not had time to consider the other Bills that had been laid before him".[24]

It is true that Britain had encouraged slavery, the British were at this time the world leaders in the slave trade, and British colonies such as Jamaica played an important part in the British economy. But in spite of occasional abortive attempts to ban the slave trade or slavery prior to the Revolution, it is absurd to suggest that New Englanders would have abolished slavery (or perhaps never have allowed it in the first place) were it not for pressure from the crown. For a century and a half after the Pilgrims landed at Plymouth, Massachusetts was decidedly *not* "hostile to slavery". Antislavery (or anti-*slave trade*) bills such as the one just mentioned were part of the general agitation against England. Once the colonies had declared their independence and the possibility of veto by the royal governor was no longer a possibility, interest in such legislation diminished.

---

21 Washburn (1858), p. 334. [Emory Washburn (1800-1877) was governor of Massachusetts in 1854-55 and then for twenty years a professor at Harvard Law School.]
22 That is, by Article I of the 1780 Constitution. (Washburn (1869), p. 3.)
23 Moore (1866), pp. 137-140.
24 Moore (1866), p. 137.

In May, 1774 a number of slaves submitted a petition to Thomas Gage, the royal governor of the colony, asking for their freedom.[25]

> The Petition of a Grate Number of Blackes of this Province who by divine permission are held in a state of Slavery within the bowels of a free and christian Country Humbly Shewing That your Petitioners apprehind we have in common with all other men a naturel right to our freedoms without Being depriv'd of them by our fellow men as we are a freeborn Pepel and have never forfeited this Blessing by aney compact or agreement whatever. But we were unjustly dragged by the cruel hand of power from our dearest frinds and sum of us stolen from the bosoms of our tender Parents and from a Populous Pleasant and plentiful country and Brought hither to be made slaves for Life in a Christian land. Thus are we deprived of every thing that hath a tendency to make life even tolerable, the endearing ties of husband and wife we are strangers to for we are no longer man and wife then our masters or mestreses thinkes proper marred or onmarred. Our children are also taken from us by force and sent maney miles from us wear we seldom or ever see them again there to be made slaves of fore Life which sumtimes is vere short by Reson of Being dragged from their mothers Breest Thus our Lives are imbittered to us on these accounts By our deplorable situation we are rendered incapable of shewing our obedience to Almighty God how can a slave perform the duties of a husband to a wife or parent to his child How can a husband leave master and work and cleave to his wife How can the wife submit themselves to there husbands in all things. How can the child obey thear parents in all things ... Nither can we reap an equal benefet from the laws of the Land which doth not justifi but condemns Slavery or if there had bin aney Law to hold us in Bondege we are Humbely of the Opinon ther never was aney to inslave our children for life when Born in a free Countrey. We therfor Bage your Excellency and Honours will give this it its deu weight and consideration and that you will accordingly cause an act of the legislative to be pessed that we may obtain our Natural right our freedoms and our children be set at lebety at the yeare of Twenty one for whoues sekes more petequeley your Petitioners is in Duty ever to Pray .

As far as can be determined, there was no response from Governor Gage to this eloquent appeal.

---

25 *Collections of the Massachusetts Historical Society*, Vol. 3, Fifth Series, pp. 432-433 (1877). On pages 434-435 a revised version of this petition is printed. ("Drawn up by a more skilful hand, as regards penmanship and orthography. – EDs.") Greene, quoting from the same petition, gives the date as 1773. (Greene (1942), p. 217.)

Occasional antislavery agitation continued, even when it was no longer entangled with other protests against England. More petitions and resolutions were adopted in the 1770s. In 1775, for instance, the Committees of Correspondence for Worcester County endorsed a petition from the slaves of Bristol and Worcester counties.

> WHEREAS the NEGROES in the counties of Bristol and Worcester, the 24th of March last, petitioned the Committees of Correspondence for the county of Worcester (then convened in Worcester) to assist them in obtaining their freedom.
> THEREFORE.
>   In County Convention, June 14th, 1775.
> RESOLVED, That we abhor the enslaving of any of the human race, and particularly of the NEGROES in this country. And that whenever there shall be a door opened, or opportunity present, for any thing to be done toward the emancipating the NEGROES; we will use our influence and endeavour that such a thing may be effected,
>   Attest. WILLIAM HENSHAW, Clerk.
> *Massachusetts Spy or American Oracle of Liberty*   June 21, 1775

As the Revolution continued in the early 1780s, antislavery sentiment grew and became more respectable, but it is unlikely that a significant number of whites in Massachusetts even thought about abolition or that they would have favored bringing slavery to an end if asked.

Those who argue that slavery came to an end in 1783 with the conclusion of the Walker-Jennison-Caldwell cases have to deal with a number of inconvenient facts. No notice at all was given to these cases in the Boston newspapers of the time, and it was many decades before they were cited in other court cases.[26] Furthermore, there exist tax lists dated "1784-5" that include the number of "servants" owned in various towns.[27] Deerfield, for instance, is shown with eight "servants" – as well as 260 cows, 204 horses, 200 oxen, 200 sheep, and 46 swine. Hadley is

---

26 "[The case] is not mentioned by name nor is its date given in any official court report until 1867, although its citation might in several cases been most apposite. Original documents still preserved in the archives of the Supreme Judicial Court in Boston reveal nothing to indicate that in the pertinent case the Court grounded its ruling on the Declaration of Rights or on any other constitutional provision." (O'Brien (1960), pp. 220-221.) I, too, have searched without success through Boston newspapers of the 1780s and 1790s for mention of these cases.
27 Massachusetts General Court: Committees: Valuations: 1784. Aggregates of the polls and of the valuation of the real and personal property in the towns of Massachusetts, 1784-1785.

listed with five servants, Hatfield thirteen, Springfield seventeen, Westfield fifteen, Amherst two, Greenfield one, and Northfield three. Unfortunately, owners' names are not listed.

And slaves continued to be mentioned in wills during the 1780s. As discussed in the Addendum to Chapter Four, for instance, Mrs. Silliman, in her 1785 will, specified that her slave Chloe should become free after her death and bequeathed to her quite an array of household possessions. In his 1787 will, Reverend James Chandler of Rowley (north of Boston) directed his wife *not* to sell his elderly slave, Sabina, but to provide for her. He then specified that his "Negro Woman Phillis", Sabina's daughter, should be freed after his death (though he stated in the will that he had already given her her freedom thirteen years earlier) and then that she be given "five Pounds lawful Money" and a few possessions. He also directed that she be paid, belatedly, the wages that he had promised her for the work she had done over the years.[28]

> I commit to my said Wife my Negro Woman Sabina, not to be by her sold out of the House, but to serve her; and to be provided for by her, as is mete. But if said Sabina shall live to be a Burden, which my said Wife shall think too Heavy for her to bear, my Will is – that my Executor assist in providing for her, as is fitting for an aged Servant that has been faithful. To My Negro Woman Phillis I give her Manumission or Freedom and five Pounds lawful Money, a Chest, & Such other Things in my House, as are known by the Family to be her Things. I give her also the Bed that her Mother & She lodge in and all the Bedding belonging to it. And I hereby testify that I gave her her Freedom when she was eighteen years old, and covenanted with her that if she would live & Serve in my Family I would give her one Pound & Six Shillings & eight Pence pr year for her Service & find her her Clothes. She has lived with, and Served me ever since and I have paid her Nothing of the Money that I promised as her wages therefore I owe it to her and order my Executor to pay it to her. I Suppose that my keeping her Child more than answers for Interest, but I release what more it might be reckond of.

---

28 Will of Rev. James Chandler, 23 May 1787, Essex County Probate, Docket 4,936. The will is quoted in a 2005 article by John C. MacLean on the website of the New England Historic Genealogical Society. Phillis, born in 1756, was the daughter of "Cesar and Sabina, 'negroes joined in wedlock and servants to James Chandler'". Phillis had been married in 1783 and then married again in 1793, after the death of her owner, when she became free. Reverend Chandler died in 1789, but Mary, his widow, lived until 1806. What happened to Sabina, how long she lived with Mrs. Chandler, is not known. (*Vital Records of Rowley* (1928); *Vital Records of Newburyport* (1911).)

In the first federal census, carried out in 1790, Massachusetts stood out as the only one of the thirteen states to report having no slaves. Some skepticism has been voiced, however, as to whether this count was accurate. Jeremy Belknap, writing shortly after the time of this census, made the following comment.[29]

> The following anecdote ... , it is believed, has never been made public. In 1790, a census was ordered by the General Government then newly established, and the Marshal of the Massachusetts district had the care of making the survey. When he inquired for *slaves*, most people answered none, – if any one said that he had one, the marshal would ask him whether he meant to be singular, and would tell him that no other person had given in any. The answer then was, "If none are given in, I will not be singular;" and thus the list was completed without any number in the column for slaves.

Curiously enough, one person who may have considered the outcome of the Walker-Jennison-Caldwell cases as having definitively outlawed slavery in Massachusetts was Nathaniel Jennison himself. According to Cushing, there is evidence that after the conclusion of the 1783 case, Jennison hurried home to Barre and took his remaining slaves (one of whom was Quock Walker's brother) to Connecticut, where slavery was still indisputably legal, and sold them.[30]

Slavery in Massachusetts did not come to a sudden end in 1780, or in 1783, or at any other time. I suggest the following as a brief summary of the complicated story recounted above.

> Slavery came to a gradual end in Massachusetts in the last two decades of the 18th century. If any blacks (or Indians) were held as slaves after about 1800, the practice was not overt. Though Article I of the state constitution of 1780 states that "All men are born free and equal", there is no evidence that those who wrote those words had any intention that they should apply to enslaved blacks. In the early 1780s, a number of court cases (the "Walker-Jennison-Caldwell cases") culminated in a 1783 case that resulted in the freeing of Quock Walker, a slave from the town of Barre. Though the judge's charge to the jury in that case did include a reference to Article I with its "free and equal" wording, there were other factors – such as a claim of a prior promise of manumission – that may also have played a role. There was no

---

29 Marcou (1847), pp. 164-165.
30 Cushing, John (1961), p. 144, note 38.

written *decision* in the case, only a jury verdict. These cases initially drew little attention and slaves were sometimes listed as property on tax lists or left in wills until at least the late 1780s, but as time went on, it slowly became accepted that slavery was illegal in Massachusetts.

But why did slavery end here while it not only survived but was on the increase in the South? This is not the place to try to give an adequate answer to this question. It is often said that it was "public opinion" that led to the end of slavery in the North. But that response obviously begs the question. Why was the supposed opinion of the public increasingly opposed to slavery – or at least unwilling to support its continuation? Surely there were a number of reasons, of which the most obvious is the fact that although slavery had played a significant role in the Massachusetts economy, it had never been as centrally important as it was in the South. For some reason, perhaps as a result of their different religious traditions as well as the differences in the economies, northerners took the words of the Declaration of Independence more seriously and were more willing to recognize the blatant contradiction involved in fighting for liberty while continuing to enslave blacks. It has been suggested – by John Adams, among others – that pressure for the end of slavery came from the increasing number of white immigrant laborers who were threatened by competition with the cheaper labor available from slaves. As Adams wrote to Jeremy Belknap in 1795[31]–

> The real cause [of the abolition of slavery in Massachusetts] was the multiplication of labouring white people, who would no longer suffer the rich to employ these sable rivals so much to their injury ... The common people would not suffer the labor, by which alone they could obtain a subsistence, to be done by slaves ... I never knew a jury, by a verdict, to determine a negro to be a slave. They always found them free[32] ... The common white people, or rather the labouring people, were the cause of rendering negroes unprofitable servants. Their scoffs and insults, their continual insinuations, filled the negroes with discontent, made them lazy, idle, proud, vicious, and at length wholly useless to their masters, to such a degree that the abolition of slavery became a measure of economy.

---

31 Belknap Papers, *Collections of the Massachusetts Historical Society*, Vol. 3, Fifth Series, pp. 401-402 (1877).

32 Adams apparently forgot the case discussed in Chapter Seven, the freedom suit of Amos Newport, the Hatfield slave who sued unsuccessfully in 1766, a case in which Adams himself had participated.

It has even been argued that the southern colonies – feeling threatened by the Somerset decision of 1772 in England that seemed to presage the possible end of slavery in the English colonies – had entered the fight for independence in order to *preserve* slavery.[33]

As the American Revolution came to an end, slavery existed in every state, north of the Mason-Dixon Line as well as south. One might think that it would be a simple matter to make a list of the seven original northern states[34] and find the dates on which slavery ended in each state. The Massachusetts story is certainly complicated, but for none of the northern states is there a simple answer even to the question of "When?" New Hampshire, like Massachusetts, never did adopt legislation outlawing slavery. Slavery gradually disappeared in New Hampshire during the final decades of the 18th century and the early decades of the 19th, with three New Hampshire slaves still being listed in the federal census of 1830 and one in 1840.[35]

Other states adopted *post nati* laws, providing for a gradual (usually *painfully* gradual) end to slavery. In New York, the "Gradual Abolition Act" of 1799 provided[36] –

> That any child born of a slave within this state after the fourth day of July next shall be deemed and adjudged to be born free: Provided nevertheless, That such child shall be the servant of the legal proprietor of his or her mother until such servant, if a male, shall arrive at the age of twenty-eight years, and if a female, at the age of twenty-five years.

Nothing in this law provided for freeing slaves born *before* 1799. Thus a child born in 1798 who lived to an age of 103 might remain a

---

33 Blumrosen and Blumrosen (2005). James Somerset was the slave taken to England by his owner in 1769, who finally gained his freedom in the English courts in 1772. The Somerset decision, a fairly narrow decision, was quickly misinterpreted on both sides of the Atlantic. White slave owners feared that it would lead to the end of slavery in England and its colonies; blacks hoped fervently for the same outcome. Somerset's famous trip to England, the voyage that eventually led to the Somerset decision, began in Boston.

34 New Hampshire, Massachusetts, Connecticut, Rhode Island, New York, New Jersey, and Pennsylvania. Vermont only became a state (the 14th) in 1791. Maine was part of Massachusetts until 1820 and became a state as part of the "Missouri Compromise".

35 For the numbers of slaves reported in the federal census for all states from 1790 to 1860, see *Negro Population in the United States, 1790-1915*.

36 The texts of the 1799 and 1817 New York laws are printed in *Laws of the State of New York*, and that of the 1817 law is also printed in *Statutes on Slavery*, Vol. 1, pp. 85-106. The most significant provisions of these two laws are included in *Jim Crow New York* (2003), pp. 53-72.

slave into the 20th century. And a girl born in 1798, still enslaved in, say, 1835 might give birth to a son who would not become free until 1863. These possibilities were modified by the law of 1817, which left unchanged the age of freedom for those born between 1799 and 1817 but reduced the age at which children born *after* 1817 would become free to twenty-one years for both males and females and also provided that all those born before July 4, 1799 would become free on July 4, 1827.

> That every child born of a slave within this state, after the fourth day of July, in the year of our Lord one thousand seven hundred and ninety-nine, shall be free, but shall remain the servant of the owner of his or her mother, and the executors, administrators or assigns of such owner, in the same manner as if such child had been bound to service by the overseers of the poor, and shall continue in such service, if a male, until the age of twenty-eight years, and if a female, until the age of twenty-five years; and that every child born of a slave within this state after the passing of this act [i.e., after 1817], shall remain a servant as aforesaid until the age of twenty-one years and no longer.

> That every negro, mulatto or mustee[37] within this state, born before the fourth of July, one thousand seven hundred and ninety-nine shall, from and after the fourth day of July, one thousand eight-hundred and twenty-seven, be free.

Under the terms of this law, a child born to an enslaved mother in, say, June, 1827, would remain a "servant" until 1848. The number of New York slaves listed in the federal census declined from 21,193 in 1790 to 10,088 in 1820, then to 75 in 1830 and just four in 1840.[38]

The process of emancipation in New Jersey was even more gradual than in New York. It was in 1804 that New Jersey began the slow process of emancipation with "An Act for the Gradual Abolition of Slavery", whose first section provided that[39] –

---

37 Mustee – A not very well defined term but one that was used in various ways at different times to describe someone of mixed racial descent. See Melish (1998), pp. 37-38 for more discussion of the use of this term in colonial New England.

38 The New York law was not completely clear as to the status of, for instance, a young woman on the verge of becoming free who gave birth to a child in 1847. Would that child be free? Or would that child perhaps in turn be held as a servant until age twenty-one (until 1868), and so on, *ad infinitum*? In spite of the theoretical possibilities, no New York slaves were listed in the federal census of 1850 or in later years. See Melish (1998), Chapter Three for discussion of the ambiguities associated with various *post nati* statutes.

39 The texts of these and other New Jersey laws are available on the website of the New Jersey Digital Legal Library – http://njlegallib.rutgers.edu/slavery.

> Every child born of a slave within this state, after the fourth day of July next, shall be free; but shall remain the servant of the owner of his or her mother, and the executors, administrators or assigns of such owner, in the same manner as if such child had been bound to service by the trustees or overseers of the poor, and shall continue in such service, if a male, until the age of twenty five years; and if a female until the age of twenty one years.

In 1820 New Jersey adopted "An Act for the Gradual Abolition of Slavery, and Other Purposes Respecting Slaves" whose first section simply reiterated the provisions of the 1804 law and then went on with some minor modifications of the other sections of the law.

These laws did nothing to free those born into slavery prior to 1804 and continued to leave a long apprenticeship awaiting those born after 1804 to enslaved mothers. Then in 1846 New Jersey adopted "An Act to Abolish Slavery", which begins in promising fashion.

> BE IT ENACTED by the Senate and General Assembly of the State of New Jersey, That slavery in this state be and it is hereby abolished, and every person who is now holden in slavery by the laws thereof, be and hereby is made free ... and the children hereafter to be born to all such persons shall be absolutely free from their birth, and discharged of and from all manner of service whatsoever.

But then comes the "Subject, however ... " section.

> Subject, however, to the restrictions and obligations hereinafter mentioned and imposed ... That every such person shall, by force and virtue of this act, and without the previous execution of any indenture of apprenticeship, or other deed or instrument for that purpose, become and be an apprentice, bound to service to his or her present owner, and his or her executors or administrators; which service shall continue until such person is discharged therefrom, as is hereinafter directed.

The provisions of this New Jersey law have been described with the Orwellian term "lifetime apprenticeship", and those held in bondage under this law were listed in the federal census, quite logically, as "Slaves". The 19th-century census records show New Jersey's slave population declining from a high of 12,422 in 1800 to 2,254 in 1830, then 674 in 1840, 236 in 1850, and – astonishingly – the last federal census before the Civil War, in 1860, still showed 18 slaves in New Jersey. For New Jersey, as for the southern states, slavery was only definitively ended with ratification of the 13th Amendment to the United States Constitution in 1865.[40]

Vermont became the 14th state in 1791, and Vermonters boast that slavery was outlawed from the day of statehood by the first article of Vermont's constitution. What that article actually says, though, is somewhat less than an outright prohibition of bondage.

> Article 1st. All persons born free; their natural rights; slavery prohibited
> – That all persons are born equally free and independent, and have certain natural, inherent, and unalienable rights, amongst which are the enjoying and defending life and liberty, acquiring, possessing and protecting property, and pursuing and obtaining happiness and safety; therefore no person born in this country, or brought from over sea, ought to be holden by law, to serve any person as a servant, slave or apprentice, *after arriving to the age of twenty-one years*, unless bound by the person's own consent, after arriving to such age, or bound by law for the payment of debts, damages, fines, costs, or the like. [Italics added.]

The words "after arriving to the age of twenty-one years" are difficult to overlook. To be sure, servitude for life is one of the defining characteristics of slavery, and therefore someone bound to the age of twenty-one is not truly a *slave*. The last clause ("unless ... bound by law for the payment of debts ..."), though, would seem to be an invitation to abuse. And certainly slavery had existed before the time of statehood in the area that subsequently became the state of Vermont. In Chapter Five we described the purchase of Caesar by Charles Phelps of Hadley from William Williams of New Marlborough in 1770, as well as the sale of Peg to a Bennington owner in 1772 and her repurchase by Phelps in 1778.[41]

Although Vermont did not become a state until 1791, results for the census carried out in that year were included in the reports of the federal census of 1790. Melish observes that until 1870 the printed reports of the

---

40 By early December, 1865 the amendment had been approved by three-fourths of the states and had thus been ratified. In New Jersey, the amendment was first rejected in March, 1865 and then belatedly approved in January, 1866.

41 Vermont's admission as a state had been delayed by controversies over competing claims to the territory. New Marlborough – now called Marlboro and, like Bennington, a Vermont town – was described in the 1770 bill of sale as being in the "Province of New York". Before Vermont became a state in 1791 (having briefly been known as the "Republic of Vermont"), portions of what is now Vermont were claimed by both New York and New Hampshire.

1790 census assigned sixteen slaves to Vermont. At that time the "mistake" was discovered and the description of those sixteen persons was changed to "Free Other".[42] What their actual status was is now impossible to determine.

In the next chapter, we will discuss – very briefly – the gradual ending of slavery in Massachusetts in the last two decades of the 18th century and then the ways in which memory of the very existence of slavery in colonial times largely disappeared.

---

42 Melish (1998), p. 64.

CHAPTER NINE

The 1800s and Beyond – Deliberate Amnesia

By the early and mid-1780s, there were indications that slavery in Massachusetts was on its way out, even though there had been neither legislation to that effect nor a definitive court case. Fewer "Slaves For Sale" advertisements or notices seeking runaways appeared in Boston newspapers. The latest Massachusetts bill of sale I have come across was written in November, 1784.[1]

> Boston November 15th 1784 I have this Day sold to Mr Samuel Pitts of Boston a Negro Boy Named Poppy, Nine years old, for and in the full Consideration of Thirtyfive pounds Lawfull money for which Sum I promise to warrant and Defend against the Lawfull Claims of all and every Person or persons whatever as Witness my Hand.
>
> Samuel Ireland   Witness Joseph Giddinge

And the latest Massachusetts runaway notice that I know of is this one, also from the fall of 1784.

> Ran away from the Subscriber the 30th ult, a light coloured Negro Lad, named OSMER, about 16 Years old; a likely Countenance; of a middle Size; a Black-Smith by trade, he lately sheared the Wool off his Head. Whoever will take up said Negro, and return him to his Master, or secure him, so that he may be obtained, shall receive ten Dollars reward and all necessary Charges paid.
>
> N.B. All Masters of Vessels and others are cautioned against harbouring or carrying of said Negro.   Ebenezer Richardson, jun   Billerica, Sept. 29, 1784.
>
> *American Herald*   October 25, 1784

Some care is required in reading such advertisements and notices. Sometimes what appears at first glance to be a bill of sale for a slave is actually an indenture agreement or a sale of the "time remaining" of an

---

1 Sheridan (1963). (The original copy of the bill of sale is in the Special Collections Department of the University of Kansas Library.)

indentured servant and, similarly, a runaway notice may actually be for an indentured servant who had run away.

Many owners (and slaves) could see which way things were going in Massachusetts. Quite a few slaves simply walked away from their owners, and many of those owners did not bother to try to reclaim their property, instead posting notices like these.

> Ran away from the subscriber, on the night of the 16th of December, a NEGRO GIRL named DIDO, about 22 years of age, having with her a large bundle of clothing; I therefore forbid all persons harbouring or trusting her the said Negro on my account, and thereby avoid trouble, as I will not pay any thing of her contracting,   MARGARET TUFTS, New-Braintree, Jan. 10, 1783.
>
> *Massachusetts Spy or Worcester Gazette*   January 22, 1784

> RAN away from the Subscriber in Wrentham, three Negro Servants, viz. Ruben Cudgo, and Lethie and Peggy Cudgo. These are therefore to forbid any Persons harbouring said Servants, as the Subscribers will not pay one Farthing for the Support and Maintenance of them, from the Date hereof.
> HANNAH BOYDEN, and JAIRUS BOYDEN. July 25, 1785.
>
> *American Herald*   August 1, 1785

Instead of advertisements offering slaves for sale or notices from owners seeking slaves to purchase, one was apt to see blacks, probably former slaves, seeking employment, or whites, probably former owners, seeking servants.

> Wants a Place, A Negro Man, who understands driving a Charriot and taking care of Horses.
> Inquire of the Printer.
>
> *Continental Journal and Weekly Advertiser*   March 3, 1785

> WANTED, in a Family, A LIKELY NEGRO MAN, About 18 or 20 years of age, to take the Care of a Horse. – One must come with an unexceptionable Character, then may he enter into immediate Employ.
> Apply to the PRINTER.
>
> *American Herald and General Advertiser*   February 16, 1784

At least by 1800, slave ownership seems to have been considered illegal in Massachusetts. It is possible that some of those who had been slaves continued to be held as slaves in fact if not in name; if so, such cases are probably impossible to document. No doubt some Massachusetts slave owners sold their slaves to buyers in states where slavery continued to be legal. Some of those who had been enslaved in the Connecticut Valley stayed on, living with those who had owned them. Jenny and Cato, for instance, slaves of Reverend Ashley, remained with the Ashley family in Deerfield until they died – Jenny in 1808, Cato in 1825. Many of the former slaves and their children probably left the primarily agricultural towns such as Deerfield and Hadley, moving to larger towns or perhaps farther, to cities such as Boston. In part because so few slaves had surnames, it is extremely difficult to determine with any certainty where former slaves went or where they found new homes. Some former slaves took as surnames the names of their former owners; Chloe, for instance, the slave Mrs. Silliman of Deerfield freed by the terms of her 1785 will, was married as "Chloe Syllaman" in 1794. Some newly freed slaves chose their own surnames, as Hebar *Honestman* and his wife did when they became free early in the 18th century and moved to Ashfield.[2] Napthalo, formerly a slave of Joseph Dickinson of Sunderland, became Napthalo *Freeman*, and Dinah *Freedom* of Greenfield, married in Deerfield in 1794, was probably a former slave.[3]

With slavery continuing and ever increasing in the South, northern blacks were always at risk of being captured and sold into slavery in the South. The danger was greater in Pennsylvania, for instance, which shared a border with the slave states of Delaware, Maryland and Virginia. Even in western Massachusetts, blacks were always at risk. In a notorious 1840 case in Amherst, Angeline Palmer, an eleven-year old girl, an orphan who had been bound out as a pauper to the Shaw family of Belchertown, was rescued by a group of three black Amherst men – Lewis Frazier, Henry Jackson, and William Jennings – who had reason to believe that her mistress was planning to take her along on a trip to the South and sell her into slavery. Technically, Angeline Palmer had been kidnapped, and the three "kidnappers" were charged with assault, abduction, and unlawful imprisonment. After short jail terms (during which visitors brought them gifts of food and clothing), they were released and generally regarded as heroes for their success in rescuing Angeline.[4]

---

2 See the discussion in Chapter Four.
3 See the discussion in Chapter Five.
4 The story of Angeline Palmer has been told in detail by Smith. Henry Jackson was the grandson of Peter Jackson, who was probably born about 1746 during the "Middle Passage", on a slave ship en route from Africa to the southern American colonies. (Smith, James (1999), pp. 22-31. See also pp. 20, 75-76, 81, 88-90, 93-94.)

A decade later, in 1851, Angeline married Sanford Jackson (no relation to her rescuer, Henry Jackson). Angeline probably died sometime in the 1850s, and Sanford Jackson was married twice more, once in 1859 to Emily Mason and then again in 1860 to Nancy Newport, while still married to Emily – Amherst's earliest known case of bigamy. Sanford enlisted in the 54th Massachusetts Volunteer Infantry Regiment (listed as "single"), was wounded in the assault on Fort Wagner in July, 1863, and died of his wounds two months later. Apparently neither Emily nor Nancy knew of the other's existence until they both filed pension applications as Sanford Jackson's widow.[5]

A significant community of free blacks, including some who had escaped from slavery in the South, grew up in Northampton, especially in the village of Florence, which became a center of abolitionist activity. Sojourner Truth[6] – born a slave in the Hudson Valley – came to Florence in 1843, attracted by the Northampton Association of Education and Industry, a utopian community that had been formed the previous year.[7] Although the Northampton Association disbanded after only a few years, Sojourner Truth stayed on in Florence until 1857, dictating her book,[8] buying a home, and turning her talents as a speaker to antislavery and women's rights.[9]

Antislavery agitation increased enormously after the passage of the draconian Fugitive Slave Law of 1850, which in effect put the burden of proof on a black person to prove that he or she was *not* an escaped slave. Even among those whites opposed to abolition, there were many who were outraged at the idea that their own officials could be forced to aid southern slave owners in the recovery of their "property". Throughout

---

5 "Jackson, Sanford 33, sin. [single]; teamster; Amherst. 4 Mch 63; died of wounds 13 Sep 63 Gen. Hos. Beaufort, S.C. Wounded 18 Jly 63 Ft Wagner." (Emilio (1891), p. 341.) See also Smith, James (1999), pp. 42, 50, 86-87, 106.

6 Sojourner Truth was born about 1797 as a slave, "Isabella", in Rosendale, New York, about ninety miles north of New York City. She left her owner in late 1826, six months before she would have been freed by the provisions of the New York laws of 1799 and 1817. The same laws, however, would not free her children until much later – not until 1847 in the case of Sophia, born in 1826. Her son Peter, born in 1821, was illegally sold to an Alabama owner in 1827, whereupon Sojourner went to court to regain custody of her son, who then became free long before reaching the age of twenty-one specified in the law of 1817.

7 Clark (1995).

8 Truth (1850).

9 Painter (1996).

Statue of Sojourner Truth in Florence, Massachusetts, created by sculptor Jay Warren and unveiled in 2002. Further information is available at the website of the Sojourner Truth Committee – www.sojournertruthmemorial.org. (Author's photograph.)

the North, black people, whether free blacks or fugitive slaves, were increasingly at risk. A remarkable display of black concerns and of courage on the part of black citizens of Florence and Northampton – some of whom were themselves fugitives or former slaves and all of whom were in danger simply because they were black – is shown by a notice that appeared in the *Northampton Courier* on October 15, 1850.

To the Citizens of Northampton.

The undersigned, fugitives from Southern Slavery, respectfully call your attention to the law recently enacted by the Congress of the United States, and approved by the President, which requires the officers of Government, aided and assisted by all good citizens, to seize upon, and convey back, those persons guilty of no crime, save their love of liberty, to a state of bondage worse than that existing in any part of the known world, denying its victims all social, political, and religious rights, reducing them to chattelism, and articles of merchandise, mercilessly separating families, and refusing them the Bible, and the attainment of all knowledge.

Aided and directed by a kind Providence we have effected our escape from this deplorable servitude and fled to Massachusetts for an asylum and refuge, confidently believing she would not betray the wanderer, nor deliver up the oppressed.

For our orderly, peaceful, and quiet behavior in our adopted State, we fearlessly challenge investigation; by our industry and sobriety we have many of us accumulated property, and under the free, fostering, and liberal policy of this noble commonwealth, have become citizens, and eligible to any office in the gift of the people. The enactment of this cruel and unrighteous law has thrown us into a state of alarm and consternation, for fear we may be torn from our families and friends and again doomed to a tyranny far worse than death.

We therefore respectfully invite the inhabitants of the town of Northampton, irrespective of party, or sect, to assemble in public meeting in the Town Hall, on Wednesday eve, the 23d inst., at 6 1-2 o'clock, to express their opinions and adopt such measures as they may deem proper to prevent Massachusetts from being made slave hunting ground,—the purity of the Judiciary from being soiled by legal bribes, and the public Treasury from being robbed to perpetrate these gross and enormous wrongs.

BASIL DORSEY,	JOHN WILLIAMS,
WM. C. RANDELL,	LEWIS FRENCH,
JOSEPH WILSON,	WM. HENRY BOYER.
GEORGE WRIGHT,	HENRY ANTHONY,
LOSENBERRY,	WM. WRIGHT.

Northampton Courier   October 15, 1850

Long before 1850, the first antislavery society in Massachusetts was founded in 1823 at Williams College, a college whose initial funding came in part from the 1755 bequest of a slave owner, Ephraim Williams.[10] (Williams College was founded in 1793; its first black student graduated in 1889.) At the college's Fourth of July celebration in 1827, a member of the society gave an address and a "Hymn to the Liberated Slave" was sung. (Celebrations on that day were shared with the Temperance Society. This collaboration between opponents of slavery and alcohol was quite common at this time.) Antislavery groups in the 1800s were badly split between those who favored colonization, solving the problem of slavery by "returning" freed slaves to Africa, and those, like abolitionist William Lloyd Garrison,[11] who were strongly opposed to colonization. The wording of the "Hymn" sung at Williams in 1827 makes it clear that at least the author of that hymn favored colonization.[12]

> We are bound for the land of our fathers afar,
> And the blue wilds of ocean exulting we roam –
> For hope tells of kindred that watch for us there,
> And glad bosoms bounding to welcome us home.

The Williams College Anti-Slavery Society participated in annual Fourth of July celebrations at least until 1831. How long the society lasted after that year and what its activities were – these are matters on which no information has survived.

At Mount Holyoke College (founded in 1837 as the Mount Holyoke Female Seminary, attended briefly by Emily Dickinson), there is no record of any formal antislavery organization. Shortly after the college was founded, a man said to be an "admirer" of the institution urged that it be "as freely open for the reception of colored young ladies as ... for others".[13] The trustees, however, refused the plea, and it was not until 1883 that Mount Holyoke had a black alumna. During the decades leading up to the civil war, there is no evidence that the faculty did anything to encourage antislavery activities. As is often the case, though, the students were ahead

---

10 This discussion of antislavery activities at Amherst, Mount Holyoke, and Williams Colleges is based largely on Brigham (1985), Cole (1940), Perry (1899), Rudolph (1956), Rudolph (1983), Spring (1917), and Tyler (1873).

11 William Lloyd Garrison, the famous Massachusetts abolitionist, founder and editor of *The Liberator*, the weekly abolitionist newspaper that he published from 1831 to 1866. See, for instance, the recent biography by Mayer (1998).

12 Perry (1899), p. 485.

13 Cole (1940), p. 53.

of the faculty, with increasing levels of protest and antislavery agitation after passage of the Fugitive Slave Law in 1850 and the Kansas-Nebraska Act in 1854.

Amherst College was founded in 1821, and its first black student, Edward Jones, graduated in 1826. Amherst undergraduates formed an antislavery society in 1833 – in fact, Amherst at this time had *two* societies dedicated to ending slavery, one way or another. The Anti-Slavery Society, sympathetic to Garrison who advocated immediate abolition, was regarded as extremely radical by the faculty and a majority of the student body. The second society was called the "Amherst College and Amherst *Colonization* Society". By the fall of 1834, the Anti-Slavery Society comprised approximately one third of the Amherst students, but they were forced to disband after President Humphrey informed them that "the Society was alienating Christian brethren, retarding and otherwise injuring the cause of religion in College, and threatening in many ways the prosperity of the Institution".[14] Evenhandedly, the president also insisted that the Colonization Society disband, though – with townspeople and faculty as well as students being members – it seems likely that in fact he was only asking them to cease their on-campus activity.

Three years later the college's Anti-Slavery Society was back – the request to form such a society was "cheerfully granted" by the faculty, though the president and the majority of the faculty remained firm in their opposition to the radical views of Garrison. The Amherst students, not surprisingly, had some difficulty deciding precisely where they stood on these issues. Though in its earlier incarnation, the college Anti-Slavery Society had described itself as an auxiliary of Garrison's Massachusetts Anti-Slavery Society, this time the students explicitly decided not to subscribe to Garrison's newspaper, *The Liberator*. By this time, Garrison was vigorously criticizing Massachusetts ministers, publishing essays that rejected their authority, questioning the authenticity of the Bible,[15] and this undoubtedly helped to persuade the Amherst students to keep their distance. The students' views remained relatively radical, however, as they adopted the affirmative in answer to questions such as "Is slave holding always a sin?" and "Is it the duty of Christian churches to exclude slave holders from their communion and slaveholding ministers from their pulpits?", while choosing the negative in response to the

---

14 Tyler (1873), p. 247.
15 See, for example, Stewart (1976), p. 89 and Mayer (1998), pp. 226-236.

question "Can an abolitionist consistently belong to a Colonization Society?" On the question "Does the Constitution of the United States, properly interpreted, sanction slavery?" the group was evenly divided. Surely antislavery activity and debate must have continued at Amherst, especially after passage of the Fugitive Slave Law in 1850, but the records from the years after 1841 have not survived.

Although there was at least some antislavery agitation at all three western Massachusetts colleges (Williams, Mount Holyoke, and Amherst), few if any – students or faculty – seemed ready to welcome freed slaves into American society as equals. And the underlying view of the colonizationists was that everyone, black and white, would be better off if the slaves were liberated and promptly sent to Africa – whether Africa was their birthplace or not.

But the subject of this book is that of slavery in the valley, of the 18th century. The stories of the antislavery societies, of abolitionism, of William Lloyd Garrison, of the "Underground Railroad", of Sojourner Truth, are stories for a different book, as are the accounts of the struggles of free blacks in the 19th century for education and voting rights.

And the story of Massachusetts slavery, as far as the 1800s are concerned, is one of *forgetting*. It sometimes seems as though soon after 1800 the residents of Massachusetts (at least the white residents, especially those who wrote the history books) quickly set out to erase from their collective memory the inconvenient fact that until the late 1700s slavery was a flourishing institution here. Charles Sumner was just one of those who managed to forget, in his 1854 speech in the United States Senate that was quoted in Chapter Two – "In all her annals, no person was ever born a slave on the soil of Massachusetts."[16] Historian Alden Bradford wrote in 1835 – "There were some instances of negro slavery in the colony at an early period, and even to the time of the revolution; but they were very few, and public sentiment appears to have been unfavorable to the practice." And then, even more astonishingly – "The slave-trade was never permitted by the government of Massachusetts."[17] We prefer to remember the "good things" – the efforts to help slaves escape from the South, the abolitionist speeches and writings of Garrison and others (while also forgetting the hostile reception that abolitionists like Garrison received in many quarters, the fact that many ministers refused to let him speak

16 Sumner (1854).
17 Bradford, Alden (1835), p. 51.

in their churches, that he was nearly killed by a Boston mob). This process of forgetting, a process I often call "deliberate amnesia", gives a distorted view of history, it tends to render invisible the many, many blacks and Indians whom New Englanders had enslaved. Slavery has sometimes been referred to as the "Peculiar Institution" – New England slavery might be termed the "Forgotten Institution".[18]

In the late 1800s and early 1900s, a large number of local histories were published, histories of many of the towns in the valley. For the most part those histories paid little attention to the slavery that had existed throughout the valley in the 1700s, mentioning slavery, if at all, primarily in connection with 19th-century abolitionism, the "Underground Railroad", and the Civil War. Sheldon's history of Deerfield is an honorable exception, with an 18-page section on "Negro Slavery".[19]

In Trumbull's history of Northampton, a two-volume work of over 1300 pages, the only mention of slavery in Northampton consists of five lines in a report on a 1764 census of the town – "In addition there were ten negroes, five males and five females. Apparently they were nearly all slaves, and were distributed in the following families:– Mrs. Prudence Stoddard, widow of Col. John, one female; Lieut. Caleb Strong, one male; Joseph and Jonathan Clapp, one each; Joseph Hunt, one of each sex. There was one negro at Moses Kingsley's, not a slave, another at Zadoc Danks, and Bathsheba was then living near South Street bridge." Elsewhere in the book there is a report of the execution of Jack, a slave belonging to an owner in Wethersfield, Connecticut, who burned down a Northampton house and was executed in Boston by hanging (to be followed by burning his body), together with a Roxbury slave, Maria, also convicted of arson, who was burned alive. Trumbull writes simply – "both of these negroes were slaves" – and then adds a laconic footnote – "Many slaves were burned alive in New York and New Jersey, and in the southern colonies, but few in Massachusetts."[20]

The history of Hatfield by Wells and Wells[21] is perhaps typical of the town history genre, with some scattered acknowledgment of the fact that slaves were owned here but presented in such a way that no

---

18 Melish tells the story of New Englanders' forgetting in detail. (Melish (1998).) That is the focus of her book, *Disowning Slavery*, but her first chapter provides an excellent introduction to slavery in New England.
19 Sheldon (1895), pp. 888-905.
20 Trumbull, James (1898-1902), Vol. 1, pp. 376-377 and Vol. 2, p. 328.
21 Wells and Wells (1910), pp. 129, 196-197, 312-313.

one can really get any idea of the extent of slave ownership or of the general acceptability and importance of slavery. The authors include a record of a very early tax assessment list, from 1694, showing the values put on various pieces of property, for instance, "horses, 40s., 2 years old, 20s., 1 year old, 10 s.; hogs, 5s.; sheep, 3s.; negroes, 2s." No explanation is offered for the mysterious fact that slaves were assessed at a lesser value than were horses, hogs, and sheep. This is followed by these two sentences – "Mr. Williams [the minister] had negro slaves and possibly other inhabitants did also. During the eighteenth century many were owned in town." It would be difficult to compose a more inadequate description of slavery in colonial Hatfield.

Later in the Hatfield history we find a completely misleading paragraph about the reason for the existence of slavery here (with an incorrect statement about the date of its ending) – "Slavery was abolished in Massachusetts in 1781, but even before that many had liberated their slaves. It was maintained in the colonies by the crown and so, although the institution was held in abhorrence by many of the northern colonists, it could not be abolished till the success of the Revolution was assured." The same paragraph goes on to recount a supposedly amusing anecdote in "Negro dialect", and then we read about the antislavery sentiments of Hatfield citizens in the decades before the Civil War, the "Underground Railroad", and Hatfield volunteers in the Civil War. There are scattered references to houses occupied by blacks in the 1800s, including that of "Amos Newport, another colored man, whose father was kidnapped when a child and brought from the coast of Africa",[22] and finally a photograph of a dilapidated house ("a picturesque feature") with the caption "Negro Cabin on the Road to Northampton".

Carpenter and Morehouse's history of Amherst contains a brief mention of Amherst's slaves – "In 1765, there were six negroes in Amherst; three at least were owned as slaves, one by Josiah Chauncey, one by John Adams and one by Ephraim Kellogg. There were other slaveholders in earlier years. In 1738, Zechariah Field had a slave valued at £130. Ebenezer Kellogg owned slaves. Richard Chauncey, John Ingram, Sr. and Daniel Kellogg had each a negro, probably a slave."[23] There are

---

22 The "Amos Newport" referred to by Wells and Wells was actually the grandson, not the son, of the Amos Newport who was born in Africa and whose unsuccessful freedom suits were described in Chapter Five. (Smith (1999), pp. 101-102.)
23 Carpenter and Morehouse (1896), p. 59.

also a few scattered references to the military service of Caesar Prutt (whose life was described in Chapter Five) though without mention of the fact that for most of his life he was owned by Josiah Chauncey.

Carpenter and Morehouse's history also contains an astonishing table – astonishing because it appears to be a deliberate falsification of an historical document. A portion of this table is shown on the next page.[24] This is alleged to be a presentation of an Amherst tax valuation list, from the year 1759 when Amherst was first set off from Hadley, with the names alphabetized but with other information preserved – taxpayers' names and columns for the numbers of "Polls, Horses, Oxen, Cows, Hogs, Sheep, Personal Estate, Houses and Lands, Real Estate, and Total". When I first saw this list in Carpenter and Morehouse, it seemed to me – on the basis of many other valuation lists that I had seen – that something was missing. And indeed, when I went to the Special Collections Department at the Jones Library and inspected surviving original valuation lists, I soon found the document from which Carpenter and Morehouse had worked. A portion of the original list is shown below, following the Carpenter and Morehouse table.

The names and numbers are all the same (except for the order of the names), but there is one column in the original table that was not included by Carpenter and Morehouse – "Negro & faculty".[25] This portion of the original valuation list shows both Elisha Ingram and Josiah Chauncey as owners of one "Negro". It is almost impossible to believe that the omission of that column was an accident. Although other town histories (with the exception of Sheldon's history of Deerfield) present a very incomplete and distorted view of slavery in their towns (if indeed mentioning it at all), concealing more than they reveal, this is the only instance I have come across of what appears to be an intentional falsification of the record.

The process of forgetting did not end in the 19th century. It seems that many Massachusetts residents would like to believe that not only are we now more virtuous than anyone else but that we (our predecessors here) always have been. If this means covering up the unhappy fact that

---

24 Ibid., pp. 598-599.
25 Valuation lists, in Amherst as in other towns, often listed slaves and "faculties" (valuable skills, tavern licenses, etc.) in the same column. A second column, "Mills", is also mysteriously missing from Carpenter and Morehouse's table; perhaps this is an indication that in fact Carpenter and Morehouse were simply careless. Still, omission of the "Negro and faculty" column seems much more significant, more difficult to excuse as possibly accidental.

VALUATION LIST, 1759.

NAMES.	Polls.	Horses.	Oxen.	Cows.	Hogs.	Sheep.	Personal Estate.	Houses and Lands.	Real Estate.	Total.
Allis, John	1							5	6 : 5	6 : 5
Baker, Elijah	1	1	2	2	1		9 : 8	44	66 : 0	75 : 8
Belding, Hezekiah	1	1		2			5 : 0	11	15 : 8	20 : 8
Blodgett, David	1									
Boltwood, Solomon	2	2	3	6	1	6	20 : 6	40	84 : 0	104 : 6
Boltwood, William	1	1	2	4	1	9	13 : 15	18	34 : 0	47 : 15
Brooks, John	1	1		1			3 : 10	2½	4 : 0	7 : 10
Chauncey, Josiah	1	2	3	4	1		65 : 8	32	55 : 0	120 : 8
Chauncey, Richard	1	1		3			26 : 10	18	27 : 0	53 : 10
Church, Joseph	1	1		3	1		16 : 18	8	19 : 0	35 : 18
Clapp, Widow Sarah		1		2			5 : 0	18	30 : 10	35 : 10
Clark, Simeon	1	1	2	3		13	11 : 19	20	57 : 0	68 : 19
Cleary, Joseph	1	1		2	1		5 : 8	25	44 : 0	49 : 8
Colton, Eli	1									
Cooke, Moses	1	2	2	3			12 : 10	14	28 : 0	40 : 10
Cowls, Jonathan	3	2	4	5		15	31 : 15	35	70 : 0	101 : 15
Cowls, Oliver	1	1	2				6 : 0			6 : 0
Dickinson, Ebenezer	2	2	2	6			15 : 10	32	57 : 14	73 : 4
Dickinson, Ebenezer (2)	1	1		1			3 : 10	8	19 : 10	23 : 0
Dickinson, Gideon	1	1		4			8 : 0	20	35 . 10	43 : 10
Dickinson, Jonathan	2	2	5	4			20 : 0	25	54 : 0	74 : 0
Dickinson, Nathan	2	2	3	5	4	23	22 : 3	40	65 : 10	87 : 13
Dickinson, Nathan (2)	1		2	1			5 : 10	2	2 : 0	7 : 10
Dickinson, Nathaniel	1	2	3	5		11	19 : 3	32	62 : 12	81 : 15
Dickinson, Noah	1	1	2	3			10 : 10	12	21 : 0	31 : 10
Dickinson, Reuben	1	1		3			6 : 10	9	16 : 0	22 : 10
Dickinson, Simeon	1	1	2	4			12 : 0	14	26 : 12	38 : 12
Eastman, Joseph	1	2	4	5			19 : 10	24	59 : 6	79 : 0
Edwards, Jonathan	1	1	2	2			9 : 0	22	36 : 16	45 : 16
Elmer, Edward	1	1		2	1		5 : 8	20	33 : 0	38 : 8
Field, John	2	3	8	2	1		25 : 8	50	103 : 0	128 : 8
Goodale, Isaac	3	1		2			25 : 0	7	17 : 0	42 : 0
Guilford, Paul	1									
Harwood, Benjamin	1									
Harwood, Eleazer	1									
Harwood, Peter	1	2		2	1	6	8 : 6	15	13 : 9	21 . 15
Hastings, Thomas	1	1	2	4	1		17 : 8	20	33 : 10	50 : 18
Hawley, Moses	1	1		1	1		3 : 18	1	1 : 0	4 : 18
Hawley, Samuel	1									
Howe, Abner	1	1		1			18 : 10			18 : 10
Hubbard, Isaac	1	1		1			3 : 10			3 : 10
Ingram, Elisha	1	2	4	3			32 : 10	28	58 : 8	90 : 18
Ingram, John	1	1		1	1		3 : 18			3 : 18
Ingram, Philip	1			2			3 : 0	10	17 : 0	20 : 0
Ingram, Reuben	1	1	2	2			9 : 0	10	19 : 10	28 : 10
Ingram, Samuel	1	3	3	4	1		18 : 8	35	73 : 10	91 : 18
Keet, John	1	1	2	1			7 : 10	15	25 : 10	33 : 0
Kellogg, Daniel	1	3	2	5			37 : 10	27	54 : 5	91 : 15
Kellogg, Ebenezer	1	2	2	2		11	12 : 13	18	30 : 12	43 : 5
Kellogg, Ephraim	2	2	4	6	1	10	22 : 18	30	70 : 0	92 : 18
Leonard, Aaron	2	1		2	1		5 : 8	5	9 : 0	14 : 8
Mattoon, Ebenezer	1	2	2	4			14 : 0	34	57 : 0	71 : 0
Moody, Nathan	2	1	2	3		5	11 : 5	15	28 : 10	39 : 15

Part of the 1759 Amherst tax valuation list, as printed by Carpenter and Morehouse (1896), p. 598.

Part of the 1759 Amherst tax valuation list. Elisha Ingram (line twelve) and Josiah Chanucey (the bottom of the page) are both listed as owners of one "Negro" valued at £20. (Courtesy of the Special Collections Department, Jones Library, Amherst.)

slavery flourished here in colonial times, suppressing the evidence, then so be it, apparently. Even from some very recent histories it is impossible to learn about slavery in colonial Massachusetts. It is perhaps unsurprising, though regrettable, to find histories of the United States with inadequate treatment of slavery in the North, but it is remarkable that a book completely devoted to the history of Massachusetts could be published in 2000 with no mention whatever of the fact that Indians and blacks were enslaved here in colonial times. Look for information about slavery in Brown and Tager's *Massachusetts – A Concise History.*[26] One will find a number of references to "opposition to [southern] slavery". Massachusetts, you will learn, "had a reputation as a hotbed of abolitionism and as the leading opponent of returning fugitive slaves. Massachusetts abolitionists and others were soldiers in a second American revolution founded on the principles of the first." True enough, but from this 360-page book you will never learn that any Massachusetts residents were slave owners or involved in the slave trade. The only hint that just possibly slavery might once upon a time have existed here is to be found in a mysterious remark – "In Massachusetts, where slavery had been outlawed by the constitution of 1780 ... " Quite aside from the fact that the remark is wrong, what is a reader supposed to make of this statement, coming as it does in a book where no mention of slavery in Massachusetts has been made? Why would the state outlaw something that had never existed? Carpenter and Morehouse falsified a document by omitting a column from a tax valuation list. Books such as that of Brown and Tager falsify history by omitting all mention of slavery in Massachusetts.

Any books purporting to be histories of Massachusetts that say nothing about the role of slavery in the first century and a half after the arrival of the Pilgrims in 1620 are at the very least incomplete and inadequate. We can only hope that future histories of our state will treat our colonial past more accurately.

---

26 Brown and Tager (2000). One and a half pages are devoted to the "Fifty-fourth Regiment of Massachusetts Volunteers of African Descent", pages devoted primarily to its commanding officer, Colonel Robert Gould Shaw. Lorenzo Greene's *The Negro in Colonial New England* (Greene, 1942) is one of the items listed under "Further Reading". It is described as treating "the minority, non-European inhabitants of Massachusetts". Even here, though Greene's book deals almost exclusively with *slavery*, there is no allusion to the fact that slavery had ever existed in the state. There is no evidence that the content of Greene's book had any influence on Brown and Tager's text. (Passages from Brown and Tager that are mentioned or quoted above appear on pages 183-185, 194-196, 334.)

CHAPTER TEN

Why This Book Was Written

With all the very real problems faced by this nation and by the world in the 21st century, why should we be interested in this old (and very local) history? It was not merely a fascination with old documents or curiosity about my neighborhood that motivated the writing of this book. The history of the United States is inextricably linked with that of slavery – in the North as well as in the South, in rural New England as well as in the cities. Slavery was introduced by English settlers only a few years after their arrival at Jamestown and Plymouth. Slavery was in no way simply a regional phenomenon. For the first century and a half after Jamestown, black slaves were owned throughout the American colonies. As the American Revolution came to an end in the early 1780s, slavery was legal and being practiced everywhere in the new nation, in every one of the thirteen original states, although by that time it was gradually (*very* gradually) coming to an end in the North. For another eighty years slavery flourished in the southern states, and it was not until yet another century after the Civil War that the nation began to address seriously its obligation to ensure full political and social equality for the descendants of America's slaves.

I must say that I have very little patience with those who say – "Well, we have to understand that things were different back then." Slavery is wrong now and it was wrong then, and those New England ministers, at some level, *knew* it was wrong.

Lincoln understood that the North as well as the South bore a responsibility for slavery. The final sentence of Lincoln's second inaugural ("With malice toward none; with charity for all …") is the passage most often quoted from that address, but there is another sentence that eloquently calls attention to the entire nation's blame.

> If we shall suppose that American slavery is one of those offenses which, in the providence of God, must needs come, but which, having continued through His appointed time, He now wills to remove,

and that *He gives to both North and South this terrible war as the woe due to those by whom the offense came*, shall we discern therein any departure from those divine attributes which the believers in a living God always ascribe to Him?

Slavery was a nationwide phenomenon, built into our economic and social life. An important exhibit at the New York Historical Society in 2005-2006 brought attention to the important place of slavery in the history of New York City.[1] In recent years, more and more people have learned that many of the most prominent citizens of colonial Boston were slave owners and were among those who made handsome profits in the African slave trade. Even in the seemingly most unlikely places such as the Connecticut Valley of Massachusetts, black slaves were ubiquitous, owned as property by many of the leading citizens. Americans, brought up to think of our country as a beacon of liberty throughout the world, need to be aware of these sobering facts. There are many things to be proud of in our past, but there are also parts of our history of which we must be ashamed. The United States continues to live with the legacy of slavery. Knowledge of the history of slavery, of how thoroughly it is embedded in our nation's history, of how pervasive and almost universally accepted it was, can help us all to deal with that legacy. This book deals with just one facet of this subject, but if it sheds some new light on the history of slavery, it will have served its purpose.

---

1 Berlin and Harris (2005). See also Lepore (2005).

APPENDIX I

Jonathan Ashley's 1750 Sermon to the Deerfield Slaves

On at least one occasion, January 23, 1749/50, Deerfield's Reverend Jonathan Ashley gave a special sermon to the town's slaves.[1] A transcript of his notes was published in an historical journal in 1867 – *The Historical Magazine and Notes and Queries concerning the Antiquities, History and Biography of America*, Vol. 1, Second Series, pp. 142-143 (1867). That article is transcribed below, complete with the incorrect heading referring to John Ashley, rather than Jonathan, and an incorrect date of birth.[2] It should be pointed out that *X* is a common abbreviation for *Christ*. Thus *X* should be read as *Christ*, *Xtianity* as *Christianity*, *Xts* as *Christ's*, etc. The words in square brackets in the text below were inserted by the editor of *The Historical Magazine*.

REV. JOHN ASHLEY OF DEERFIELD.

This distinguished minister was born in 1713, graduated at Yale College in 1730, and, on the eighth of November, 1732, was ordained Pastor of the church at Deerfield, Mass.

He was widely known and greatly respected; and few of his contemporaries exercised a greater influence in the churches.

The following notes of one of his sermons, preached at Deerfield on the twenty-third of January, 1749, are copied from the original Manuscript, in the possession of the Rev. E. H. Gillette, D.D., of Harlem, N.Y.; and will serve to illustrate the views of the Clergy of New England, concerning the duties of Masters and Slaves, a century ago. – [ED. HIST. MAG.]

---

1 Ashley's notes for this sermon are now at the Union Theological Seminary. (Proper (1997), p. 44.) George Sheldon had access to Ashley's notes, for he included excerpts in his Deerfield history (Sheldon (1895), pp. 901-902), and Bruce McClellan consulted these notes in the 1950s when he was writing *Grapes and Thorns*, his biography of Jonathan Ashley. (McClellan (ca. 1955).)
2 Jonathan Ashley was born in Westfield not in 1713 but on November 11, 1712. (Trowbridge (1896), p. 61.)

I. Cor. 7. 22. *For he that is called in yᵉ Lord, being a servant, is the Lord's Freeman; likewise also, he that is called, being free, is Christ's Servant.*

DEERFIELD January 23, 1749.

Preached on an evening Lecture to the Negroes.

God has no regard of persons in the affair of our Salvation; whosoever will is invited to come and take of the waters of life freely. *Is.* 55, beg. *Rev. 22.*

There are none of the human race too low & despicable for God to bestow Salvation upon. Yea it is the mean & base things of this world which God is pleased to elect to eternal life – whilst the rich are sent empty away, & yᵉ great and honorable are left to perish in their sins. – There are some of the children of men, however wretched and miserable yʳ case is, [*that*] have no sense of yʳ need of a Saviour – They are satisfying themselves with earthly things – They glory in the enjoyment of this world – They say who will show us any earthly good – They pant after the dust of yᵉ earth, but they have no desires after Spiritual and eternal things – Some look upon themselves [*as*] too good to trouble themselves about the pardon of Sin. Fruits of [*the*] Spirit, meekness, humility, repentance towards God are too much beneath them, so some are ready to look upon themselves [*as*] above the duties of Xtianity.

On the other hand, there are some who are tempted to think themselves beneath the offers of mercy, & they are ready to think – God will not have mercy on them, because they are such poor miserable creatures. It may be they are poor and despised – and will God think on them whom the world will take no notice of – or it may be they are ignorant, and cant know and understand like other men – and it is not worth while for them to trouble themselves much about Salvation.

Or it may be they think yʸ are Servants & yʸ han't time or advantages, & they are such poor creatures that it is not likely they shall ever obtain mercy. But let us take notice of the riches of grace to the children of men – The poor may be rich in faith and heirs of Glory – The ignorant may understand and know God in Christ, whilst the wise perish in their own understanding.

Servants who are at the dispose & Command of others, who, it may be, are despised in the world, may be the Lord's freemen and heirs of glory.

1st. I will show that Christianity allows of the relation of masters and Servants.

2dly. I will show that such as are by Divine providence placed in the State of Servants, are not excluded from Salvation, but may become the Lord's freemen.

3dly. I will show what a privilege and advantage it is to be a freeman in the Lord.

4^{thly}. Will give some Directions to such as are servants to become the Lord's freemen.

5^{thly}. Will show what motives there are for such to seek to be the Lord's freemen.

1st. I will show y^{t} Xtianity allows of ye relation of masters and Servants.

When the Gospel was first preached to ye Gentiles, & y^{y} partook of the glorious privileges of it, the Devil endeavored to puff them up with pride & to lead them into an abuse of the liberties of the Gospel. Servants who became believers, were ready to despise their unbelieving masters – and began to proclaim liberty to themselves, and declare it unlawful for such as were Xtians to be Servants. But the Apostle by the direction of God's Spirit, considers and determines this point – They who were servants were not to forsake y^{r} masters, but to abide in that Station – Nor would he have them trouble themselves about being Servants. So when Onesimus, a Servant, ran away from his master, and was persuaded to be a christian by Paul, he does not tell him to forsake his master, but sent him home to him, and tells Philemon in his epistle he would be profitable to him for time to come, – What a temptation of the Devil is it therefore to lead Servants into Sin, and provoke God; to insinuate into them they ought not to abide in y^{r} place of Servant, – and so either forsake their master or are uneasy, unfaithful, slothful Servants, to the damage of masters and the dishonor of religion – the reproach of Xtianity.

Secondly I am to show that Such as are by Divine Providence placed in the place of Servants are not excluded from Salvation, but may become ye Lord's freemen – The offers of Salvation are made to Servants as well as masters – There is no distinction among men. Whosoever will, is invited to come and be saved by X Jesus – he will cast out none if they have no money to buy – nothing that this world value – if they have no righteousness or goodness of y^{r} own, yet y^{y} shall find rest in X to y^{r} Souls. The Gospel is not sent to one nation or people, but to Gentiles as well as Jews, to Barbarians Scythians – bond and free are all alike welcome to X – tho they are under bonds to earthly masters – yet they may be free in X. Spiritual liberty is not inconsistent with a State of Servitude – men may serve their masters, and yet be free from the law of sin and death, and be free to serve X.

Thirdly I am to Show what a privilege it is to be the Lord's freeman, and it includes these things.

1st. They who are the Lord's freemen are delivered from the Covenant of works. They are not under the law, but under grace.

2dly. They are free from the condemnation of death that is passed upon them.

3dly. They are freed from the power and dominion of sin, and are enabled to Serve X.

4^{thly}. They are freed from the hands of Satan and set at liberty from his Kingdom.

5^{thly}. They are freed from the bondage of fear and have good hope through grace – a sure refuge in X Jesus, – these are great privileges were there nothing more, – but as in cities or in Commonwealths, freemen have great privileges, so it is in the will of God Xts freemen have great privileges.

6^{thly}. They are children of God, adopted into his family.

7^{thly}. They are friends of God, and have liberty of access to him at all times, to lay open their wants and grievances to him.

8^{thly}. They are entitled to all the great and precious promises which God has made to his people in his word.

9^{thly}. They who are Christ's freemen are led by the Spirit of God – his Spirit dwells in them to guide, quicken and comfort them.

10^{thly}. Xts freemen are heirs of eternal glory & y^y are training up by providences and ordinances to eternal life and happiness.

11^{thly}. Xts freemen have the holy angels to guard them & minister to them in the world.

12^{thly}. Xts freemen when they come to die enter into everlasting rest and glory. They go to be with the Lord.

Fourthly I will give some directions to you that you may become Christ's freemen.

1st. You must break off from all sin and sincerely repent of all your past wickedness.

2dly. You must believe on the Lord Jesus Christ and accept of him on the terms of the Gospel, subjecting yourselves to his Government.

3dly. You must be holy in all manner of life and Conversation – if you live in sin you are the Servants of sin & are not Xts freemen.

4^{thly}. You must watch against Sin and Keep at the greatest distance from it.

5^{thly}. You must be contented with your State & Condition in the world and not murmur and complain of what God orders for you.

6^{thly}. You must be faithful in the places God puts you and not be eye Servants – in vain to think to be Xts freemen & be slothful Servants.

7^{thly}. If you would be the Lord's freemen you must resist all temptation to sin and be exemplary in your lives and Conversation.

8^{thly}. Be constant and diligent in the uses of the means of Grace – read pray meditate – hear the word preached.

Fifthly for motive consider.

1st. If you are not Xts freemen you will be the Slaves of the Devil.

2^{ndly}. If you are Xts freemen you may contentedly be servants in the world.

3dly. X is come into the world and died to free you.

4^{thly}. God has done much for some of you to make you free.

5^{thly}. You are under good advantages to obtain your liberty by X.

6^{thly}. The time is that you know not what may be on the morrow.

7^{thly}. Think what it is to die in sin – not freed by X.

APPENDIX II

Calendar Problems – Julian and Gregorian, New Year's Day, Leap Years

There are several distinct problems associated with the construction of any calendar. The first is the fact that the length of a year, the time required for the Earth to complete one full orbit around the Sun, is not an exact whole number of days. We cannot change this fact – that is the solar system in which we live. If we want calendar dates to maintain, at least approximately, a constant relationship with the seasons from year to year, then an occasional "leap day" or something equivalent must be introduced from time to time.[1] It was known in the time of Julius Caesar that the length of a year is approximately 365-¼ (365.25) days. And so the fundamental feature of the Julian calendar is that a leap day is introduced every four years. (For many centuries now, that extra day has been added at the end of February, but it was not always thus – in the Julian calendar as originally designed, the leap day was inserted by *repeating* February 24.[2])

The difficulty with the Julian calendar is that the length of a day is not exactly 365.25 days but, more closely, about 365.24 days. A difference of only one one-hundredth of a day per year, but over the course of a century, that would add up to a whole day and in a millennium ten full days. By the 1500s the vernal equinox (the true vernal equinox, the time when days and nights are of equal length) was occurring about March 10 on the calendar rather than on March 21 – the "official" date of the equinox that had been designated by the Council of Nicaea in 325.[3] If this had been allowed to continue indefinitely, we would eventually find that the calendar date of the true vernal equinox would be in January or February, while March 21 on the calendar, the "official" equinox date,

---

1 There are calendars that are not tied to the seasons and the apparent movements of the Sun at all, for instance the purely lunar Islamic calendar. Here we discuss only the calendars in general use in England and France and their North American colonies.

2 Feeney (2007), p. 280.

3 Duncan (1998), p. 4.

would be occurring later and later in the spring. And then Easter, whose date is closely related to the official date of the equinox, would gradually become a midsummer holiday rather than a holiday near the beginning of spring.

That is, on the Julian calendar, there are *too many* leap years. If the length of the year were precisely 365.24 days, then the problem would be permanently solved by making every "century year" (a year evenly divisible by 100) an ordinary year, without a leap day. Even the figure of 365.24 days, though more accurate than 365.25, is not quite right – more precisely, the length of a year is very nearly 365.2422 days. In a papal bull issued by Pope Gregory XIII in February, 1582, it was decreed that henceforth *most* century years would be normal years. The year 1600, however, would be a leap year; 1700, 1800, and 1900 would be normal years; 2000 would be a leap year; 2100 will be a normal year, and so on.

At the same time that Pope Gregory settled the question of how frequently, on average, there should be a leap year, a one-time correction was made by omitting ten days in October, 1582. On the Gregorian calendar, the days October 5-14, 1582 never existed.

The Gregorian calendar reform was soon adopted in most of the predominantly Catholic regions of Europe but not by the English – who continued to use the Julian calendar – and of course those who left England to settle in North America followed the calendar in use in the mother country. Throughout the 1600s the Julian and Gregorian calendars differed by ten days, and then after 1700 (a leap year on the Julian calendar but not on the Gregorian) the difference increased to eleven days. Thus an event described by those living in Boston or London as occurring on, say, July 10, 1740 would have been given a date of July 21, 1740 by residents of Quebec or Paris. It was only in 1752 that England finally adopted the Gregorian calendar, omitting eleven days in September of that year (September 3-13) to put English and French dates in agreement.[4]

More confusing is the date on which a new year begins. This date is subject to human choice, and New Year's Day in principle could be at any time of the year. At the same time that the ten-day correction was

---

4 In Russia, use of the Julian calendar continued until after the Bolshevik Revolution of 1917. (By that time, the Julian and Gregorian calendars were out of step by thirteen days.) That is why the anniversary of the "October Revolution", the coup that took place on the night of October 24-25 on the Julian calendar, came to be celebrated in November, after the Russians finally adopted the Gregorian calendar.

announced by Pope Gregory in 1582, it was also decreed that on the Gregorian calendar, New Year's Day would be January 1. As for England and her colonies, one can read statements of the following sort – "According to the Julian calendar the new year began on March 25 instead of January 1." Would that it were that simple! In fact, until 1752, in England and her colonies there were *two* New Year's Days – January 1 and March 25 ("Annunciation Day"). An event that occurred between January 1 and March 25 really took place in two different years at the same time. Church records and legal documents generally followed the "March 25 convention". If one examines the records of baptisms in the Deerfield church, one finds, for instance, that Rachel Mitchel was baptized on Sunday, March 16, 1739, and then two weeks later, on March 30, 1740, Ebenezer Smead was baptized.[5] Most almanacs, though – Benjamin Franklin's *Poor Richard's Almanack*, for example – followed the "January 1 convention" and considered the year to run from January 1 to December 31.

Most Boston newspapers also took New Year's Day to be January 1. But not all – one can find examples of days on which two newspapers printed issues with two apparently different dates. The *Boston News-Letter*, for example, printed an issue bearing the date Monday, February 8, 1720; on the very same day, the *Boston Gazette* was dated Monday, February 8, 1719. Keepers of account books and diary writers did not all follow the same conventions. Some changed the year on March 25 but others did so on January 1. In the account book of William Williams, the page for the transactions recorded on March 25, 1751 is headed "Laus Deo [praise be to God] March 25, 1751 – New Years Day", but there is an entry in the diary of Reverend Stephen Williams of Longmeadow that reads – "January 1 1730/31 - a new year begins - I pray God to forgive ye sins of ye year past". Finally, in the same act of parliament in which it was decreed that eleven days in October, 1752 would be omitted, the "dual New Year's Day" problem was resolved by the announcement that beginning on January 1, 1752, New Year's Day would be unambiguously January 1.

Only occasionally did an author of a letter or a document take the trouble to be unambiguous by using "dual-year notation", writing, for instance, January 10, 1743/44. Those who did so have earned the gratitude of 21st-century historians as well as of their contemporaries. In referring to events that occurred in the winter months of years before

---

5 Deerfield minister's record book, PVMA Library.

1752, I use the "January 1 convention" or, more often, "dual-year notation". When quoting from an original source, I quote the item as written, often adding an explanatory note about the date, especially if the date is of some significance. Often, but not always, the ambiguity can be resolved by examining the context, looking at other evidence, but the opportunities for error in interpreting colonial records from the early 1700s, those with dates between January 1 and March 25 in the years prior to 1752, are obviously enormous.[6]

There is one more issue that must be addressed – which years were leap years? Suppose, say, that it is February in the year 1723/24. Will there be a February 29th at the end of the month or not? If the rule is that leap years are those evenly divisible by four, then if it is still 1723, it should not be a leap year, whereas if it is already 1724, then there *will* be a leap day at the end of the month. Fortunately – avoiding an additional bit of complexity – the English took months such as February, 1723/24 to be leap months, even though 1723 is not divisible by four. Deerfield baptism records, for instance, from winter months such as January - March, 1739/40 show clearly that February that year had twenty-nine days. And if higher authority be sought, we have Deerfield's Reverend John Williams who, in his best-selling account of the most famous attack on Deerfield, describes it as occurring on the early morning of "Tuesday, the 29th of February, 1703-4".[7] And an even more authoritative source is Isaac Newton, author of a brief scientific paper about his now-famous theory of light and colors, a paper that he submitted to the *Philosophical Transactions of the Royal Society* on February 29, 1675/76.[8]

---

6 Calendar converters, of the type that one can now conveniently find on the Internet (e.g., www.fourmilab.ch/documents/calendar/) almost all treat January 1 as New Year's Day in converting dates between the Julian and Gregorian calendars.

7 Williams, John (1707), p. 10. Deerfield celebrated the 300th anniversary of that attack on February 29, 2004. They really should have waited until March 11, just as the birthday of George Washington, born on February 11, 1731/32 according to the Julian calendar, came to be celebrated on February 22. (Until 1971, when the holiday – still legally "Washington's Birthday" but unofficially "Presidents Day" – was shifted to the third Monday in February, which is never February 22.)

8 "A particular Answer of Mr. Isaak Newton to Mr. Linus his Letter, printed in Numb. 121. p. 499, about an Experiment relating to the New Doctrine of Light and Colours: This Answer sent from Cambridge in a Letter to the Publisher Febr. 29. 1675/6." By a further happy coincidence, Newton's paper was published just a few weeks later, in the issue of March 25, 1676, New Year's Day according to the "March 25 convention". (This paper was reprinted in Cohen (1958).)

Sources and Bibliography

I – Libraries and other document repositories

American Antiquarian Society, Worcester.

Amherst College Library, Amherst.

Berkshire Athenaeum, Pittsfield.

Connecticut State Library, Hartford.

Deerfield Library. Officially two libraries in the same building – The Pocumtuck Valley Memorial Association ("PVMA") Library and the Henry N. Flynt Memorial Library of Historic Deerfield, Inc.

Forbes Library, Northampton.

Jones Library, Amherst.

Massachusetts State Archives, Boston.

Hampden County Registry of Deeds, Springfield.

Hampshire County Registry of Probate, Northampton.

Mount Holyoke College Library, South Hadley.

Norman Rockwell Museum, Stockbridge.

Smith College Library, Northampton.

Storrs Library, Longmeadow.

University of Massachusetts Library, Amherst.

Westfield Athenaeum, Westfield.

II – Published collections of documents and statistics

Acts and Resolves. The Acts and Resolves, Public and Private, of the Province of the Massachusetts Bay. Boston: Wright & Potter, 1869-1922.

Ancestry.com. (Early census enumeration data.)

Biographical sketches of the graduates of Yale College. Franklin Bowditch Dexter, ed. New York: Holt, 1885-1912.

Colonial Laws. The Colonial Laws of Massachusetts. Reprinted from the edition of 1660, with the Supplements to 1672. Containing also the Body of Liberties of 1641. Boston: Published by order of the City Council of Boston. 1889. (Another edition contains supplements through 1686 – *The Colonial Laws of Massachusetts.* Reprinted from the edition of 1672, with the Supplements through 1686. Boston: 1887.)

Documents Illustrative of the History of the Slave Trade to America (1930-1935). Elizabeth Donnan, ed. Washington, D.C.: Carnegie Institution of Washington.

Forgotten Patriots (2008). *Forgotten Patriots – African American and American Indian Patriots in the Revolutionary War.* Eric G. Grundset, ed. Washington: National Society of the Daughters of the American Revolution.

Historical Statistics of Black America (1995). Jessie Carney Smith and Carrell Peterson Horton, eds. New York: Gale Research.

Historical Statistics of the United States (2006). Susan B. Carter et al., eds. New York: Cambridge University Press.

Jim Crow New York (2003). *Jim Crow New York, A Documentary History of Race and Citizenship, 1777-1877.* D. Gellman and D. Quigley, eds., New York: New York University Press.

Laws of the State of New York. Albany. Volumes containing laws passed at the 22nd and 40th sessions of the legislature contain the texts of the 1799 and 1817 gradual abolition acts. See also *Statutes on Slavery* and *Jim Crow New York* (2003).

Massachusetts Records. Records of the Governor and Company of the Massachusetts Bay in New England. Nathaniel B. Shurtleff, ed. Boston: William White, 1853-54.

Massachusetts Soldiers and Sailors. Massachusetts Soldiers and Sailors of the Revolutionary War. Boston: Wright & Potter Printing Co., State Printers. Seventeen volumes, 1896-1908.

Negro Population in the United States, 1790-1915. Washington: Bureau of the Census, 1918. (Reprinted by Arno Press, New York, 1968 and Ross Publishing, New York, 2005.)

New Jersey Digital Legal Library. The website http://njlegallib.rutgers.edu/slavery has the text of the New Jersey "gradual emancipation" statutes.

Patriots of Color (2004). George Quintal, Jr. *Patriots of Color – African Americans and Native Americans at Battle Road & Bunker Hill.* Washington: National Park Service.

Plymouth Records. Records of the Colony of New Plymouth in New England. Nathaniel B. Shurtleff and David Pulsifer, eds. Boston: Press of William White, 1855-61.

Sibley's Harvard Graduates. Biographical Sketches of Those Who Attended Harvard College. Boston: Harvard University Press. 1933- .

Statutes on Slavery. Statutes on Slavery: The Pamphlet Literature. Paul Finkelman, ed. New York: Garland Publishing, 1988. (Reprinted by Lawbook Exchange, Clark, N.J., 2007.) Volume 1 contains the text of New York's gradual abolition law of 1817.

Vital Records. In the early 20th century, a large number of volumes of Vital Records of Massachusetts towns (with records up to 1849 or 1850) were published by the New England Historic Genealogical Society and the Essex Institute. A set of CDs containing these volumes was published in 2003 by Search & ReSearch Publishing Corporation, Wheat Ridge, Colorado. The *Western Massachusetts* CD contains additional material, e.g., James Smith's *Families of Amherst* (Smith, James (1984)).

III – Collected papers

Diary and Autobiography of John Adams (1961). L. H. Butterfield, ed. Cambridge: Harvard University Press.

Legal Papers of John Adams (1968). L. Kinvin Wroth and Hiller B. Zobel, eds. New York: Atheneum. (Originally published by Harvard University Press.)

Porter-Phelps-Huntington Papers. (The "PPH Papers" are on deposit at the Amherst College Library, Archives and Special Collections Department.)

Pynchon Papers (1982-1985). Carl Bridenbaugh, ed. Boston: The Colonial Society of Massachusetts.

Winthrop Papers (1929-1992). Boston: Massachusetts Historical Society.

IV – Books and articles.

Arms, Pliny (ca. 1840). Pliny Arms. *Deerfield History.* Unpublished manuscript, Deerfield Library. (A transcript, made by Robert H. Romer in 2005, is also at the Deerfield Library. A photocopy of the manuscript is included with the transcript. Bound with this transcript are several pages from the "Bloody Brook Address", also by Pliny Arms, pages that give a second version of the description of the whipping of Daniel Arms' slave, Titus.)

Ashley, Elihu (1773-1775). Elihu Ashley. *The Diary of Elihu Ashley.* (The original manuscript of Ashley's diary is in the PVMA Library. An edited version has recently been published – see Miller and Riggs (2007).)

Bailey, Richard (2003). Richard Bailey. "From Goddess of Love to Unloved Wife: Naming Slaves and Redeeming Masters in Eighteenth-Century New England." *Slavery/Antislavery in New England, Annual Proceedings of the Dublin Seminar for New England Folklife, pp. 44-55.*

Baker (1878). C. Alice Baker. "Ensign John Sheldon." *History and Proceedings of the Pocumtuck Valley Memorial Association,* Vol. 1, 405-431.

Ballantine (1737-1774). *Journal of Reverend John Ballantine.* (The original copy of Ballantine's journal is at the Westfield Athenaeum. A transcript is available at the library of the University of Massachusetts, Amherst. A CD was published in 2007 that includes both the original and the transcript by Heritage Books, Inc., Westminster, Maryland.)

Berlin and Harris (2005). *Slavery in New York.* Ira Berlin and Leslie M. Harris, eds. New York: The New Press.

Blanck (2002). Emily Blanck. "Seventeen Eighty-Three: The Turning Point in the Law of Slavery and Freedom in Massachusetts." *New England Quarterly,* Vol. 75 (No. 1), 24-51.

Blumrosen and Blumrosen (2005). Alfred G. Blumrosen and Ruth G. Blumrosen. *Slave Nation.* Naperville, Illinois: Sourcebooks.

Bradford, Alden (1835). Alden Bradford. *History of Massachusetts, for Two Hundred Years: From the Year 1620 to 1820.* Boston: Hilliard, Gray, and Co.

Brigham (1985). Robert J. Brigham. *Amherst College: A Pious Institution's Reaction to Slavery, 1821-1841.* (Unpublished manuscript at the Archives and Special Collections Department, Amherst College Library.)

Brown and Tager (2000). Richard D. Brown and Jack Tager. *Massachusetts – A Concise History*. Amherst: University of Massachusetts Press.

Burgan (2005). Michael Burgan. *Voices from Colonial America –Massachusetts, 1620-1776*. Washington: National Geographic Society.

Carlisle (2004). Elizabeth Carlisle. *Earthbound and Heavenbent*. New York: Scribner.

Carpenter and Morehouse (1896). Edward W. Carpenter and Charles F. Morehouse. *The History of the Town of Amherst, Massachusetts*. Amherst: Press of Carpenter and Morehouse. (The Town Meeting Records Section, with separately numbered pages, was not included in the reprint edition published by the *Amherst Journal Record* in 1959. Also omitted from the reprint edition were some photographs and the 1772 map of the town.)

Carvalho (1984). Joseph Carvalho III. *Black Families in Hampden County, Massachusetts, 1650-1855*. Boston: New England Historic Genealogical Society and Westfield: Institute for Massachusetts Studies, Westfield State College.

Clark (1995). Christopher Clark. *The Communitarian Moment – The Radical Challenge of the Northampton Association*. Ithaca: Cornell University Press.

Cohen (1958). I. Bernard Cohen. *Isaac Newton's Papers & Letters on Natural Philosophy and Related Documents*. Cambridge: Harvard University Press.

Cole (1940). Arthur C. Cole. *A Hundred Years of Mount Holyoke College*. New Haven: Yale University Press.

Commager (1949). Henry Steele Commager. *Documents of American History*. Fifth edition. New York: Appleton-Century-Crofts.

Crawford (1914). Mary Caroline Crawford. *Social Life in Old New England*. New York: Grosset and Dunlap.

Cushing, John (1961). John D. Cushing. "The Cushing Court and the Abolition of Slavery in Massachusetts: More Notes on the 'Quock Walker Case'." *American Journal of Legal History*, Vol. 5 (No. 2), 118-144.

Davis (1900). Andrew McFarland Davis. *Currency and Banking in the Province of the Massachusetts Bay*. New York: Macmillan Co. (Reprinted by Augustus M. Kelley, New York, 1970.)

Demos (1994). John Demos. *The Unredeemed Captive*. New York: Vintage Books.

Du Bois (1968). W. E. B. Du Bois. *The Autobiography of W. E. B. Du Bois*. New York: International Publishers.

Duncan (1998). David Ewing Duncan. *Calendar – Humanity's Epic Struggle to Determine a True and Accurate Year*. New York: Avon Books.

Earle (1893). Alice Morse Earle. *Customs and Fashions in Old New England*. New York: Scribner and London: David Nutt. (Reprinted by Corner House Historical Publications, Gansevoort, New York, 1997.)

Ellison (1952). Ralph Ellison. *Invisible Man*. New York: Random House.

Emilio (1891). Luis F. Emilio. *A Brave Black Regiment, the History of the 54th Massachusetts*. Boston: The Boston Book Company. (Reprinted by Da Capo Press, 1995.)

Everts (1879). Louis H. Everts. *History of the Connecticut Valley in Massachusetts*. Philadelphia: L. H. Everts.

Feeney (2007). Denis Feeney. *Caesar's Calendar – Ancient Time and the Beginnings of History*. Berkeley: University of California Press.

Felt (1839). Joseph B. Felt. *Historical Account of Massachusetts Currency*. Boston: Perkins & Marvin.

Field, Phinehas (1879). Phinehas Field. "Slavery in Massachusetts." *History and Proceedings of the Pocumtuck Valley Memorial Association*, Vol. 1, 480-486.

First Congregational Church of Amherst (1990). *250 Years at First Church in Amherst, 1739-1989*. Amherst: The First Congregational Church.

Francis (2005). Richard Francis. *Judge Sewall's Apology*. New York: HarperCollins.

Franklin (1947). John Hope Franklin. *From Slavery to Freedom*. New York: Alfred A. Knopf.

Gerzina (2008). Gretchen Holbrook Gerzina. *Mr. And Mrs. Prince*. New York: HarperCollins.

Godbeer (2002). Richard Godbeer. *Sexual Revolution in Early America*. Baltimore: Johns Hopkins University Press.

Greene (1928). Lorenzo J. Greene. "Slave-Holding New England and Its Awakening." *Journal of Negro History*, Vol. 13 (No. 4), 492-533.

Greene (1942). Lorenzo J. Greene. *The Negro in Colonial New England*. New York: Columbia University Press. (Reprinted by Atheneum, New York, 1968.)

Haefeli and Sweeney (2003). Evan Haefeli and Kevin Sweeney. *Captors and Captives*. Amherst: University of Massachusetts Press.

Haefeli and Sweeney (2006). Evan Haefeli and Kevin Sweeney. *Captive Histories*. Amherst: University of Massachusetts Press.

Hall (1988). Michael G. Hall. *The Last American Puritan – The Life of Increase Mather*. Middletown, Connecticut: Wesleyan University Press.

Hart (1927-1930). Albert Bushnell Hart. *Commonwealth History of Massachusetts*. New York: States History Co.

Hawthorne (1835). Nathaniel Hawthorne. *Old News*. (Originally published in 1835, *Old News* has been reprinted in, for instance, *The Centenary Edition of the Works of Nathaniel Hawthorne*, Vol. 11, pp. 132-160, Ohio State University Press, 1974, William Charvat et al., eds. The excerpt cited in the text appears on p. 139 of this volume.)

Isaacson (2003). Walter Isaacson. *Benjamin Franklin, An American Life*. New York: Simon & Schuster.

Jordan and Walsh (2008). Don Jordan and Michael Walsh. *White Cargo*. New York: New York University Press.

Judd Manuscripts. Sylvester Judd, author of the 1863 *History of Hadley*, wrote copiously on the history of the Connecticut Valley. The original copies, now too fragile for routine perusal, are at the Forbes Library, where microfilm copies are also kept.

Judd Manuscripts (*Selected Papers*, 1976). *Selected Papers from the Sylvester Judd Manuscripts*. Gregory H. Nobles and Herbert L. Zarov, eds. Northampton: Forbes Library. (Copies are held by the Forbes Library, the Amherst College Library, the Mount Holyoke College Library, the Smith College Library, and the University of Massachusetts Library.)

Judd (1863 / 1905). Sylvester Judd. *History of Hadley*. Northampton: Metcalf & Co. (Included is a Genealogy Section, with separately numbered pages.) After Judd's death in 1860, the original edition of his Hadley history was completed by L. H. Boltwood. A second edition, with a small amount of additional material by George Sheldon, was published in 1905. (Springfield: H. R. Hunting & Company. Reprinted by

The New Hampshire Publishing Company, Somersworth, New Hampshire, 1976.) Page references in the text are to the 1905 edition.

Kaplan (1969). Sidney Kaplan. *The Selling of Joseph*. Amherst: University of Massachusetts Press. (An edited version of Sewall's *Selling of Joseph*.)

Kupperman (1993). Karen O. Kupperman. *Providence Island, 1630-1641: The Other Puritan Colony*. New York: Cambridge University Press.

LaPlante (2007). Eve LaPlante. *Salem Witch Judge – The Life and Repentance of Samuel Sewall*. New York: HarperCollins.

Lauber (1913). Almon Wheeler Lauber. *Indian Slavery in Colonial Times Within the Present Limits of the United States*. New York: Columbia University.

Lawrence (1927). Robert M. Lawrence. *New England Colonial Life*. Cambridge, Massachusetts: The Cosmos Press.

Lepore (1998). Jill Lepore. *The Name of War*. New York: Alfred A. Knopf.

Lepore (2005). Jill Lepore. *New York Burning*. New York: Alfred A. Knopf.

MacEacheren (1970). Elaine MacEacheren. "Emancipation of Slavery in Massachusetts." *Journal of Negro History*, Vol. 55 (No. 4), 289-306.

Marcou (1847). Jane Belknap Marcou. *Life of Jeremy Belknap*. New York: Harper.

Marsden (2003). George M. Marsden. *Jonathan Edwards – A Life*. New Haven: Yale University Press.

Mason (1736). John Mason. *A Brief History of the Pequot War*. (Reprinted in *Collections of the Massachusetts Historical Society*, Second Series, Vol. 8, 120-153 (1826).)

Mather, Cotton (1706). Cotton Mather. *The Negro Christianized*. (Originally published in 1706, Mather's pamphlet has been frequently reprinted, e.g., in Ruchames (1969).)

Mayer (1998). Henry Mayer. *All on Fire – William Lloyd Garrison and the Abolition of Slavery*. New York: St. Martin's Press.

McClellan (ca. 1955). Bruce McClellan. *Grapes and Thorns – A Biographical study of Jonathan Ashley*. (Unpublished manuscript at the Deerfield Library.)

McCullough (2001). David McCullough. *John Adams*. New York: Simon & Schuster.

McCusker (1978). John J. McCusker. *Money and Exchange in Europe and America, 1600-1775*. Williamsburg, Virginia: Institute of Early American History and Culture.

McCusker (1992). John J. McCusker. *How Much is That in Real Money?* Worcester, Massachusetts: American Antiquarian Society.

McGowan and Miller (1996). Susan McGowan and Amelia F. Miller. *Family & Landscape – Deerfield Homelots from 1671*. Deerfield: Pocumtuck Valley Memorial Association.

McManus (1973). Edgar J. McManus. *Black Bondage in the North*. Syracuse: Syracuse University Press.

Melish (1998). Joanne Pope Melish. *Disowning Slavery – Gradual Emancipation and "Race" in New England, 1780-1860*. Ithaca: Cornell University Press.

Miller (1962). Amelia F. Miller. *The Reverend Jonathan Ashley House*. Deerfield: Heritage Foundation.

Miller and Riggs (2007). *Romance, Remedies, and Revolution – The Journal of Dr. Elihu Ashley of Deerfield, Massachusetts, 1773-1775*. Amelia F. Miller and A. R. Riggs, eds. Amherst: University of Massachusetts Press. (An edited version of Ashley, Elihu (1773-1775).)

Minkema (1997). Kenneth P. Minkema. "Jonathan Edwards on Slavery and the Slave Trade." *William and Mary Quarterly*, Third Series, Vol. 54, No. 4, 823-834.

Minkema (2002). Kenneth P. Minkema. "Jonathan Edwards's Defense of Slavery." *Massachusetts Historical Review*, Vol. 4, 23-59.

Moore (1866). George H. Moore. *Notes on the History of Slavery in Massachusetts*. New York: Appleton. (A lengthy unsigned review was published in the *Historical Magazine and Notes and Queries Concerning the Antiquities, History and Biography of America*, First Series, Vol. 10, Supplement II, 47-57 (1866).)

Morris (1879). Henry Morris. "Slavery in the Connecticut Valley." *Papers and Proceedings of the Connecticut Valley Historical Society*, Vol. 1, 207-217.

Newell (2003). Margaret Ellen Newell. "The Changing Nature of Indian Slavery in New England, 1670-1720." In *Reinterpreting New England Indians and the Colonial Experience*. Colin G. Calloway and Neal Salisbury, eds. Boston: Colonial Society of Massachusetts.

Nissenbaum (1996). Stephen Nissenbaum. *The Battle for Christmas*. New York: Alfred A. Knopf.

O'Brien (1960). William O'Brien. "Did the Jennison Case Outlaw Slavery in Massachusetts?" *William and Mary Quarterly*, Third Series, Vol. 17 (No. 2), 219-241.

Painter (1996). Nell Painter. *Sojourner Truth*. New York: W.W.Norton.

Palfrey (1883). John Gorham Palfrey. *A Compendious History of New England*. Boston: Houghton, Mifflin and Co. (First published in 1873.)

Perry (1899). Arthur L. Perry. *Williamstown and Williams College*. New York: C. Scribner's Sons.

Phelps, Elizabeth Porter (1763-1817). *Diary of Elizabeth Porter Phelps*. (The original copy of Phelps' diary is part of the Porter-Phelps-Huntington Family Papers collection, located at the Archives and Special Collections Department, Amherst College Library. A transcript of much of the diary was published in the *New England Historical and Genealogical Register*, 1964-1969.)

Philbrick (2006). Nathaniel Philbrick. *Mayflower: A Story of Courage, Community, and War*. New York: Viking.

Piersen (1988). William D. Piersen. *Black Yankees*. Amherst: University of Massachusetts Press.

Preiss (1976). Lillian E. Preiss. *Sheffield, Frontier Town*. Sheffield, Massachusetts: Sheffield Bicentennial Committee.

Proper (1997). David R. Proper. *Lucy Terry Prince – Singer of History*. Deerfield: Pocumtuck Valley Memorial Association and Historic Deerfield, Inc.

Pruitt (1978). *The Massachusetts Tax Valuation List of 1771*. Bettye Hobbs Pruitt, ed. Boston: G. K. Hall & Co.

Rantoul (1833). Robert Rantoul. "Negro Slavery in Massachusetts." A paper read before the Beverly Lyceum, 1833. Printed in the *Historical Collections of the Essex Institute*, Vol. 24, 81-108 (1888).

Romer (2004/2005). Robert H. Romer. "Higher Education and Slavery in Western Massachusetts." *Journal of Blacks in Higher Education*, No. 46, 98-101 (Winter, 2004/2005).

Rosenthal, Bernard (1973). Bernard Rosenthal. "Puritan Conscience and New England Slavery." *New England Quarterly*, Vol. 46 (No. 1), 62-81.

Rosenthal, James (1937). James M. Rosenthal. "Free Soil in Berkshire County 1781." *New England Quarterly*, Vol. 10 (No. 4), 781-785.

Rozwenc (1954). Edwin C. Rozwenc. "Caleb Strong: The Last of the River Gods." In *The Northampton Book*, compiled and edited by the Tercentenary History Committee (Lawrence E. Wikander, Chairman), pp. 56-74. Northampton, Massachusetts: The Tercentenary History Committee.

Ruchames (1969). *Racial Thought in America*. Louis Ruchames, ed. Amherst: University of Massachusetts Press. (This volume contains most of the text of Sewall (1700), Saffin (1701), and Mather, Cotton (1706).)

Rudolph (1956). Frederick Rudolph. *Mark Hopkins and the Log; Williams College, 1836-1872*. New Haven: Yale University Press.

Rudolph (1983). *Perspectives: A Williams Anthology*. Frederick Rudolph, ed. Williamstown: Williams College.

Saffin (1701). John Saffin. *Reply to Judge Sewall*. (Originally published in 1701, Saffin's *Reply* was lost until rediscovered by Moore, who included it in his 1866 book. (Moore (1866).) It is also included in Ruchames (1969).)

Sewall (1674-1729). Samuel Sewall. *Diary of Samuel Sewall, 1674-1729*. New York: Arno Press, 1972. (The Arno Press reprint is taken from the 1878-82 edition, published by the Massachusetts Historical Society, issued as Vols. 5-7, Series 5, of the *Collections of the Massachusetts Historical Society*. Vols. 1-3 of the reprint edition correspond to Vols. 5-7, respectively, of the 1878-82 edition.)

Sewall (1700). Samuel Sewall. *The Selling of Joseph*. (Originally published in 1700, *The Selling of Joseph* has been reprinted in, for example, Kaplan (1969) and Ruchames (1969).)

Sheldon (1893). George Sheldon. "Negro Slavery in Old Deerfield." *New England Magazine*, Vol. 8, 49-60 (March, 1893). (This article is almost identical to the "Negro Slavery" section of his 1895 history.)

Sheldon (1895). George Sheldon. *A History of Deerfield, Massachusetts*. Greenfield, Massachusetts: E. A. Hall & Co. (Included is a Genealogy Section, with separately numbered pages.)

Sheridan (1963). Richard B. Sheridan. "Slavery and Antislavery Literature." *Books and Libraries at the University of Kansas*, Vol. 2 (No. 4), 11-15.

Shurtleff (1872). Nathaniel B. Shurtleff. *A Topographical and Historical Description of Boston*. Boston: Noyes, Holmes and Company.

Silverman (1984). Kenneth Silverman. *The Life and Times of Cotton Mather*. New York: Harper & Row.

Smith, James (1984). James A. Smith. *Families of Amherst*. (Unpublished manuscript at the Special Collections Department, Jones Library, Amherst. This manuscript is one of the items included on the *Vital Records* CD published in 2003.)

Smith, James (1999). James A. Smith. *The History of the Black Population of Amherst, Massachusetts, 1728-1870*. Boston: New England Historic Genealogical Society.

Smith, John (1899). John M. Smith. *History of the Town of Sunderland*. Greenfield, Massachusetts: E. A. Hall & Co.

Smith, Mary P. Wells (1904). Mary P. Wells Smith. *The Boy Captive of Old Deerfield*. (Originally published in 1904, reprinted in 2000 by the Pocumtuck Valley Memorial Association.)

Spector (1968). Robert M. Spector. "The Quock Walker Cases (1781-83) – Slavery, its Abolition, and Negro Citizenship in Early Massachusetts." *Journal of Negro History*, Vol. 53 (No. 1), 12-32.

Sperry (1998). Kip Sperry. *Reading Early American Handwriting*. Baltimore: Genealogical Publishing Company.

Sperry (2003). Kip Sperry. *Abbreviations & Acronyms*. Second edition. Provo, Utah: Ancestry.com.

Spring (1917). Leverett W. Spring. *A History of Williams College*. Boston: Houghton-Mifflin Co.

Stewart (1976). James Brewer Stewart. *Holy Warriors – The Abolitionists and American Slavery*. New York: Hill and Wang.

Sumner (1854). *The Works of Charles Sumner*. Boston: Lee and Shepard, 1875. (The passage quoted from Sumner's June 28, 1854 speech appears in Vol. 3, p. 384.)

Sweet (2003). John W. Sweet. *Bodies Politic – Negotiating Race in the American North, 1730-1830*. Baltimore: Johns Hopkins University Press.

Temple (1889). J. H. Temple. *History of the Town of Palmer, Massachusetts*. Palmer: The Town of Palmer.Thompson, Roger (1986).

Thompson, Francis (1904). Francis M. Thompson. *History of Greenfield*. Greenfield, Massachusetts: T. Morey & Son.

Thompson, Roger (1986). Roger Thompson. *Sex in Middlesex – Popular Mores in a Massachusetts County, 1649-1699*. Amherst: University of Massachusetts Press.

Towner (1964). Lawrence W. Towner. "The Sewall-Saffin Dialogue on Slavery." *William and Mary Quarterly*, Third Series, Vol. 21 (No. 1), 40-52.

Trowbridge (1896). Francis Bacon Trowbridge. *The Ashley Genealogy*. New Haven: Printed for the Author.

Trumbull, James (1898-1902). James R. Trumbull. *History of Northampton*. Northampton: Gazette Printing Co.

Trumbull, J. Hammond (1886). J. Hammond Trumbull. *Memorial History of Hartford County*. Boston: E. L. Osgood.

Truth (1850). Sojourner Truth. *Narrative of Sojourner Truth, a Northern Slave.* (After its initial publication, Truth's autobiography appeared in various editions through the 1880s and has been reprinted many times.)

Twombly and Moore (1967). Robert C. Twombly and Robert H. Moore. "Black Puritan: The Negro in Seventeenth-Century Massachusetts." *William and Mary Quarterly,* Third Series, Vol. 24 (No. 2), 224-242.

Tyler (1873). W. S. Tyler. *History of Amherst College During Its First Half Century*. Springfield, Massachusetts: Clark W. Bryan and Company.

Washburn (1858). Emory Washburn. "The Extinction of Slavery in Massachusetts." *Collections of the Massachusetts Historical Society*, Vol. 4, Fourth Series, pp. 333-346.

Washburn (1869). Emory Washburn. *Slavery as it Once Prevailed in Massachusetts*. Boston: Press of John Wilson and Son.

Wells and Wells (1910). Daniel W. Wells and Reuben F. Wells. A *History of Hatfield, Massachusetts*. Springfield, Massachusetts: F. C. H. Gibbons.

Wells (1975). Robert V. Wells. *The Population of the British Colonies in America before 1776*. Princeton: Princeton University Press.

Wilds (1999). Mary Wilds. *Mumbet: The Life and Times of Elizabeth Freeman*. Greensboro, North Carolina: Avisson Press.

Williams, John (1707). John Williams. *The Redeemed Captive Returning to Zion*. (Originally published in 1707, the book is still in print as of 2009. Bedford, Massachusetts: Applewood Books. Also available as a Kessinger Publishing reprint edition.)

Williams, Stephen (1715-1782). *Diary of Stephen Williams*. (The original copy of Williams' diary is at the Storrs Library in Longmeadow. A microfilm copy of the typewritten transcript and an index to the transcript are held at the Deerfield Library.)

Wilson, Robert J. (1981). Robert J. Wilson. "Early American Account Books: Interpretation, Cataloguing, and Use." Technical Leaflet 140, published by the American Association for State and Local History.

Wilson, Thomas (1855). Thomas Wilson. *Historical Address Delivered at Palmer, Mass., July 5, 1852*. Lowell: S. J. Varney, Printer.

Winthrop (1630-1649). John Winthrop. *The Journal of John Winthrop, 1630-1649*. (1996 edition). Richard S. Dunn, James Savage, and Laetitia Yeandle, eds. Cambridge: Harvard University Press. (An 1853 edition, edited by James Savage and published with the title *History of New England from 1630 to 1649* (Boston: Little, Brown and Co.), contains some material not included in the 1996 edition.)

Wright (1970). Wyllis E. Wright. *Colonel Ephraim Williams – A Documentary Life*. Pittsfield, Massachusetts: Berkshire County Historical Society.

Zilversmit (1967). Arthur Zilversmit. *The First Emancipation: The Abolition of Slavery in the North*. Chicago: University of Chicago Press.

Zilversmit (1968). Arthur Zilversmit. "Quok Walker, Mumbet, and the Abolition of Slavery in Massachusetts." *William and Mary Quarterly*, Third Series, Vol. 25 (No. 4), 614-624.

Acknowledgments

Many people have contributed to my research and to the writing of this book – faculty colleagues, fellow researchers, librarians, and many others, including those who have attended talks I have given on this subject or walking tours I have led and who have volunteered information or asked good questions.

Staff members at a number of libraries and document depositories have given invaluable assistance – David Bosse and Martha Noblick at the Deerfield Library, Tevis Kimball and Kate Boyle at the Jones Library, Daria D'Arienzo and her staff at the Amherst College Library, Elise Bernier-Feeley and others at the Forbes Library, Cindy Brennan, Jon Benoit and Jackie Penny at the American Antiquarian Society, and Carl Sturgis at the Storrs Library. Registrar David Sullivan's staff members at the Hampshire County Registry of Probate were always willing to interrupt their work to retrieve copies of ancient wills and probate inventories for my perusal.

Among those who read and commented on all or part of various drafts and chapters were Anthony Gerzina, Gretchen Gerzina, and Joanne Pope Melish (with all of whom I have been sharing information and documents since 2002), Donald Born, Mary Born, Penny Johnson, Martha Noblick, Betty Romer, David Romer, and Steve Strimer. Martha Noblick – Deerfield's most valuable resource – merits a special word of thanks. Martha gave a critical reading to a draft of the entire manuscript, and – more importantly – over the years she has patiently retrieved manuscripts that I requested and has always been on the alert for information that might be useful to me, introducing me to others who visited the Deerfield Library, sending me an email when she came across a document that she thought I would want to see. On one occasion when I thought I was on vacation and innocently accessed my email from an Internet Café in Verona, I found a message from Martha telling me about some important tax valuation lists she had just found. Any researcher who visits the Deerfield Library knows how helpful Martha Noblick can be and how generous she is with her time and expertise.

Throughout my time on the faculty, Amherst College has provided the atmosphere that supports scholarly research and the time and facilities to make it possible. I want to thank the College for a grant that helped me in this research by paying for some of my expenses for travel, copying, and acquisition of research materials.

Bruce Aller devoted his artistic talents and his care and thoughtfulness to the creation from my rough drawings of the two maps that now grace the pages of this book. And for her careful and expert work on the index I am indebted to Jodi Simpson.

Steve Strimer — friend, colleague, publisher, editor — has encouraged this work from the beginning, reading manuscript drafts and then carefully turning my computer files into a finished book while tolerating my need to occasionally split an infinitive or to begin a sentence with a conjunction.

Finally — Betty Romer. It is impossible to adequately describe my indebtedness to Betty Romer and the contributions she has made to this book. Painful though the subject of slavery is, she has aided and abetted this research from the beginning. She has read and criticized countless drafts of this book — sometimes a chapter, sometimes a paragraph or two, and more times than she or I can remember the entire manuscript. This is a better book because of the care and attention that she has lavished upon it.

Robert H. Romer   Amherst, Massachusetts   June, 2009

Index

Slaves are indexed under their given name (or surname, if any), with the surname of their owner in parentheses. If necessary to avoid ambiguity, the owner's initial is included. A slave who passed from one owner to another by sale or inheritance or who became free is listed with the name of the owner with whom he or she is most closely identified in this book.

The three lists that precede the alphabetical index refer to the Bills of Sale, Estate Inventories, and Wills that are quoted in the text. Reproductions of excerpts from many of the originals of these documents are included in the text.